Queer Silence

Queer Silence

ON DISABILITY AND RHETORICAL ABSENCE

J. Logan Smilges

UNIVERSITY OF MINNESOTA PRESS
MINNEAPOLIS • LONDON

Chapter 3 was previously published as "White Squares to Black Boxes: Grindr, Queerness, Rhetorical Silence," *Rhetoric Review* 38, no. 1 (2019): 79–92; reprinted by permission of the publisher, Taylor & Francis Ltd., http://www.tandfonline.com.

Published by the University of Minnesota Press
111 Third Avenue South, Suite 290
Minneapolis, MN 55401–2520
http://www.upress.umn.edu

ISBN 978-1-5179-1408-0 (hc)
ISBN 978-1-5179-1409-7 (pb)

A Cataloging-in-Publication record for this book is available from the Library of Congress.

Printed in the United States of America on acid-free paper

31 30 29 28 27 26 25 24 23 22 10 9 8 7 6 5 4 3 2 1

Contents

Introduction

Unspeakably Queer

I'm sitting on an old couch. It's soft from wear, and the cushions give out beneath me. I feel smaller and skinnier than I already am. The room is warm and intentionally so. A heater buzzes in the corner. A fern wilts sadly beneath a lamp. There's a bookcase with one shelf full of books and three shelves filled with baseballs, each encased in glass. Across from me is a portable whiteboard, the kind with wheels that football coaches use to diagram plays in movies. My therapist sits beside it. He has one knee draped over the other, a clipboard in his lap, and a pen tapping against his thigh.

This is my third session with Joe, but he's not really my therapist. Or, rather, he's not a therapist, really. Joe is a conversion therapist hired by my parents to make their child less gay. Preferably straight, otherwise committed to celibacy. The first session had been a diagnostic meeting. I remember spending the last thirty minutes alone in the waiting room while Joe discussed my prognosis with my parents. We all left in good spirits. The second session was just between Joe and me, but it was largely a continuation of the first, albeit with more graphic questions. "How often do you lust over men, John? And how often do these lustful fantasies lead to masturbation? Approximately how many of your homoerotic masturbatory sessions lead to orgasm?" I answered each question in earnest. I was in fact quite committed to getting better, straighter.

This third session is supposed to be when the therapy starts. I sit in the sunken couch, and Joe stares at me. I'm crying, which is predictable. I'm a sad, anxious, feminine boy with undiagnosed complex post-traumatic stress disorder, obsessive-compulsive disorder, and autism;

we are a species who cry. At sixteen, I am scared and ashamed. Kids at school call me "fag"; Joe says it's same-sex attraction. The former bites worse than the latter.

"Same-sex attraction is reversible," Joe tells me, and I believe him. "If you want to be good, if you want to follow God's law, if you really want it, you can change."

But I continue to cry because even though I want to be good, even though I want to change, I'm not good enough, and I'm not changing at all. Earlier just that day, I lusted over the boy next to me in Algebra II. At least, I think I lusted. I'm not really sure. I didn't have a masturbatory session, so does it still count as lust? Probably. Still crying.

Joe pats my knee and then stands to use the whiteboard. He writes DAD and JOHN in bold letters. "Do you love your dad?" he asks me.

"Well, yeah, of course," I respond, sniffling.

"Do you want to be like him when you get older?"

I don't answer right away. My dad is mean, violent. A bully. "Maybe, like, some parts of him."

"Why only some parts?"

"I don't know."

"Your dad is a man, isn't he?" Joe frowns.

"Yeah." I nod.

"And you want to be a man, don't you?"

I nod again, even though now that I'm thinking about it, I'm unsure. Something about Joe's insinuation that I am not yet a man makes me excited, and I feel guilty immediately.

"So if you want to be a man, why wouldn't you want to be like your dad?"

"I dunno. We're just different, that's all."

"And isn't that difference why you're here?"

I say nothing.

"Look, John." Joe sits back down. "You're struggling right now because you're confused about who you are. You're a man in the making. You hear me? You're going to be a man someday. Once you believe that, the rest of this stuff"—he opens his arms widely, gesturing to the extent of my homoerotic affliction—"will figure itself out. If you spend all your time worrying about how you feel and who you want, you will never be happy. You will be alone, just wandering through life. The gay lifestyle is like that, John. It is lonely and sick. It's full of men who don't know who they are, men who never had anyone tell them, 'You're a man! Start acting like one!'" Joe leans forward and puts his hand on my knee. My pulse quickens, and my groin aches. "Who are you, John?"

I don't know what to say. I didn't feel any of the things I was supposed to feel. I didn't like girls. The thought of being a man unnerved me. I couldn't even imagine having sex with a girl as a man. I place my hand lightly on top of Joe's, thinking it's what he wanted. I tremble.

Joe stands and pushes me back against the couch, leaving a finger in the center of my chest. "Who are you?" His finger presses harder into me.

"I don't know." And I don't. I cross my knees to cover the tent growing through my shorts.

Joe grabs both my shoulders. "You're a man, John. Say it."

"I'm a man."

"You're a man."

"I'm a man."

"You're a man."

The day on which this scene occurred, some afternoon in June 2010, was the day I like to believe that I started writing this book. Following that session with Joe, I continued in conversion therapy for another eighteen months and wouldn't come out as gay or trans for another four and five years, respectively. I wouldn't receive any of my diagnoses for another six years (not that diagnoses are necessary for a disability identity). And I wouldn't physically write the first sentence of this project for another ten years. But I like to believe I started writing that day when I was sixteen because it was then, in a humid room on a shabby couch, that I realized the power of silence. It was then that I learned that absence could be generative, that what remains undone, unseen, unheard, and untouched could be not only transformative but world-building. And more than that, I learned that my trans, (neuro)queer bodymind held the capacity to wield these world-building absences strategically, in ways that helped me to survive in spite of the conditions of my childhood, which were bent on moralizing and subsequently pathologizing how I moved, spoke, longed, lusted, and loved. As I argue here and throughout the following pages, what occurred that afternoon was not merely Joe's attempt to police me into a docile state of ashamed submission but also my resistance to his attempt, a resistance born and bred by a queer silence.

In this book, I propose *queer silence* to name both the surprising potentialities of silence to generate meaning from absence and the ways people on the margins of society tap into these potentialities in order to build community, navigate hostile spaces, and resist forms of institutional and state-sponsored violence. This definition is indebted to, even as it departs from, existing work on *queer* and *silence* as independent concepts. I use *queer* to reference a political position rooted in the dissension occasioned by an inequitable power relation. Following many queer studies scholars, I do not reduce *queer* to "some homogenized identity," such as lesbian, gay, bisexual, transgender, or asexual, but understand it as a space for marginalized populations to coalesce across lines of difference.[1] Queer silence is not code for gay silence. Even so, I acknowledge that the anti-identitarian impulse of queer studies is a colonial fantasy, one fueled by futile attempts to empty the field of its specific historical, geographic, raced, classed, gendered, and disabled contexts.[2] I am thus inclined to locate *queer*'s use value neither in its mainstream, identitarian uptake nor in its intellectualized, anti-identitarian critique. Instead, I value *queer* for both its capacity to dissent from, reject, and resist normativity as well as how this capacity fosters a range of situated and local hungers for worlds that are new, different, and better. This is a *queer* informed by José Esteban Muñoz as "a utopian kernel and an anticipatory illumination."[3] As a kernel, it is pure potentiality. As anticipatory, it is on the cusp of its own becoming. *Queer* as trajectory, as orientation toward futurity, as desire.

Silence, as I understand it, attends to the rhetoricity of queerness, the way *queer* signifies what would otherwise remain nameless and neglected. More broadly, silence catalyzes signification, at once holding space for a sign's precipitation and orienting audiences toward the appropriate modality for its emergence. It is thus the route *queer* takes on its journey from contingent abjection to substance in its own right. Silence mobilizes *queer.* But silence is also queer all on its own. Borrowing from Erin J. Rand's description of queerness as a "general economy of undecidability,"[4] I argue that silence is similarly unstable and uncontainable, serving as "both the condition of possibility for agency *and* that which can never be expressed through form."[5] Silence, though meaningful, is inarticulable; it can only find its articulation through the nonverbal modalities to which it draws attention. When a person is silent, we might read their silence not only as an absence of speech but also as an invitation to consider other ways they are signifying. Silence is a gesture toward visual, material, haptic, and other embodyminded modalities that can signify in tandem with or independently from the verbal register. The absence of speech might cue us to further inspect how else an object (or subject) is speaking. In this way, I position silence as a rhetorical absence: a lacuna that harkens to meaning found elsewhere.

Queer silence, as the imbrication of the queerly silent and silently queer, is the coming together of silence's endless referentiality and queerness's utopian entelechy. Queer silence captures the ways that queer people pursue the worlds they long for with/in silence. Sometimes this silence is loud and includes conventional forms of verbal speech, but it is always a silence enriched by the capacity of queer people to take hold of our queerness—to harness the significations that mark us for abjection and reappropriate them toward new ends. Indeed, the bodyminds of queer people have long been layered in significations that bear no connection to verbal speech. Queer folks signify, whether we're speaking or not. What convinced my parents to enroll me in conversion therapy, for instance, was not a speech act on my part (e.g., "Mom, Dad, I'm gay.") but my visual, haptic, and embodyminded significations: my obsession with scarves, my swishy gait, my sensitiveness, and the extra time I spent dawdling in the men's locker room after swim practice. Queer silence is how I held onto the idea that I might not yet be a man, even as Joe coaxed me into admitting that I was. It is a strategy queers use to make do with the bodyminds we have. It is how we make ourselves heard when nobody is listening.

Unfortunately, among the groups who are least likely to listen to queers are themselves self-identified LGBT people who attempt to shore up their own homo- and transnormativity by distancing themselves from those who cannot or will not approximate white and nondisabled sexual and gender norms.[6] This book is particularly invested in the relationship between *disability* and *queer,* both as racialized identity categories and as subject positions offering unique epistemologies. *Disability,* as I use it, is a broad term that encompasses a wide variety of embodyminded difference, including physical, intellectual, cognitive, psychiatric, and sensory impairments, as well as forms of neurodivergence, D/deafness, disease, and chronic illness that may be less readily associated with disability. I lean into *disability*'s capaciousness not because I believe it is the "correct" term that reveals a biological or medical truth about people but because its singularity exposes the breadth of ableism, the way ableism stretches and folds itself into nearly every domain of life. Like *queer, disability* refers to a colonial construct that is commonly employed by the medical-industrial complex to demarcate racialized thresholds of embodyminded variation. But again like *queer, disability* has been reclaimed by some people as a source and signifier of pride. Disability activism and disability justice movements have worked to usurp the authority of medicine that distinguishes normative instantiations of human difference (we call it "diversity") from abnormal ones (we call it "pathology"). This form of disability critique resembles queer studies' commitment to "resist state regulation" in all its many iterations, especially those that rely on a medical model to valorize the white cis-hetero-ablenormative bodymind.[7]

Indeed, it is in part because of their shared histories of (resisting) pathologization that disability and queerness have been thought together with increasing enthusiasm over the past two decades. Their intersection not only provides a useful site for coalitional organizing—ways of critiquing medical sovereignty on multiple fronts—but also works to destabilize both terms' coherence as independent categories. Abledness and heterosexuality are revealed as mutually reinforcing, thereby rendering disability and queerness as "unstable, distributed, lively."[8] Disability betrays the compulsory abledness entangled with heterosexuality that, in turn, exposes the queerness of disability.[9] To be disabled is to occupy one's bodymind queerly. This reading of disability is most often referred to in the context of crip theory, popularized by Robert McRuer's eponymous book, which politicizes the queerness of disability while also ensuring that disability's queer politics are not reducible to queerness. That is, crip theory contends with disability's nonconformance as resonant but not synonymous with the place of queer in queer studies. While McRuer's work has seen its fair share of critiques,[10] there has been relative consensus on his central observation that, to some degree, disability and queerness are contingent. And while I take no issue with his argument, per se, I am interested in situating it alongside the oft-neglected history of queer/disability's relationship within the purview of medicine and pathology. This is a relationship that far precedes the inventions of queer studies and disability studies, let alone their hybridization, and this project is a testament to the ongoing effects of their intimate histories in both fields. Prior to the institutionalization of disability and queer, I show that the relationship between the two categories was both secured and contested by gay activists' repeated attempts to divest homoeroticism from disability, not out of their concern for medicine's disciplinary function but because they feared disability's apparently intractable stigmas as deficit, deviance, and death.

This fear on behalf of gay activists not only led to missed opportunities for productive coalitions but also, as I argue below, dictated the terms by which queer studies would eventually come to (dis)regard disability. Despite the generativity of crip theory, I contend that there has yet to be sustained attention paid to the effects of homosexuality's pathologization on the figure of disability in queer studies. That is, in spite of the excitement surrounding the critical and political affordances of thinking queer and disability together, this excitement seems to forget that queer and disability have known each other for a long time. When the pathologization of homosexuality is discussed in the field of queer studies, it is almost always done so in the past tense or in the service of tracing negative affect. To talk about the pathologization of homosexuality is to talk about the invention of homosexuality as a social category,[11] to talk about histories of gay activism,[12] to talk comparatively between the history of sexuality and the contemporary medicalization of gender nonconformance,[13] or to talk about legacies of shame, melancholia, and despair.[14] Rarely does queer studies address the ongoing pathologization of homosexuality as it occurs now in conservative and religious circles across the United States, as well as in parts of Southeast Asia, South America, and Africa.[15] And more rarely still does it attempt to reconcile the violently ableist and sanist legacies of gay liberation with their effects on the place of disability in the field of queer studies today—effects that continue to link disability to self-loathing and pain. Among my primary goals with this project is to offer queer silence as a rhetorical methodology for opening up the intersection of queer and disability in light of their historical contingencies, thereby allowing for alternative crip futurities in queer studies that do not deny the violence of pathologization but still hold the field accountable for its dispossession of disability.

I specify queer silence as a rhetorical methodology because it is attentive to the flux of *queer*'s meaning from moment to moment and place to place, as it shifts in tenor and substance, at times demarcating disability more or differently than sexuality. While the field of rhetorical studies has long been associated with argumentation and civic debate, I draw on queer, disability, and feminist approaches that use a wider net to reveal the meaning-making strategies enacted by minoritarian populations to defend themselves against dominant discourses.[16] Typically speaking from a place of simultaneous invisibility and hypervisibility, where their voices are ignored even as their bodies are more intensely scrutinized, these queer, disabled, gender nonconforming, and racialized populations tap into the visual, material, and haptic modalities illuminated by queer silence to make known what would otherwise remain unheard. These nonverbal modalities demand an approach to rhetoric that is less situational than affective and ecological, tracing the "choreography"—to borrow from Erin Manning—of bodyminds as they see, hear, smell, taste, and touch one another, leaving dynamic impressions in real time.[17] Rhetoric, in this sense, is less about the linear exchange of information from a single rhetor to an audience than it is about the production of meaning between and among living, breathing, and moving things and people. I will flesh out the contours of this rhetorical model a bit more later on and extensively in chapter 1, but it suffices to summarize here that the rhetoricity of queer silence lies in its openness to the many forms that *queer*'s meaning might take and to the many itinerancies of its movement.

The organization of this book is roughly chronological. While the body chapters focus on queer silence in the present and recent past, the epilogue looks toward the future. In this introduction, I want to attempt a brief and partial history of silence in gay activism that focuses on the role and figuration of disability vis-à-vis homosexuality and, later, *queer.* In subsequent chapters, the subject of disability flickers in and out of the primary argument, but throughout, the specter of disability haunts this project. The specter of disability might be best understood in terms of a supplementary methodology to rhetoric that, as Julie Avril Minich proposes, attends more closely to the norms and conditions that produce the category of disability than to the fact of disability itself.[18] Sami Schalk, reflecting on Minich's work, explains that disability studies is most generative when it "is not dependent upon defining an object of analysis (no matter how expansive the definition), but rather focuses on the method of analysis instead."[19] To recruit disability as a methodology alongside rhetoric is to dial out from the list of embodyminded conditions typically recognized as disabilities in order to better contextualize the processes by which disability comes to be named and, equally important, to illuminate those bodyminds rendered (non)normative through disability's invention. In this book, disability as methodology allows me to think disability as a technique of *queer*'s incarnation.

Queer silence throws into relief the conceptual entanglement of disability and silence that occurred within multiple gay activist movements from the 1960s through the 1990s, when gays who didn't speak might as well have been mad or dead. The effects of this entanglement seeped into the nascent field of queer theory, and they continue to linger, influencing how the wider field of queer studies overlooks or overdetermines disability's pivotal role in its own formation. In consideration of these ongoing effects, I argue for *queer*'s return to its original pathology, for a circling back to the people, spaces, discourses, and affects that once defined it. This (re)turn effectively calls for queer studies to shift its attention away from legible forms of queerness toward the vast and shifting realms of the illegible, away from what people are saying to what they aren't, away from who is speaking to who is remaining silent, and away from speech entirely toward the ways silence has been signifying all along. Part of this shift in attention requires renegotiating the field's relationship to disability, so as to acknowledge it not only as a parallel line of lived experience or as an intersecting vector of marginalization but also as a necessary condition for *queer*'s own emergence. In calling for queer studies to reconcile with silence, I am thus demanding it also take stock of its own histories of disability, as well as those variations of queerness that themselves seem disabled, broken, inefficient, and incapacitated. This is the realm of queer silence: worlds of uncomfortably *queer,* excessively *queer,* illegibly *queer,* and not quite *queer* enough.

Historicizing Silence

We might begin these interrelated projects by examining two instances when disability figured prominently, though admittedly not favorably, in queer history. Following Christopher Nealon's observation that modern conceptions of queer identity emerged from "a determined struggle to escape the medical-psychological 'inversion' model of homosexuality that was dominant in the United States in the first half of the [twentieth] century," I analyze two examples of gay activists working to extract homosexuality from the realms of illness and disease, ultimately with the hope of categorically distinguishing homosex from disability.[20] While these two examples are not the first or only of their kind, I believe they have been among the more influential on the role of disability (and silence) in the field of queer studies. In both, *disability*'s perceived deviance exceeds *queer*'s power of reclamation, operating "as the trope and embodiment of true physical difference."[21] Silence functions as tolerance or, worse, endorsement for disability's aberrance. Disability, in these instances, is simply too queer, and silence is too suspicious. Disability's pathological stigma is too deeply entrenched, its material-discursive reactions too complex. Disability is crazy. Disability is dying. Disability, unlike homosexuality, cannot be recovered or recuperated. Disability is dangerous company—too dangerous even for sex—and silence leaves a person's allegiances entirely up to the imagination. As a result, in each example, activists use and demand speech to reject disability in favor of a purer, less threatening, more aesthetically pleasing, and more easily intellectualized variation of homosexuality. More than that, these activists rhetorically position the experience of disability against queer sexualities, so that *disability* is not only different from *queer* but also maintains a constitutive tension. Indeed, it is only in the absence of disability, I suggest, that *queer* remains coherent.

In the early 1960s, Frank Kameny, a prominent homophile organizer and president of the Mattachine Society's D.C. chapter, began arguing for the removal of homosexuality from the *Diagnostic and Statistical Manual of Mental Disorders* (*DSM*). Central to Kameny's position was that homosexuality was a perfectly natural variation of human sexuality and thus should never have been categorized as a mental illness.[22] Historian Regina Kunzel notes that this line of argument "became the defining project of the emerging gay rights movement," quickly growing into what seemed "necessary to the political intelligibility of gay people."[23] While the sexological invention of homosexuality in the mid-nineteenth century may have paved the way for a gay subject position, it was the concerted effort to depathologize homosexuality that explicitly politicized this position. The early gay rights movement was convinced that distancing itself from medical authority was necessary in order to become the face of a disenfranchised community, and the primary method used to erect this distance was to deny any and all relationship between homosexuality and disability, especially mental illness.

Perhaps surprisingly, Kameny acknowledged the possibility for solidarity across sexual and disability lines, even as he ultimately refused it. In a 1965 essay for *The Ladder: A Lesbian Review,* he writes:

> There are those who say that the label appended [to homosexuality] really doesn't matter. Let the homosexual be defined as sick, they say, but just get it granted that even if sick, he can function effectively and should therefore be judged only on his individual record and qualifications, and it is that state of being-judged-as-an-individual, regardless of labels, toward which we must work.[24]

Though the perspective espoused in this passage does not include the kind of structural critique typically occasioned by queer/disability coalitional arguments today, it nevertheless avoids juxtaposing homosexuality against the "sick." Kameny goes on, however, to dismiss this position as a "woefully impractical, unrealistic, ivory-tower approach" that is entirely too risky for the future of gay liberation.[25] He explains:

> Homosexuality is looked upon as a psychological question. If it is sickness or disease or illness, it becomes then a mental illness. Properly or improperly, people ARE prejudiced against the mentally ill. Rightly or wrongly, employers will NOT hire them. Morally or immorally, the mentally ill are NOT judged as individuals, but made pariahs. If we allow the label of sickness to stand, we will then have two battles to fight. . . . One such battle is quite enough![26]

Notably, Kameny skirts the question of whether homosexuals should ally themselves with their disabled comrades by focusing instead on the difficulty such a strategy would entail for gay activists. It is much easier, he claims, to punch down—to make an appeal for the liberal inclusion of sane homosexuals by reinforcing the exclusion of disabled people—than it is to punch up by taking neoliberalism to task for demanding consumerism in exchange for subjectivity. "We cannot," he assured, "declare our equality and ask for acceptance and for judgement as whole persons, from a position of sickness."[27]

Kameny's argument was not purely hypothetical. In addition to preaching the efficacy of his position, he insisted that other homosexuals be vocal about their own mental health. This insistence stemmed from Kameny's certainty that homosexuality was not a disability and his belief that any argument for equality required "an affirmative, definitive assertion of health."[28] In fact, Kameny fully admitted that if good evidence were to exist for the pathology of homosexuality that gay people would "have a moral obligation to seek cure," implying that a medical model is the only ethical answer to disability.[29] In the absence of such evidence, Kameny pleaded that the homophile movement collectively and loudly maintain a position of total and absolute able-mindedness: "I feel that for the purposes of strategy, we must say this and say it clearly and with no possible room for equivocation or ambiguity."[30] Equivocation and ambiguity, here, are the products of silence—what happens when people do not "say this and say it clearly." Silence was to risk being further subsumed into disability and toward cure. To speak, however, was to demand acceptance by demonstrating mental fitness.

In 1971, Kameny had the chance to demonstrate this fitness for himself when he attended the annual meeting of the American Psychiatric Association, along with the Gay Liberation Front. To a room full of psychiatrists, he shouted, "We're rejecting you all as our owners. We possess ourselves and we speak for ourselves and we will take care of our own destinies."[31] And come the revised *DSM-II* in 1973, when homosexuality was replaced by "sexual orientation disturbance," his strategy vis-à-vis speech worked: being gay was no longer a mental illness. Homosexuality was formally depathologized, and as historian Douglas C. Baynton points out, "once gays and lesbians were declared not to be disabled, discrimination [against them] became less justifiable."[32]

Approximately fifteen years later, one winter night in 1987, Kameny's insistence on queer speech resurfaced when six gay activists plastered "SILENCE=DEATH" posters across New York City. Against a solid black background, a fuchsia triangle hovers over the words that appear in bold, white letters. Beneath them, in much smaller font, reads:

> Why is Reagan silent about AIDS? What is really going on at the Center for Disease Control, the Federal Drug Administration, and the Vatican? Gays and lesbians are not expendable . . . Use your power . . . Vote . . . Boycott . . . Defend yourselves . . . Turn anger, fear, grief into action.[33]

This poster, which has since become one of the most well-known icons for AIDS Coalition to Unleash Power (ACT UP) and AIDS activism more broadly, revived Kameny's assumption that political activism only works with a united front.

As Avram Finkelstein, one of the creators of the poster, recalls, "SILENCE=DEATH" was intended to be "a conversation starter."[34] Its purpose was not only to hold the government, the medical-industrial complex, and the Church accountable for their failure to respond in an appropriate and timely manner to AIDS but also to "inspire action" among the people who were most at risk of seroconversion. Not unlike Kameny's insistence that homosexuals had an individual responsibility to fight their pathologization, the "SILENCE=DEATH" poster placed similar pressure on people to advocate for themselves or otherwise risk certain death. The silence mentioned in the poster functions as a reminder of institutional violence and state-sponsored neglect, as well as a call to arms. To resist silence, and thus to speak, became an imperative for gay people in particular. If they were going to survive, they had to demand it. Silence, by contrast, was understood as complicity with Reagan, the CDC, the FDA, the Vatican, and—perhaps most importantly—with the virus itself. Silence took on connotations of cowardice, shame, internalized hatred, and unimaginable privilege that afforded some people access to lifesaving drugs while allowing others to go without. For most people, to remain silent was to accept death—whether your own or that of your community. The "SILENCE=DEATH" poster made explicit a binary division between speech and silence that had undergirded queer life for the past several decades. One could not be both silent and alive. To live was to speak.

While the anxieties that surrounded this particular political and cultural moment began to fade by the mid-1990s after HIV had been named, testing protocols had been established, and protease inhibitors had been made more widely available in the United States, there is yet a distinct rhetorical effect of the first wave of the AIDS crisis that remains. Finkelstein refers to this phenomenon as "AIDS 2.0," "its storytelling."[35] Rhetoricians and historians might call AIDS 2.0 a kind of historiography that provides not an objective account of AIDS history (as if such a thing were possible) but rather a carefully crafted, deeply racialized, and markedly ableist narrative about AIDS. This narrative, as Black, transnational, and queer of color scholars point out, rests on "making the Global North the default referential point" and denying the AIDS crises that are ongoing throughout the Global South.[36] AIDS 2.0 celebrates the unmitigated success of single-axis visibility politics, effectively reducing the multiple geographies and temporalities of AIDS activism to a simple teleological arc, wherein white cis men narrowly but victoriously resist death. Finkelstein writes:

> [AIDS 2.0 is] a parable that "proves" the system works in a way so predicated on the presumptive neutrality of whiteness, male physiology, pharmaceutical intellectual property rights, and a deregulation-mad political landscape that it turns its back to the

parts of the pandemic that continue to rage, offering a sense of resolution in its place.[37]

Though the creation of HIV-management biotechnologies is an important part of AIDS history, it is only one part and certainly not the end of the story. As Finkelstein hints, the technical availability of protease inhibitors is not the same as guaranteeing access or education to use them.

AIDS remains a persistent and fatal threat for many populations, some living in the United States, who are Black, poor, incarcerated, disabled, or some combination thereof.[38] Bracketing AIDS as a historical event not only "obscures [its] continued biopoliticization"—the way resources for prevention and treatment are stratified along racial, class, disability, and geographic lines—but also fails to capture the multidimensionality of AIDS's social life.[39] Cindy Patton explains that the crisis of AIDS has never been only about the virus or health care; rather, it has also included "the uneven distribution of rights and relationships (including spiritual), and even the distribution of the idea of 'crisis' itself."[40] These variable and violent distributions mitigate the life chances of already marginalized persons, and the historical framing of AIDS 2.0 purports to neutralize their harm. *AIDS was so last century,* we are meant to believe, despite, as Nishant Shahani writes, "those queer subjects who still inhabit the here and now."[41]

The temporal discontinuities produced by AIDS 2.0's triumphalist account—those that subtend "the here and now" with a vision of AIDS-as-history—embed an overcoming narrative that belies the experiences of people still living with AIDS today. In narratives that include or are about disability, overcoming functions as a trope typically used to bypass structural critiques of ableism for more palatable stories of individual achievement. Rather than attending to the cultural and material obstacles that make life more difficult for people with disabilities, overcoming narratives decontextualize disability as an internal condition that can only be mourned or celebrated, depending on a person's effort and capacity to realign themselves with normative standards of fitness, productivity, and desirability.[42] Those who successfully overcome their disabilities are viewed as inspirations while those who do not are either pitied or made to feel guilty. Within the context of AIDS, the overcoming narrative pits sexual health against HIV positivity, protecting normative (homo)sexuality from the taint of the virus.

In her analysis of safer-sex campaigns launched during the 1980s to combat the transmission of HIV among gay men, Karisa Butler-Wall argues that "ideals of mutual care, affection, and responsibility were marshaled to defend 'the community' against the threat of illness and disability, thereby marginalizing seropositive individuals and coding behaviors that might lead to seroconversion as dangerous and antisocial."[43] Similar to the homophile movement's positioning of homosexuality contra disability in the 1960s and 1970s, these safer-sex campaigns fixed the boundaries of homonormativity at the explicit disavowal of HIV, which threatened to confuse good and responsible homosexuals with the "queers, addicts, and sex workers out of control [who] would infect everyone."[44] And even though more radical queer organizations, such as ACT UP, were vocal about the homophobia implicit in this disavowal, their retorts did more to exceptionalize AIDS as queerly stigmatizing than they did to disrupt the quotidian forms of ableism experienced by many people with disabilities.

For instance, in his vitriolic essay "1,112 and Counting" that helped to catalyze momentum for the fight against AIDS, Larry Kramer cautions that "if we don't get angry" about AIDS, then "something worse will happen" than "the obvious losses" of life.[45] This something, it turns out, is the disability stigma produced when gays are "blamed for AIDS, for this epidemic."[46] More horrifying to Kramer than the growing death toll was the idea that the gay community was "being called [AIDS] perpetrators, through our blood, through our 'promiscuity,' through just being the gay men so much of the rest of the world has learned to hate."[47] I understand Kramer's fear as ultimately about disability because his priority was not caring for people with AIDS or even preventing its further transmission but addressing the alleged shame of contagion, refusing the disgrace that accompanies AIDS. This is a disability stigma: when the infected is blamed for the infection. Indeed, it was Kramer's anxiety over the threat of being disgraced that—in his mind—helped to transform AIDS into the "issue that has, ironically, united our community in a way not heretofore thought possible."[48] Disability—or, rather, its threat—assisted in the production of a queer counterdiscourse surrounding AIDS, a discourse premised on "generat[ing], visibly, numbers, masses"[49] that would later blossom into that mode of "anti-homophobic inquiry" called queer theory.[50] Not unlike how it was previously disowned to preserve homosexuality's intelligibility apart from pathologization, disability was once again cast off to ensure the coherence of a queer constituency against the destructive force of AIDS. In both cases, disability functioned in the negative, generating forms of queer social life out of its constitutive absence. As Lisa Diedrich puts it, "Illness making queer as much as sexuality."[51]

And herein lies the coming together of silence and disability. The compulsion for queer people to speak, to offer what Michel Foucault called "the truthful confession," has long been rooted in the desire to extricate homosexuality from disability.[52] First with regard to pathologization and then again in the context of AIDS, speech—as verbal, visual, material, or embodyminded presence—has repeatedly been used as a rhetorical tactic to safeguard normative homosexuality via its differentiation from sickness, mental illness, and disability more generally. Indeed, the "infinite task of telling" has been the central tool used to remap pathological homosexuals as rational gays and lesbians and, later, as disenfranchised queers.[53] This is the process, as Foucault tells us, of "transforming sex into discourse."[54] Speech has characterized nondisabled queers as agents deserving of their autonomy from the medical-industrial complex and as subjects who were unfairly called "the cause of AIDS."[55] To be clear, I am not arguing that gays should be beholden to a medical model of homosexuality or that AIDS was a legitimate mark of queer (ir)responsibility; instead, I am illuminating how the history of antihomophobic activism has relied on speech to claim liberal personhood in contradistinction to disability's (and disabled people's) objectifying silence.

Even within queer studies, wherein *queer* is invoked to shirk institutionalized forms of recognition, liberalism rears its head by claiming queer—through speech—as a political orientation. Despite its frequent citation as nonidentitarian and thus, allegedly, outside the strictures of liberalism, *queer*'s politics mandate its stability as a category that is made legible by way of speech. That is, *queer* has to be named in order to be recognized, and until an object is recognized as queer, it simply isn't.

Judith Butler predicted this problem early in the field's history when they famously warned that "if the term 'queer' is to be a site of collective contestation . . . it will have to remain that which is, in the present, never fully owned, but always and only redeployed, twisted, queered from a prior usage."[56] Butler knew that any articulation of *queer*—any speech act that identifies *queer* as queer—necessarily demands a degree of shared legibility that risks undermining the term's initial promise to "never be fully anticipated."[57] It would only be through "insurrectionary" uses of the term, those "without prior authorization," they argued, that *queer* would be able to retain its critical edge.[58] Over time, however, insurrection and unauthorization have taken on their own disciplinary lives, working against *queer*'s openness to the "radical democratic contestation" that once defined it.[59]

Queer's institutionalization is perhaps the most pressing problem facing the utility of queer studies today. The field's instinct toward democratization is rubbing up against its own disciplinarity, leaving one to wonder whether *queer* still means (or has ever meant) what it was intended. As Kadji Amin argues, "queer mobility and indefinition function within Queer Studies as both *a disciplinary norm* and *a front*" that allege *queer*'s infinite malleability even as they make evident the field's situatedness within specific historical and cultural contexts.[60] These contexts are not only dominated by whiteness, settler logics, cissexism, and ableism but also hinged, as I argue, on the role of speech to secure a claim to civic life.[61] By "civic," I am referring to the democratizing impulse inherent to any discourse, queer or otherwise, that mandates shared signs or modes of signification. This is the relational role of language: to create a community around a shared symbol system.[62] Even if *queer* is "redeployed, twisted, queered from a prior usage," as Butler insists it must be, it can only be redeployed, twisted, and queered so far—to the extent that it remains decipherable to others. *Queer* is always already named *queer* as such and thus traffics in a liberal, colonial economy, wherein legibility begets autonomy begets self-determination. This variation of "queer liberalism," as coined by David L. Eng, valorizes a select few iterations of rhetorical action, such as speech, as "the mark of presence and inclusion" at the expense of other ways of being and doing that are rooted in silence.[63] Such enthymematic reasoning neglects the multiplicity of meanings that speech might carry, including those that mark absence and exclusion. It also denies the queerness of objects and attachments that cannot be readily absorbed into queer studies' existing theoretical framework.

Queer's politicization relies on its uneven distribution, and it is in the process of distributing—of allowing some objects to become queer while dismissing others—that the field's inherent liberalism is exposed. That *queer* can be stratified, despite its allegedly unshakable commitment to the abject and marginal, suggests that queer studies underestimates the rhetorical effects of normativity, the ways that language is not only a product of power but also its producer. This is the performative work of *queer*: to append an object with queerness is to shape both the object and *queer* itself, delimiting the latter's "future linguistic life"—all other appendages as well as the scope within which they may dissent or reinvent *queer*'s meaning within the jurisdiction of the field.[64] Surely, anyone can stamp queerness onto anything, but that does not, by itself, guarantee a thing is queer. There is the issue of legibility, as I said, which is ultimately an issue of respectability. Who has the power to wield *queer*'s power?

This is a question I return to at length in the epilogue, but the answer has much to do with the critical difference between a marginalized politics and what we might call a politics of marginalization. Whereas the former refers to those people, practices, beliefs, and modes of being *on* the margins, the latter denotes the institutionalization *of* the margins. *Queer* is meant to signify the former—a place of abjection—but queer studies often takes shape as the latter, acclimatizing *queer* to fit the needs of academia's corporate interests in diversity. Heather Love anticipates my concern by accusing queer studies of "fail[ing] to acknowledge the distance queer scholars have climbed up the hierarchy of credibility."[65] This hierarchy refers to the liberalization of *queer* as it enters the academy, as it is thought and theorized, and as its nonnormative impulses are slowly but steadily domesticated in the service of a cohesive discourse. The process of domestication, I argue, is an effect of *queer*'s speechification, its translation into an accessible register that can be conveniently politicized and aestheticized, offering queer scholars their "remarkable ability to combine insider cachet with outsider attitude."[66] Regardless of the fact that queer studies opposes the tenets of liberalism in theory, the field's demand that *queer* be conversant shows that it shares liberalism's rhetorical mechanics.

These are mechanics that secure speech's political power by emptying silence of its own. Silence, unlike speech, cannot name *queer.* Silence cannot call itself or its practitioners *queer.* Silence is discreditable. Silence is absence, and absence is linked to incapacity or refusal and thus to disability or denial: to not speak *queer* because you can't or won't speak *queer.* Certainly, the relationship between silence and disability calls to mind literal disabilities that pertain to the production of speech, but it also emphasizes the figurative imbrication of these terms, what James Berger calls "dys-/disarticulation," which "describes the *problem* of how to imagine an outside to a social-symbolic order conceived as total and totalizing."[67] The rhyming of silence and disability depends on both reading disability as deficit (disarticulate) and disregarding the conditions that make speech accessible, let alone liberatory, for some people and not others (dysarticulate). The interplay here between silence and disability, what we might call "silence=disability," functions as a barometer by which *queer*'s political effects are evaluated. As foregrounded above, queer speech marks progress and pride, whereas silence indicates madness or death. Within queer studies, this binary rubric serves as a structuring grammar for the field. It dictates that the queer subject, though not necessarily nondisabled, must nevertheless be spoken into existence in such a way that elides the dys-/disarticulate, the pathological, and thus the disabled conditions of *queer*'s emergence.

Both silence and disability are rendered virtually unthinkable as objects of sustained queer critique because their absence is foundational to queer studies. How to observe the place of silence or disability in the field when *queer* is itself a spoken repudiation of disability? Where to locate silence in a field measured by speech? Where to find disability in a discourse generated by its invisibilization? Among the aims of this book is to reveal what is omitted or otherwise left unthought in queer studies when we forgo the field's historicity in the contexts of silence and disability. Even as I applaud queer studies' current investment in the contingence of *disability* and *queer*, this book inquires about the degree to which that contingence serves as a theoretical substitution for the more daunting task of reconciling with the field's ongoing dispossession of *disability.* And more specifically, this book explores how that substitution continues to obfuscate or foreclose alternative ways of understanding the two categories' interanimation.

Queer silence is my final methodology, charged by the synergy between disability and rhetoric. By attending to contemporary implications of silence=disability, queer silence takes seriously the rhetorical role of *disability* in *queer*'s history, revealing variations of the *queer/disability* entanglement that exist outside the prevailing "*political horizon*" of queer studies.[68] Queer silence does not deny that queerness and disability are mutually reinforcing, but it does situate *queer/disability*'s present relationship within a genealogy of queer ableism that is predicated on the silencing of disability. Thus the work of queer silence is, in part, to make a crip intervention in the way disability—or, rather, its absence—structures queer studies. Queer silence reverses the original emphasis of McRuer's *Crip Theory* to hasten queer studies' "return to *old* locations, to shameful sites" that are resonant of the field's pathological origin: not *disability*'s queerness but *queer*'s disability.[69] I hope that such a return precipitates the crip reconciliation that queer studies desperately needs, one that joins recent calls for the field to face the history of its own institutionalization.[70] This is a history that in the ongoing process of disavowing disability implicitly fuses it to the infrastructure of the field.

My intentions with this book, though, move beyond the specific relationship between *queer* and *disability* to trace a range of silences as they are strategically performed by a variety of queer populations. I am not suggesting that queer silence is ever not about disability but rather that disability is internal to the methodology of queer silence. *Disability,* here, is like *queer* insofar as both are ways of thinking and knowing—at once irreducible to identity and yet molded by embodyminded experiences. As Merri Lisa Johnson and McRuer write, "disability knowledge—embodied and relational—is *about* disability . . . and extends *beyond* disability."[71] Therefore, the interanimation of silence=disability not only reveals *disability*'s centrality to homosexuality and other minoritized sexual and gender configurations but also exposes the generative capacity of silence to illuminate a broader array of meaning-making forms that are typically dismissed or ignored by queer studies. Indeed, if we can establish *disability* as the bedrock of *queer,* might we not also identify silence as the origin of speech, the wellspring of signification? Rather than reducing silence to the inversion of speech, can we not envision a model that recognizes speech as silence's progeny? Might the queerness of silence lie in its potential to resist its own erasure? To all of these questions, I answer with a resounding *yes*: silence is what makes *queer*'s disability speak.

Reclaiming Silence

My approach to silence in this book is informed by a number of conversations in feminist theory and Black feminism, disability studies, and rhetorical studies that address both literal, aural silences and figurative, metaphoric ones. This range of perspectives not only highlights the raced, disabled, gendered, and sexualized dimensions of silence but also cleaves the concept away from any single disciplinary framework, offering an elastic model that remains adaptable to different contexts. Sometimes I discuss silence in its traditional, verbal form, but I also acknowledge other silences across the sensorium, like visual silences, haptic silences, and embodied silences. For me, *silence* refers simply to the space of rhetorical absence. Given the long-standing prioritization of speech over silence in queer studies and in Western culture more generally, I am drawn to silence's subversive potential, even and perhaps especially when deployed as a metaphor, to throw into relief the range of meaning-making modalities that fill our world. Silence is not merely absence; it's meaningful absence.

Admittedly, this definition exists in stark contrast with how *silence* is usually defined alongside or in opposition to speech. In *Silence, Feminism, Power: Reflections at the Edges of Sound,* Sheena Malhotra and Aimee Carrillo Rowe admit that within "the Western tradition, reiterated from Aristotle to Audre Lorde, . . . silence [is] a site of reform and . . . voice [is] the ultimate goal of and means to achieve empowerment."[72] For marginalized people, this prevailing dichotomy purports speech as the only possible route to agency. People are expected to speak up and speak out to signal their subjectivity or membership to a community, regardless of the consequences they may face for doing so or of the fact that not everyone uses verbal speech to communicate. In the first case, speaking entails a degree of vulnerability that some marginalized folks cannot afford. Coming out, for instance, continues to be risky and often dangerous for many queer and trans people, and doing it on a whim isn't always possible. In the second case, speech has never been humans' only form of communication. Despite the "audiological perspective," as described by Brenda Brueggemann, that "imagin[es] the human world only and always in terms of sound," there are in fact many ways to engage with people that rely on other sensoria, such as with sign languages and facilitated communication.[73] The correlation of speech with power is antithetical to the embodyminded and material conditions that constitute many people's lives, and it does less to support and uplift marginalized populations than it does to enforce colonialist and ableist norms that demand the individualization of a person beholden to a particular group identity prior to recognizing them as fully human.[74]

It is for this reason that Wendy Brown argues that speaking up and speaking out can sometimes edge into virtue signaling, where the occurrence of a speech act matters more than the repercussions from it.[75] "The work of breaking silence can metamorphose into new techniques of domination," she writes. "Our confessions become the norms by which we are regulated."[76] Echoing Foucault, Brown worries that confessional speech acts—such as when Kameny claims a homosexual identity before decrying its inclusion in the *DSM*—evidence not pure liberation but a chimera entwined with surveillance. To come out as a marginalized subject is to accept, at least in part, the categorical terms proffered by an institution. While both Foucault and Brown admit that a degree of confession is necessary to build community around a social identity, Brown problematizes the extent to which "breaking silence" is compulsory for marginalized people. She asks, "amidst this cacophony of expression, confession, coming out, claiming a voice and telling all, where in this cult of the personal . . . can a political space be claimed to break a political silence?"[77] That a silence might be political is itself noteworthy, a departure from the outstanding assumption that all silences are either enforced or complicit with enforcing the silence of others. And to insist on "a political space" for silence, even if it is eventually broken, is to suggest an ethics of silence; it's to acknowledge there may be reasons beyond fear, weakness, or capitulation that a person would choose to be silent. "It would seem," Brown proposes, "that our capacity to be silent in certain venues might be a measure of our desire for freedom."[78] Such a desire is precisely what calls queer silence into being. Though no silence (or speech act) is ever entirely willed into existence independently of the material-discursive forces that constitute both a subject and their positionality, queer silence clings to the potential that absence can do work.

The work of absence signals the capacity—however partial and mediated—of queer silence to reject the compulsion to confess. This rejection extends not only to speech but also to other forms of mandated signification, such as visibility. Similar to the dichotomy between speech and silence, the bifurcation of visibility and invisibility presumes the supremacy of visual presence over the alleged oppressiveness of invisible absence. Jenell Johnson and Krista Kennedy write that "visibility, rhetorical agency, and political action are understood as tightly interlinked," despite the fact that visibility can sometimes "lead to surveillance, doxing, deportation, firing, and even violence or death."[79] Again like the unmitigated celebration of speech, visibility is touted as unilaterally beneficial to marginalized populations, even though the lived experience of being visible can be less than liberating. By attending to the potentialities of rhetorical absence, including invisibility and silence (among other absent sensoria), I am holding space for a variation of what Johnson elsewhere calls "dispublicity," where absence might be understood "not as a personal failing but as a result of the complex meeting of bodyminds and material/discursive environments."[80] This is a coming together of people and their conditions that puts pressure on how terms like *activism, advocacy,* and *politics* are typically envisioned. It is a reconciliation that exposes "entirely new ways of being together" and wholly alternative paths to making meaning.[81] The work of absence, in the end, is the work of invention.

In classical rhetoric, invention is the first of five canons, followed by arrangement, style, memory, and delivery. To invent, rhetorically speaking, is to take stock "in any given case the available means of persuasion," so that a rhetor might assemble an effective speech.[82] Feminist rhetoricians have picked up on the inventive work of absence, noting that "the available means of persuasion" sometimes do not include speech or visibility, particularly for folks whose race, gender, sexuality, or disability make conventional forms of rhetorical action inaccessible.[83] Absence thus becomes a rhetorical strategy, a way of making meaning when the conditions would otherwise render it impossible. Writing specifically about verbal silence, Cheryl Glenn assures that it "is meaningful, even if it is invisible."[84] Despite the fact that the silences of any marginalized group "often goes unremarked upon if noticed at all," there is a potentiality inherent to silence that does not depend on recognition to effect material change.[85] In Glenn's words, "Neither speech nor silence is more successful, communicative, informative, revealing, or concealing than the other. Rhetorical success depends upon the rhetorical situation."[86] The shift in emphasis here from the signifying mode (speech versus silence) to the rhetorical situation (meaning-making context) recalls why rhetoric is relevant to the project of queer silence: the signifying potential of absence does not come to mean on its own but is activated by the commingling of a rhetor and their conditions. Queer silence is a relational project.

By "relational," I mean that no individual rhetorical situation can be separated out—materially, geographically, or temporally—from the collective rhetorical situation that is the evolution of meaning itself. Jenny Rice refers to this relational rhetoricity in terms of "ecologies," where the "the elements of [a] rhetorical situation simply bleed."[87] While rhetorical scholars will sometimes isolate instances of rhetorical exchange for the purpose of analysis, it is nevertheless the case that "bodies carry with them the traces of effects from whole fields of culture and social histories."[88] Rhetorical ecologies thus expand the focus of rhetorical studies to include not only frame-by-frame interactions but also more robustly contextualized discursive flows. "An ecological, or *affective,* rhetorical model," Rice writes, "is one that reads rhetoric both as a process of distributed emergence and as an ongoing circulation process."[89] Meaning is produced in a cycle of exchange where the roles of rhetor and audience are dynamic, in flux, and responsive to their environment. As it pertains to absence, Rice's ecological rhetoric sheds light on how neither silence nor invisibility can be tacitly linked to voicelessness because it is only in situ that either can come to mean at all. Absence, like presence, is contingent.

Consider, for instance, the anecdote with which I open this

chapter about an appointment I had with my conversion therapist, Joe. In our exchange, there are moments of speech and silence, presence and absence, all of which mean something. Regarding my speech, a reader can track my confession: "I'm a man." Joe elicits from me an admission of my designated category, an identity that is intended to smooth over any disjunctures among my sex assigned at birth, gender, and sexual orientation. Joe's intention here is to produce a discourse, in the Foucauldian sense, that muddies the boundary between my material self and my culturally constituted, rhetorical significations. Joe "trace[s] the meeting line of [my] body and [my] soul, following all its meanderings."[90] To be "a man," for Joe, means to be a cis, heterosexual man, and my confession is meant to be the first step toward self-actualizing as such. However, when I am not speaking, not confessing, I am still signifying. My silence during Joe's speech—when he pokes my chest, when he grabs my shoulders—means something too. I argue that my verbal silence in those moments intensifies my embodyminded and material significations: my legs crossed at the knee, my quickened breath, my soft wrists, my growing erection. These physical states take on meaning in that room as they undermine what I articulate verbally, speaking back to Joe's cisheterosexism. While my confessional speech act is certainly part of the rhetorical situation, a broader framework reveals my silence as a gesture toward alternative signifiers that also help constitute the rhetorical ecology.

These alternative signifiers can be mapped by what I call the *rhetorical matrix,* which positions silence—as rhetorical absence—at the center of all meaning making. Once again, *silence* in this framework may refer to a lack of speech, but it could also refer to any absent form of signification (haptic, material, visual, etc.). By defining *silence* broadly, I emphasize the virtual impossibility of arhetoricity. If a thing exists—in the sense that it has taken on an ontological quality, distinguishing it from pure matter—the rhetorical matrix assures that it must mean something in some way. For even if an object is verbally silent, it nevertheless possesses embodied, material, visual, or affective dimensions that also hold the potential to signify. Returning to my experience in conversion therapy, the rhetorical matrix urges any reading of my verbal silence with Joe to be done in tandem with readings of how else I was signifying. My breath, wrists, and dick all also carried signs; they too were meaningful and were made all the more so through my verbal silence. Absence and presence must be considered multimodally, so silence in one mode amplifies the rhetorical presence in others. My verbal silence turned up the volume on my signifying body. Silence within the rhetorical matrix shifts the position of absence from meaning's total negation to its original referent.

Admittedly, the embodied significations I identify above—my limp wrist, for instance—were not intentional. I did not necessarily will them into being. Yet, borrowing from Rice, we can understand my bodymind as participating in a larger ecology of meaning making where my limp wrist comes to mean irrespective of whether or how I intend it. My wrist is a product of my *rhetorical energy,* which is the phrase I use to describe the constellation of signifiers and significations that inform how an object comes to mean. While other scholars in rhetoric have likened rhetoric to energy, noting their parallel forms of sporadic movement,[91] my use of the phrase makes a dramatic departure from how it is customarily understood within the field. My invocation emphasizes the gap between how a person wants something to signify and how it actually does signify to those on the receiving end of the signification(s). Just as sometimes what we mean to say is not what comes out, or how we mean to sound is not how we are heard, so too do any of our significations exist only partially within our control. The meanings associated with my queerness, transness, and disabilities, for example, all contribute to a rhetorical energy that radiates from me. It's a composition of affective discourses that I do not entirely choose but that nevertheless contribute to how I am seen, heard, and understood by others.

In the chapters that follow, I explore how queer people use silence to harness and wield their rhetorical energy. Racialized, gender nonconforming, and disabled populations, as well as those who experience other or multiple forms of subjection, are all layered in meaning that signals their embodyminded departure from a normativity structured by white cisheteroableism. Their rhetorical energy thus speaks for them, regardless of whether they're talking, regardless of whether they intend to mean at all. In the example I offer, I frame my bodymind as a form of resistance to Joe's cisheterosexism, but it is also the case that the embodyminded rhetorical features I celebrate (my crossed legs, soft wrists, hard cock) are the same features that brought me into the precarious space of conversion therapy in the first place. Rhetorical energy is, then, something that spills out of a person not because they want it to but because they exist in a cultural context wherein their bodyminds have taken on what Debra Hawhee describes as a "vivid, weighty, kinetic presence," a discursive heft.[92]

The rhetorical matrix, centering silence as it does, tracks the contours of rhetorical energy's fluctuating intensity and motion across signifying modalities. As Joe and I both oscillate between forms of signification and silence—speech, touch, movement, etc.—the rhetorical matrix charts our interactions as collisions of rhetorical energies. It interprets our modulating significations as the effect of multiple discourses in tension with one another: affective intensities playing out as verbal, visual, and haptic meaning. While Joe and I are consciously engaging each other, rhetorical energy exists well beyond our intentions, and the rhetorical matrix works to capture its unpredictable movement. Queer silence, drawing together the rhetorical matrix and rhetorical energy, recuperates my stutters and whimpers not as mere compliance, and thus the extent of my rhetorical action, but as absences of verbal speech gesturing toward other action, toward the indefatigable resilience of queerness itself.

I recognize that the intervention I am making with queer silence may to some feel like splitting hairs. What, after all, is so impressive or resistant or political about a boy boning up to a man who's yelling at him? "It sounds like," a friend told me after reading an early draft of this introduction, "you just feel bad about not speaking up when you had the chance, like you're looking for a way to excuse the fact that you didn't act." At the risk of seeming pedantic, I'd like to trouble the assumption that queers who are impressive, resistant, or political are the only ones worth thinking about, especially when all these terms are so frequently bound up with forms of speech and visibility that make already marginalized persons more vulnerable. By linking queer silence to a politics, or by noting its potential to be deployed as a form of resistance, I am working to open up the grammar of activism to include the everyday work that some of us do to survive. In Black feminism, this is the work of refusal, of rejecting the face value of your rhetorical energy. Tina Campt writes that "practicing refusal" is "a quotidian practice of refusing the terms of impossibility that define the black subject in the twenty-first-century logic of racial subordination."[93] The "terms of impossibility" refer to the significations layered onto Black people that make life unlivable, and the "practice of refusing" gestures to the role of silence, to the ways of making meaning outside the ones already prescribed. "Refusing the impossibility of black futurity in the contemporary moment demands extremely creative forms of fugitivity," says Campt. "It is as brave an act as looking into the eyes of police officers surrounding you, seeing the certainty of a lifetime of incarceration, and deciding to create an alternate future ('line of flight') than the one they have in store."[94] As one might imagine, deciding to create an alternate future is not as easy as building one; likewise, the power of queer silence lies not in its guarantees but in its potentialities, its maybes. Reading queer silence alongside practices of refusal emphasizes not only the racialization of silence—the ways people of color and Black people in particular are disproportionately silenced and at risk of violence for speaking—but also the queerness of refusal, the fact that saying *no* or nothing at all is often unthinkable.

And yet, queer silence's unthinkability is perhaps what renders it such an effective mode of resistance. It not only rejects conventional signs and signifiers but also destabilizes the very subject position needed for those signs and signifiers to emerge.[95] Queer silence severs the ties between agency and traditional, speech-based forms of activism, echoing Diane Davis's claim that agency is but a "fragile link between rhetorical practice and civic responsibility."[96] Despite rhetoric's long history as an ethical alternative to violence (making speeches is better than going to war, or something like that), Davis argues in *Inessential Solidarity: Rhetoric and Foreigner Relations* that the implicit connection between rhetoric and civic duty overdetermines agency as the precondition for human existence. A more accurate understanding of agency, for her, positions it as the effect of a person's relationality: it's through our solidarity that we grow an agential capacity. Drawing on Emmanuel Levinas, Davis argues that a "responsibility to respond," or our need to recognize another subject as a subject, is what triggers our own subjectification, "rather than the other way around."[97] A person must be relational before they can be considered agential. The fact that a person is in relation, and thus responsible for someone else, makes them into subjects in the first place. "This underivable obligation to respond that is the condition for any ethical action whatsoever," she writes, "amounts to a preoriginary *rhetorical* imperative."[98] This preoriginary rhetoricity is "the condition for symbolic action" because before a person can intentionally signify, before they can claim the agency necessary to make meaning, they first must locate themselves within a social context.[99] Agency is little more than an elaboration of the theory of mind. It is an acknowledgment that one is not the only one, that I am not the only I.

This book builds on Davis's thesis to propose rhetorical energy as a corrective to the idea that agency can only be evidenced by a select few rhetorical modes and modalities (e.g., speech, visibility, etc.). While Davis's preoriginary rhetoricity describes the agency of a given subject in relation, rhetorical energy is akin to a preoriginary rhetoric, contextualizing the stuff of signification prior to its condensation into legible meaning. This suggests that signs, too, only signify in relation. Davis writes, "agency is always already for-the-other: it is not spontaneous or self-determined or heroic but thoroughly rhetorical, responsive, assigned."[100] Rhetorical energy is likewise assigned, operating as an underlying or preoriginary force behind signification. The flow of discourses through my body not only affect how others read me but also constitute me as having a bodymind to be read. Rhetorical energy is the stuff of culture as it swarms around my living matter, instantiating me as a signifying subject.[101] Rhetorical energy is my essence before it is mine.

Situating Silence

In the chapters that follow, queer silence comes alive as the animation of rhetorical energy across the rhetorical matrix. To make silence do work, queer people mobilize their unchosen energy toward acts of resistance, toward ways of surviving and sometimes thriving in spite of the precarious positions, rhetorical and otherwise, that they inhabit. Silence=disability comes into play as a haunting reminder of silence's inherent queerness, of the ways that disability was jettisoned to make room for, first, "homosexuality" and, shortly thereafter, "queer" to emerge as respectable, legible categories. The queerness of silence is thus not an exclusively sexual queerness but a crip one, a mad one, a disabled one that calls attention to the bodyminds living, dying, speaking, and silencing outside the narrow margins of homonormativity.

To begin, the first chapter, "To Speak of Silence," grounds this book with a series of genealogies for its central concepts: queer silence, rhetorical energy, and the rhetorical matrix. Given their interdisciplinarity, chapters 2 through 5 require something of a glossary that provides a shared vocabulary for queer studies, disability studies, and rhetorical studies readerships. Chapter 1 offers just this: a "queer methodology" culled together from multiple fields and critical conversations that "attempts to remain supple enough" to suss out queer silence's roaming and sometimes random appearances.[102] Additionally, chapter 1 addresses the intimacy between rhetorical energy and affect. Though rhetorical energy is affective, I argue through disability studies, mad studies, and queer of color critiques that it is irreducible to affect, at once too deeply embodyminded and too ephemeral. This chapter foreshadows how the remainder of the book will take up rhetorical energy and the rhetorical matrix as guiding heuristics to explain some of the ways queer silence is engaged and deployed.

Chapters 2 through 5 each offer a case study of queer silence, but more importantly, each nuances what silence can be and do. These chapters are not only examples but also building blocks that, when read together, scaffold a more comprehensive picture of silence's queer potentialities. The first of these chapters, "White Squares to Black Boxes," tracks silence as it calls forth other modalities of absence and presence beyond the verbal register. Attending to the work of "blank profiles" on Grindr, a dating app for queer and trans people, I show how rhetorical energy operates through visual and digital media. On the app, users have the option to upload profile pictures that make themselves visible to others, but many racialized, trans, and disabled users choose not to do so, resulting in blank profiles or profiles without identifiable users. I refer to this phenomenon as visual silence, where users attempt to regulate the rhetorical energy of their bodies by making themselves literally invisible. I also introduce rhetorical quieting as a way to illuminate how even invisible queer bodyminds cannot be dequeered. Instead, I argue that blank profiles speak to the resilience of queer materiality, acting as portals through the app and into "real" life.

"Queer(crip) Masquerading," the third chapter, introduces silence to the realm of identity, exposing how a stable notion of queer politics belies the itinerancy and unpredictability of queerness itself. Specifically, I delve into the world of ex-gays—a term adopted by some participants in conversion therapy—who manipulate their rhetorical energy so that their homoerotic desire might be read as a disability. Rather than "praying the gay away," as it is commonly joked about online, ex-gays are encouraged to pathologize themselves as mentally disabled by rehearsing antiquated theories of psychotherapy to elicit the pity generated by disability's rhetorical power within evangelical Christianity. While there is no question that the ex-gay cooptation of disability is troubling for its implicit heterosexism and dependence on medical and moral models of disability—wherein disability is subordinated to the purview of medical and religious establishments—it nevertheless showcases the queer potentiality of silence, its capacity to reshape itself to work within the constraints of a given context. Silence sustains the queerness of ex-gays, harnessing the malleable properties of absence, a queer resistance to its own eradication.

The malleability of absence appears again in the fourth chapter, "Disidentifying Silence," where I explore the temporality of silence and how trans elders, in particular, latch onto it as a way of navigating their transitions. Rooting my argument in Jess T. Dugan and Vanessa Fabbre's photoethnographic project *To Survive on This Shore,* I merge trans studies, trans of color critique, and critical age studies to unveil how popular representations of trans life rely on biological and deterministic models of gender that are often at odds with elder trans folks' experiences. Despite the importance of respecting trans people and the field of trans studies as distinct from queer folks and queer studies, I contend that the marginalization of trans elders within mainstream trans discourse renders them queer. Trans elders often tell stories of transition that are neither linear nor particularly predictable, and these narratives exist in stark contrast to what I call the transnatural model, which frames gender identity as a static characteristic that is inherent to all people. I propose *trans silence* as a way of naming gender variance that exceeds or resists transnormative temporalities. Trans silence exposes not only the deep-seated ageism that structures transnormativity but also the racism and ableism that is inherent to transnaturalism, thereby obfuscating the trajectories of trans of color and disabled trans people's transitions. This chapter ends with a series of speculations on the nexus of trans studies and disability studies, where silence=disability serves as a helpful guide for addressing ongoing conflicts between the fields.

The fifth chapter, "Neuroqueer Intimacies," takes up the purchase of queer silence for cross-movement work. By bringing together Jennifer C. Nash's model of "intimacy" and M. Remi Yergeau's discussion of "neuroqueer," I propose that the collectivities enabled by queer silence are at once avowedly intersectional and acutely suspicious of identity's role in coalitional projects. The indispensability of identity to community formation notwithstanding, queer silence charts alternative routes to world-building that rely less heavily on knowing who you are and more on how you want to live. This chapter offers up three examples of disability performance art, including fashion shows by the Radical Visibility Collective, the ramp-based choreography in DESCENT by Alice Sheppard and Laurel Lawson with Kinetic Light, and an aerobatic performance by Rodney Bell for Sins Invalid, each of which showcases the kind of neuroqueer intimacies afforded by queer silence. These intimacies, though brimming with radical, rhetorical potential, don't always change the world. They don't always look or feel like activism, resistance, or defiance. They aren't always very noisy or even visible. But these intimacies, grounded in a reclamation of silence, plumb absence for its impulse to the otherwise, its tendency toward something new, different, better, and disabled. Neuroqueer intimacies are what happens when we embrace silence as a mode of collective liberation.

In lieu of a summative conclusion, I end the book with an epilogue entitled "Shameful Disattachments and Queer Illegibility" that brings full circle the narrative about my experience in conversion therapy. This time, however, I appear not in a clinical setting but in the sanctuary of a church, where I attempted to kill myself shortly after finishing my treatment. Rather than try to reclaim my suicide attempt or the shame that drove me to it as examples of queer silence, I frame them as exigencies to consider what silence might tell us about the field of queer studies. Despite the fact that the field touts shame among its affective ideals, I show how queer shame's liberatory potential depends on the exclusion of pathological shame, such as my own. Building on Amin's notion of an "attachment genealogy," which seeks to "deidealize" queer studies' prized objects, I propose a disattachment genealogy to reveal how my suicidal shame, as well as *queer*'s other disavowals, have worked to produce and sustain the field's existing attachments.[103] In addition to expanding the scope of queer studies to pursue new affects and objects, it is also worth attending to those that were necessarily discarded in an effort to politicize *queer* in the 1990s and to preserve its coherence for queer studies. Refurbishing and recapacitating *queer*'s prior disavowals may indeed pose challenges to queer studies' methodological consistency, but I suggest that there is value in sacrificing *queer*'s legibility—in admitting that we don't always understand why a thing is queer. Perhaps by opening *queer* up to its own silences, we can begin listening to the people, positionalities, and politics that have until now been forcibly absented.

1

To Speak of Silence

The original title for this book was *Gaydar Theory,* which I had thought to be a wildly clever way of hooking readers into thinking about silence. What better way to escape the conventionally queer connotations of silence as death and disability than to lead readers on with the inside scoop about how queers, fags, punks, butches, dykes, and sissies suss one another out without having to speak a word? While the language of gaydar theory did not last, chiefly because it seemed to bind queer silence to sexual minorities rather than letting it pursue a wider array of deviant attachments, I am still interested in using gaydar as an example of how queer people continue to rely on silence, regardless of its dubious reputation. Among my primary aims with this book is to reorient queer studies to the relationship between silence and queer, so that the first connotations that come to mind are not delimited by the affective attachments produced by gay movements of the mid- to late twentieth century. I want to open up the relationship between silence and *queer* because *silence,* like so many other words, says a lot more than it initially leads on. Depending on the circumstance, silence can indicate power or weakness, resolve or restraint, ignorance or wisdom, anger or empathy, indifference or interest, and resistance or respect, to list just a few. It is through this flexibility that silence gains its rhetorical force, so that when it is paired with *queer* or deployed by queer people—gays picking each other up in the dark—its potential meaning is nearly limitless.

Unfortunately, the openness of silence, its potential to mean, is often prematurely foreclosed by presumptions about its relationship to voicelessness, to limited representation, and to invisibility. As I show in this chapter, some queer and feminist scholars fear that those who are silent must have been silenced; they worry that a lack of speech evidences a lack of agency. Sometimes, these fears are justified: the overwhelming absence of Black and brown people, disabled people, Indigenous and Native people, women, and queer and trans people from positions of political and economic power in the United States suggests that these populations do not have a culturally sanctioned public voice. Such limited representation is both a violence in itself as well as a justification for other violences, whether they be executed through underfunded social services or hypermilitarized police forces, that target marginalized populations, keeping them down, taking their voice, enforcing silence. Among those who occupy multiply marginalized positions, these experiences of oppression, invisibility, and silence are often more prevalent and more harmful. Existing at the margins of the margins entails the threat of rhetorical erasure, leaving people voiceless among the invisible, unheard among the unseen. It is understandable that in these contexts silence carries a bad reputation. No one wants their pain, let alone their existence, to be effaced.

Yet, I contend that there is an important distinction between silence and effacement, just as there is a difference between visibility and equity. I argue that while effacement entails a diminished rhetorical capacity, the rhetorical or meaning-making potential of silence cannot be stamped out. No matter the context behind a given silence—whether willfully deployed or violently enforced—it always signifies something. I posit that this resilience marks silence as a resource or rhetorical opportunity with which some marginalized people resist the very mechanisms by which they are rendered silent in the first place. It is not that I dismiss the disastrous, material damage that silencing has on vulnerable populations, such as the effects that silence had while homosexuality was pathologized or during the early years of the AIDS crisis, but that I recognize and hope to celebrate the ways these populations have turned and continue to turn silence back on itself, appropriating it toward their own survival.

I pay particular attention to the ways queer folks are uniquely attuned to this strategy of resistance, given how our bodyminds signify irrespective of our intention. Importantly, as I explained in the introduction, my definition of *queer* is informed by disability, trans, and queer of color scholars who identify the ways heteronormativity is contingent on dis/ability, gender expression and assignment, race, class, geographic location, and other lines of identity and experience in addition to sexuality.[1] Thus, my attention to queer people throughout this project is less an attention to persons strictly identified as LGBTQ than to the much wider and uneasy category of people who fall outside abled, white cisheteronormativity. I will explain how this definition of *queer* influences my methodology at the end of this chapter, but here I want to emphasize the claim that for queer people, broadly conceived, silence can be an opportunity to enact alternative forms of meaning making that move beyond or beside the verbal register. What I am calling queer silence, then, is not the absence of speech but a gesture toward embodyminded, material, visual, and extralinguistic realms of meaning production. These multiple and varied realms call for a model of signification, of rhetoric, that does not merely juxtapose silence with speech but acknowledges how they exist in tandem, coterminously.

In my first attempt to think through this coterminous model, I referred to it as a speech–silence continuum to demonstrate the simultaneity of silence and signification and to explain how a person might be both silent and speaking through nonverbal rhetorical forms (Figure 1).[2] In this model, a black, double-sided arrow stretches horizontally with the phrase "Rhetorical Signification" running along its side. Near the top arrow reads "Speech," and near the bottom arrow reads "Silence." Over time, however, I've realized that the visual image of a continuum reasserts speech's dominance over other modes of meaning making, suggesting that all signification must blossom out of silence and into verbal speech. I am more confident in a modified version of the continuum model that I call the *rhetorical matrix,* which still insists on the necessary role of silence in rhetorical theory, but it resituates other forms of signification (e.g., embodyminded, material, visual, etc.) so they are not defined in relation to verbal speech alone. While I had tried to divest both speech and silence from verbal rhetoric with the continuum model, the rhetorical matrix more clearly positions silence in the middle of the many forms and modes that signification might occupy, equidistant from all possible routes to meaning making (Figure 2). In this model, the phrase "Signifying Modalities" appears

FIGURE 1. Speech–silence continuum model. Created by J. Logan Smilges.

Signifying Modalities
Verbal
Yet Unimagined
Embodyminded
Silence
Visual
Material
Digital

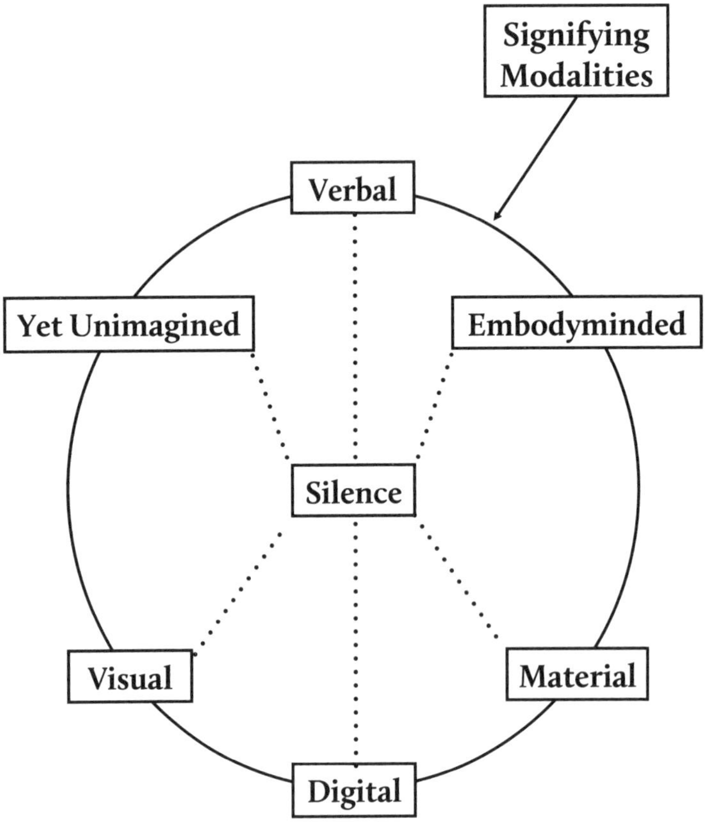

FIGURE 2. Rhetorical matrix model. Created by J. Logan Smilges.

within the outline of a black box with an arrow pointed toward the outline of a black circle. Six words, each encased by the outline of their own black box, line the edge of the circle: "Verbal," "Embodyminded," "Material," "Digital," "Visual," and "Yet Unimagined." From each of the words, a dotted line extends toward the center of the circle where the word "Silence" appears in a box. This new framework not only more clearly articulates the variety of potential signifying modalities but also visually represents them in a way that does not privilege orality over, say, haptic signification. The rhetorical matrix highlights the pervasiveness of rhetoric, revealing the conditions of possibility for the emergence of any signification. It testifies to that well-worn phrase of first-year writing instructors that "rhetoric is everywhere."

For queer people, the rhetorical matrix illuminates the sheer intensity of our significations. It reveals what I call *rhetorical energy,* or the flow of discourses that move around, through, and among queers. These discourses, circulating in a kind of feedback loop, both constitute and are constituted by queer bodyminds. Rhetorical energy is unpredictable and dynamic, and its intimacy with queers produces something akin to what Jonathan Buehl calls a "rhetorical assembly," an "emerging form that temporarily fixes a diverse range of relations among concepts, institutions, symbol systems, and media."[3] Recognizing that queer people often signify beyond any formal disclosure of an identity or any intentional speech act, rhetorical energy captures the meaning that spills out of us. It is an acknowledgment that many of us live in social, political, religious, and cultural contexts where our mere existence is a powerful rhetorical force. Our survival (not to mention death) exudes an aura of signification that—transferred from the white supremacist, cisheteropatriarchal, ableist discourses shuttling around and through us—radiates outward as a queer resistance to the governments, institutions, organizations, and individuals who render us silent. Rhetorical energy, as the matrix model reveals, is a striking, unwieldy, sometimes terrifying intensity that, not bound to any particular mode of signification, sweeps across them all. Like a discursive hurricane, it storms through space, time, and matter, swirling around the queer people who stand at the center of the eye. It is affective inasmuch as it signifies without or perhaps in spite of any single rhetorical purpose or message. Rhetorical energy means a lot to everyone but no one thing to anyone. It is the potential for meaning itself, the seedling of all signification.

The rest of this first chapter teases out the intricacies of both the rhetorical matrix and rhetorical energy. Working together to illuminate queer silence, the two concepts drive the import of the remaining chapters in this book, and it is only through their interanimation that *Queer Silence* can execute the argument I intend to make. While each concept is valuable on its own, in my mind they predict each other: two separate concepts that synergize to reveal queer silence. For reasons of clarity, I elaborate on each one individually before bringing them together in the final section of this chapter. First, I begin with a genealogy of the rhetorical matrix in feminist theory, feminist rhetorics, and queer rhetorics. Given that the intervention this book seeks to make is in queer studies, I introduce rhetorical scholarship to offer a working vocabulary of rhetorical terms, such as *signification, modality,* and even *rhetoric,* that inform my analyses in later chapters. In the second section, I situate rhetorical energy on the border between rhetoric and affect theory, using disability studies, mad studies, and queer of color critiques to demarcate space between the two fields. As it did in the introduction, disability helps to transition the focus of this project from abstracted theories of signification to the material conditions of signifying bodyminds. In the final section, I extend the conversation on embodymindedness to the particular queer people and variations of *queer* that are at the center of *Queer Silence,* including those that escape the confines of queer studies and bridge the neighboring fields of trans studies and disability studies. These bridges are meant not to reassert the infinite mobility of *queer,* which risks othering transness and disability as the ne plus ultra of nonnormativity, but to instead draw on the insights of trans and disability scholars who attend to the fleshy realities of those who are silent. It is a turn toward the materiality of silence that rejoins rhetorical energy with the rhetorical matrix and that transitions to the remaining body chapters, each of which examines one or more instances of queer silence at work.

Rhetorics of Silence

Some fifty years ago, Jacques Derrida concluded that silence is at the foundation of all signification, that it "bears and haunts" meaning.[4] Nine years after him, Michel Foucault elaborated, arguing that "there is not one but many silences . . . that underlie and permeate discourses."[5] These two premises—there are multiple silences that, together, undergird signification—are where my own theorization of silence begins. As I explain above, silence is meaningful, even if it does require a different analytic than speech. While Western philosophers since Aristotle have recognized silence as a part of the human experience, few have regarded it as anything but the leftovers from or precursor to language. Even among those scholars who have credited silence as something substantive, such as Derrida, it has been in the service of exalting speech's emergence.[6] Foucault perhaps comes the closest to my own perspective when he acknowledges that silence "functions alongside the things said," though even he attends more closely to spoken, rather than unspoken, rhetorical strategies.[7] The most attentive and careful considerations of silence have come more recently from queer and feminist scholars who note the fundamental role silence plays in the lives of many marginalized people. Feminist rhetoricians Cheryl Glenn and Krista Ratcliffe, for instance, have spearheaded new conversations that challenge "the marginalized status of silence" and argue that it is "as important to rhetoric and composition studies as the traditionally emphasized arts of reading, writing, and speaking."[8] Glenn's scholarship, in particular, has pushed silence into the center of rhetorical studies, refusing to let it—along with the marginalized groups who use and experience silence regularly—remain outside the purview of the field.

In *Unspoken: A Rhetoric of Silence,* Glenn frames silence as "an absence with a function," arguing that it cannot be read as simply the lack of speech, for it is only in contrast with silence that speech can be understood in the first place.[9] As Glenn puts it, "Speech and silence depend upon each other: behind all speech is silence, and silence surrounds all speech."[10] When we speak, we are not uttering a single, uninterrupted chain of sound but are always relying on moments of silence to divide our words, express emotion, and convey attention or deference to other people. Silence is substance, an act that can work alongside speech or entirely alone, conveying its own messages. "In much the same way we inhabit spoken discourse," Glenn writes, "we inhabit silence: in a kaleidoscopic variety of rhetorical situations."[11] Silence is every bit as powerful as speech, offering people a host of strategies for rhetorical action.

One fascinating feature of silence for Glenn is that it is complexly intertwined with issues of agency, subjectivity, and intentionality. She writes, “The question is not whether speech or silence is better, more effective, more appropriate. Instead, the question is whether our use of silence is our choice (whether conscious or unconscious) or that of someone else.”[12] Glenn specifically considers the ways that silence is both gendered and racialized, used by dominant groups to maintain their power and subordinate groups to resist that power. She identifies a variety of ways that both the ruling class and marginalized populations have deployed silence, emphasizing that it is never “simply passivity” but that it can also be used to achieve as many ends as speech, whether they be dominant and oppressive or “resistant and creative.”[13] In sum, Glenn conceives of silence as a space of possibility, an untapped reservoir of energy, that beckons attention as a rhetorical art.

In his review essay of *Unspoken,* Victor Vitanza latches onto the notion of possibility and potential, writing that the book “lies not in the past, but lies in the future.”[14] He frames Glenn’s model of rhetorical silence as a call, a promise, for other rhetorics of silence. He praises the text but determines that it “is on the way . . . leaving the future open for still more revisions,” that it “de/monstrates responsibility for an other rhetoric.”[15] This positioning of *Unspoken* not as the seminal work on rhetorical silence but as the exigence for further work explains the explosion of scholarship on the topic since the piece’s publication. In addition to Ratcliffe’s work on rhetorical listening, scholars from a variety of disciplines have expanded on Glenn’s ideas, thinking about how silence is used in their own fields. Some of them have even noted the relevance of silence to queer issues, introducing sexual/ized silences in addition to Glenn’s gendered and racialized ones.

Thinking about the dimensions of silence in lesbian culture, Lynne Huffer, in *Are the Lips a Grave? A Queer Feminist on the Ethics of Sex,* likens silence to lesbianism itself. “To speak about lesbianism,” she writes, “is to speak about silence.”[16] For her, lesbians are akin to silence because of a “queer feminist, postidentitarian landscape” where claiming the category of “lesbian” has fallen out of favor.[17] Following an analysis of French author Colette’s reading of lesbianism in Proust, Huffer concludes that what we take to be queers’ silence may simply be our own failure to hear queer people. As she puts it, “those who speak from the place of the other are, in fact, not silent at all, but unheard.”[18] Like Glenn, Huffer distinguishes silence from empty absence, arguing instead that silence is produced by an unwillingness to engage. She writes, "The category of the unread, the unheard, the illegible is not the static result of a finite movement of reading or hearing"—that is, absence—"but the perpetually produced fallout of obliterating interpretive acts."[19] Queer silence does not always indicate an absence of rhetorical action but may instead point to the existence of signifying acts that go unattended again and again. By acknowledging the rhetorical dimensions of silence and what is perceived as silent, Huffer predicts a recuperative turn in queer feminist studies: "the restoration of a fissured ground whose promise is a different history."[20]

Taking up this call for recuperative projects, Sheena Malhotra and Aimee Carrillo Rowe's collection *Silence, Feminism, Power: Reflections at the Edges of Sound* captures "a host of silent practices."[21] In their introduction, Malhotra and Carrillo Rowe draw together feminist considerations of silence from a variety of fields, concluding that silence can be both "repressive" and "resistive" but that, ultimately, the difference between the two kinds is less important than the efforts we make to "develop an authentic listening to silence."[22] Much like Huffer's plea to heed lesbian silences, Malhotra and Carrillo Rowe urge us to "consider how feminists (white and of color) deploy, rewrite, and move through silences in multiple and often productive ways."[23] They insist that while different silences may resemble one another, they are "inscribed through diverse tones and textures," calling forth multiple perspectives on what exists "at the edges of sound."[24] It is indeed this gesture toward multiplicity, echoed by Vitanza's comment that "there are other notions of the unspoken," that invites the intervention I make with *Queer Silence*.[25]

One common characteristic that links together Huffer's, Malhotra and Carrillo Rowe's, and Glenn's works is that silence is characterized as an alternative to speech. Though Glenn situates silence and speech "in a reciprocal rather than an oppositional relationship," this reciprocity presupposes that the two are dyadic, that they establish each other by way of their dichotomy.[26] In other words, most of the existing scholarship on silence assumes that if one is not speaking, they are silent, and that if one is not silent, they are speaking. This dichotomy serves as something of a counterintuitive foundation for me to explore the roles silence plays in visual, material, and embodyminded rhetorical action, where silence might be understood as speech's multimodal excess. Nishant Shahani argues that the oppositional relationship between speech and silence produces a chiasmus where not only does the existence of speech imply the existence of silence but also vice versa: the existence of silence prefigures speech.[27] Conceived multimodally, the presence of silence—or any absence—implies the simultaneous presence of other rhetorical signification. This is especially true for queer people, whose verbal silence often emphasizes our nonverbal significations. Just as Paula Treichler deems AIDS an "epidemic of signification," queer rhetoricians point out that queers are themselves heavily signified, carrying the contradictory connotations of sickness, dirtiness, and immorality, as well as freedom, pride, and love.[28] *Queer,* in this sense, speaks all on its own.

In "Queer Rhetoric and the Pleasures of the Archive," Jonathan Alexander and Jacqueline Rhodes make use of the queer bodymind's rhetoricity, pairing it with the forms of activism used by organizations like ACT UP and the Lesbian Avengers to offer a model for queer rhetoric. For Alexander and Rhodes, queer rhetoric "articulate[s] resistance to regimes of sexualized normalization" by "disrupt[ing] and rerout[ing] . . . discursive power."[29] For them, queer rhetoric combats heteronormativity by subverting it, upsetting it. It is a rhetoric that appropriates combative, masculinist discursive practices as strategies of resistance. One example that Alexander and Rhodes offer is recorded in *The Lesbian Avengers Eat Fire, Too,* a documentary about the origins of the queer feminist organization, when a few of the Lesbian Avengers eat fire to call for solidarity and promote visibility among lesbian feminists. Alexander and Rhodes write that fire-eating "insist[ed] on queer speech, while overturning the sexist notion that women are necessarily nurturing and thus not interested in revenge or vengeance."[30] To eat fire was to enact queer rhetoric because it countered and disrupted expectations on multiple levels. It privileged an embodied performance over verbal articulation and framed the participating women as strong, powerful individuals who could "resist the fear of being 'consumed' by others' hatred."[31] Their rhetorical power emanated from and was swallowed back into their bodies; they were at once consuming fire and being fire themselves.

Dan Brouwer identifies another example of such embodied queer rhetorical action in the prevalence of HIV/AIDS tattoos throughout the 1980s and 1990s. In "The Precarious Visibility Politics of Self-Stigmatization: The Case of HIV/AIDS Tattoos," Brouwer focuses on "self-stigmatization—or the conscious and willful marking of oneself as 'tainted'—as a particular communicative and performative strategy grounded in visibility politics," centering his analysis on the tattoos that people wore to display their serostatus.[32] Ranging from solid black plus signs on their shoulders to pink triangles on their chests to "Silence=Death" on their forearms, the tattoos were used by many gay people as "counter-texts" that "emphasized the vitality, the communion . . . , and the publicness of people with HIV/AIDS."[33] The tattoos were a way of making the HIV-positive body visible so its rhetorical power would be amplified. The tattoos served to draw attention to the HIV-positive body, like fire-eating, to counter the discourses surrounding both homosexuality and HIV/AIDS that aimed to shame and silence gay people. Brouwer notes that these counterdiscourses were an "assertive reminder" of the presence of HIV-positive people and thus encouraged both gay and straight individuals to educate themselves on HIV/AIDS and the gay population more generally. In this sense, the tattoos manifested themselves on the HIV-positive people not merely as messages but as intensifiers of the embodied signification already present and as catalysts for future rhetorical action.

Taken together, these approaches to queer rhetoric reveal the tremendous rhetorical power bundled up in queer people. It is a power of embodied potential that often manifests itself visually, seeping up or settling down onto the skin. It is a rhetoric that captures, as Alexander and Rhodes write, "the fullness of being, in all of its outrageous drives, desires, kinks, and embodied possibilities."[34] However, embedded in this model of queer rhetorics—indeed, at its very foundation—is the assumption that only visible and visibly queer bodies can signify. They presume that only identifiably queer bodies can speak. But what of those bodies who did not join ACT UP or the Lesbian Avengers? What of those bodies who did not reveal their serostatuses with tattoos? What of those bodies whose queerness is a by-product of their sexual or gender illegibility? What of those bodies whose queerness is produced not necessarily by their orientation toward particular sexual objects but by their racialized or disabled incapacity to approximate white cisheteronormativity?

It is in response to these questions that the necessity for a nonbinary model of speech/silence becomes clearer. For if we can acknowledge the multimodal array of significations that queer rhetorics reveal (e.g., embodyminded, visual, material, etc.), we must be prepared to acknowledge their attendant silences as well. That is, if we can imagine verbal silence, we must also be able to imagine embodyminded silence, visual silence, and material silence—all of which can exist independently of one another. Indeed, it reasons that if one form of signification is silent, another is emanating significations at full capacity. Pairing feminist approaches to silence with queer readings of nonverbal rhetorics makes evident that speech and verbal silence are not dichotomous; they do not demarcate the boundaries of meaning and nonmeaning. They are but two options in a sea of signifying potentials. A jointly queer–feminist rhetorical approach sketches out a theory that centers silence, celebrates nonverbal significations, and opens queer studies to new forms of meaning making. This is a theory of the rhetorical matrix that calls forth, calls forward, and beckons toward rhetorics yet unimagined.

From Matrixes to Energies

Underpinning these rhetorics is rhetorical energy, the phrase I use to describe the signifying aura that surrounds marginalized people. Queer people, especially, experience the weight of rhetorical energy in contexts where the sheer number of discourses informing our collective and individual existences are too many to count. Rhetorical energy is a way of conceptualizing how these discourses interact with material bodies and how signification can precede or exist independently of any given person's intentions to signify. The quality of being rhetorical, as the matrix model reveals, is not so much about whether one wants to signify but about how they do anyway. Rhetoricity often just is. Moreover, the kind of signification entailed by rhetorical energy is not legible in the way in which rhetorical theory is accustomed. As was the case in the anecdote I offered in the introduction about my experience with conversion therapy, rhetorical energy is not definable, transcribable, or narratological; you can't pin or pen it down. The power of rhetorical energy is in its unpredictability, its versatility, and its dynamism. The rhetorical matrix holds space for rhetorical energy because, unlike classical models of rhetoric, the matrix is less interested in the intelligibility of a particular sign than in the simple presence of meaning. I use "meaning" here similar to how Joddy Murray defines *nondiscursive rhetoric*: as that which can "escape the confines of any single medium."[35] Rhetorical energy does not signify like a book or a song that can be read or listened to, but it does mean insofar as it produces rhetorical effects.

In *Non-discursive Rhetoric: Image and Affect in Multimodal Composition,* Murray voices concern that nondiscursive rhetorics have been "largely eclipsed by a strong bias toward alphacentric, or word-based, discursive symbol systems," and thus rhetorical scholarship has failed to engage forms of signification that are not easily reducible to letters on a page.[36] For Murray, nondiscursive rhetorics include "all of the sensual ways" that meaning can be expressed, and he acknowledges that often these ways are unconcerned with delivering a decipherable message to an audience.[37] Instead, nondiscursive texts are "built on layers of unuttered and at times unutterable, meaning and affectivity."[38] The nondiscursive, then, is a realm wherein rhetoric can be sensed, even if it cannot necessarily be understood. Rhetorical energy exists in a similar realm because it, too, resists any straightforward decoding. Like the nondiscursive, rhetorical energy is most easily explained in terms of affect, as a kind of impression that resists any single interpretation. It is not that rhetorical energy cannot be understood or even that it cannot carry legible signification but that its decipherability and effects are contingent on context.

My own rhetorical energy, for instance, varies considerably from when I am teaching a graduate seminar about queer rhetorics on campus to when I am working out at a boxing gym downtown to when I am on the streets protesting. Since the discourses surrounding my queer sexuality, my trans nonbinary embodiment, my disabilities, and my whiteness are radically different in each case, we can expect the reception of my rhetorical energy to be different as well. Factors including race, gender, class, geography, disability, and sexuality all play into rhetorical energy, just as they would in conventional rhetorical analysis, but they do not come to signify in an articulable way. Rhetorical energy is too indeterminable to be generalized beyond any single experience in a single moment. As soon as you try to piece it apart, it's already gone.

In this respect, it is helpful to think about rhetorical energy alongside affect theory by scholars such as Brian Massumi, Jonathan Flatley, and Teresa Brennan, despite the fact that it ultimately departs from this body of work. As Chris Ingraham points out, "Rhetorical energy is paramount to affectability precisely because the dynamism at play in becoming differently affectable is so active and multilateral."[39] Even though Ingraham's understanding of rhetorical energy—perhaps better described as the energy of rhetoric—is different from my own, I agree with him that rhetorical studies would do well to acknowledge the rhetorical dimensions of people's "prior *affectability.*"[40] It is not only that people are affective but that our affectivity is at the core of our signifying potential.

Affect, as distinct from emotion, can be understood as impression or being impressed upon.[41] It's a feeling or sense that is not nameable or fully graspable. Affect is "real, material, but incorporeal," as Massumi puts it.[42] In *Parables for the Virtual,* Massumi equates affect with "intensity," arguing that so long as intensity remains abstract or "virtual," then affect provides bodies with an unbridled potential to signify.[43] So long as affect is not reduced to emotion (e.g., intensity→sadness), then it maintains its meaning-making power. Affect is nondiscursive in that it resists not only verbal legibility but all legibility. "In the instant of the affective hit," Massumi explains elsewhere, "there is no content yet. All there is is the affective quality, coinciding with the feeling of the interruption."[44] This interruption is the impression or intensity one faces in an affective encounter. It is a moment of suspended feeling, or when feeling is itself suspended—frozen on the surface of the skin before consolidating into a recognizable emotion, thought, or memory.

The conceptual purchase of affect, for me, lies in this moment of indeterminability, what Massumi calls the "autonomy of affect," which can be measured by "the degree to which [affect] escapes confinement in the particular body whose vitality, or potential for interaction, it is."[45] In other words, the importance of affect is in its potential, in its liminality, and in its contingency. It is a signifying medium that, much like *queer,* is useful only if it remains untamable. And its use value, again like *queer,* lies in the tension between its presence and absence, its tangibility and intangibility, as well as its here-and-now-ness and far-off-and-away-ness. Affect's power is in its slippage: "It is the edge of virtual, where it leaks into actual, that counts. For that seeping edge is where potential, actually, is found."[46] Rhetorical energy is affective because of that same seeping edge, the one at the cusp of embodyminded and immaterial rhetorics, where the flux of discourses streams right through the body and into the virtual. This virtual space hovers over and haunts bodies, a string of significations swirling around our heads. Our rhetorical energy gushes forth with us stumbling after it, leaving affective remnants behind for someone else, with their own signifying halo, to trip over and feel flow through them, an intensity on its way out.

Coincidentally, the image of a person tripping over affect is in line with what I imagine to be rhetorical energy's most rhetorical feature: its potential to interact with others' energies. Flatley, in *Affective Mapping: Melancholia and the Politics of Modernism,* describes affect with this same potential in mind: "Where *emotion* suggests something that happens inside and tends toward outward expression, *affect* indicates something relational and transformative."[47] The relational capacity of rhetorical energy lies in the commingling of discourses when people are in proximity to one another. Aside from any verbal, discursive exchange, there also exists an interaction of discourses at the level of the virtual or the "real but abstract."[48] When two or more bodies come into contact with each other, their rhetorical energies collide—all of the nondiscursive rhetorics come smashing together. In these moments, we experience a series of affective intensities that do not register consciously but still inform the way we see the world. Stereotypes, stigmas, biases, unspoken opinions, and attitudes toward other people, places, objects, and ideas can be confirmed or interrogated. The virtual exchange between individuals is necessarily as important to consider as any verbal dialogue. Rhetorical energy captures the unspoken conversations that occur subconsciously, the effects of semi-autonomous, affective significations. When two people meet—or pass casually on the street or swipe across a dating profile—their energies are inevitably altered, perhaps significantly, perhaps not. But in all interactions, we are changed.

In thinking about the sociability of rhetorical energy, I am taken by Brennan's "transmission of affect" that maps the trajectory of affect from being "social in origin" to "biological and physical in effect."[49] This trajectory brings into relief both affect's relational dimensions as well as its individual, material implications. Even as affect is experienced socially, between and among us, its effects are deeply personal and embodyminded. How my affect alters you may be very different from how your affect alters me, despite the fact that our unique alterations are produced from the same interaction. Brennan calls this individuated transmission "the line of the heart," a kind of "horizontal line of transmission" that is reminiscent of genetic inheritance.[50] Just as parents pass on biological traits to their offspring, so too do each of us fundamentally change one another's biologies with each interaction, each affective transmission.[51] Brennan is not speaking metaphorically. For her, affect is life itself unmoored from the symbols we typically use to encode our bodyminds, such as sociopolitical identities, medical diagnoses, or institutional labels. By moving away from "the different alphabets of the flesh," we can begin to sense a fuller range of embodyminded relations.[52] "Symbolization is the means for transformation," she writes, "as the process whereby energy is locked up in an alphabet in which it cannot speak . . . is released back into the flow of life by words, or by the strange chemistry of tears."[53] In other words, the language of affect is a kind of antilanguage that attempts to name what is necessarily unnamable about the movement and transformation of our flesh.

Rhetorical energy bares stark resemblances to Brennan's work. Like the transmission of affect, rhetorical energy is both social and biological. It is inarticulable and fleshy. Its effects are unpredictable. But unlike Brennan's affect, or Flatley's, or Massumi's, rhetorical energy is not outside of language, discourse, or signification. Rather, rhetorical energy is better understood as multiply discursive, containing more than one fleshy alphabet at any given time. Rhetorical energy is inarticulable not because it has no symbols or signifiers but because it has too many that are flowing too quickly in and out of too many bodies.

Rhetorical energy names not "the line of the heart," contra Brennan, but the lines of many hearts. It is the coming together of every body in every interaction; the rhetorical situation infinitely expanded—all of the universe a stage, all of us its rhetors. Every meet-cute enough to explode the discourses that inform our being in the world.

The distinctions I draw between rhetorical energy and affect are informed by disability studies, mad studies, and queer of color critiques that insist that affect's mobility and virtuality belie the situatedness of affect theory itself. Jasper J. Verlinden argues that the sociality of affect, in particular, illustrates that "the materiality and the historical conditions of emergence of the technologies that shape our understanding of affect must matter as well."[54] To imagine affect as social without attending to its technologies or conditions is to necessarily disregard our own subject positions as the people responsible for naming, studying, and thus normativizing affect. Verlinden points out that affect theory routinely invokes neuroscientific claims about the normative functioning of human brains in order to "demarcate the limits of how affect *normally* works," despite "the sanist and ableist histories of the neurotechnologies that enable and delimit the conditions for the productions of scientific knowledge about the brain in the first place."[55] Affect theory's investment in nondiscursivity glosses the field's genealogy of discursive practices meant to domesticate queer affects. The process of domestication includes not only identifying aberrant affects but also implicitly endorsing state-sponsored technologies of pathologization and incarceration. As Rachel Gorman argues, domesticating affect rests on positioning madness "at the horizon of whiteness," as the threshold between rational white subjectivity and racialized emotional chaos.[56] The people most likely to incur penalties for their affectivities are disabled, mad, racialized, or some combination thereof, and the assignation of each penalty rhetorically "relocate[s] white supremacist affect in the affected communities."[57]

Returning their focus to the field of affect theory, Tanja Aho, Liat Ben-Moshe, and Leon J. Hilton explain that "historical processes of racialization, settler colonialism, and heteronormative able-nationalism," which inform the carceral violences used to discipline nonconforming affects, also structure neuroscientific technologies. These technologies, laced with white cisheteroableism, feed affect theory—if not by direct citation then by implicit assumptions about how brains function.[58] Despite affect's celebrated virtuality, the concept of affect itself is indebted to deeply oppressive schools of thought and forms of genocidal violence. Similar to the way *queer*'s touted mobility tends to disguise its own affective attachments—something I address in the epilogue of this book—*affect,* too, promises a degree of versatility or conceptual flexibility that neglects to account for its own history and ideological inheritances.

Rhetorical energy is meant to fill this gap between affect's virtual sociality and its material effects, acknowledging that affect doesn't affect everyone in the same ways. Rhetorical energy is denser around queer people for the very reason that we deviate from the norm; affect hits different when you are different. The violence that attends nonconformance—in all its many variations and raced, gendered, disabled, classed, and sexed manifestations—is often occasioned by the mere existence of a queer person occupying the wrong space at the wrong time. This is an affective problem in that queer people don't have to do anything to incur violence against us; we just have to be and let our rhetorical energies do the talking. Attending to rhetorical energy helps to map out the multiple and conflicting discourses that beget violence, along with other kinds of interactions among queer people and between queers and normative others, tracking discourses as they radiate off our bodyminds and mingle with the energies of people around us.

Rhetorical energy also opens up the grammar of affect to better capture queer people's unique affectivities and orientations to affect. I am thinking especially of mad, neurodivergent, and otherwise disabled people whose perceptions of sensation and stimuli can differ dramatically from nondisabled folks. Anand Prahlad, for instance, writes at length about his experiences as an autistic person with synesthesia. He not only treasures close intimacies with people and objects based on their combination of sounds, textures, smells, flavors, and colors but also feels an uncanny alertness to the liveliness of rhetorical energy in the world around him. His skin "crackl[es] like a loose electric wire," allowing him to "see by touching the skirts of objects," to feel people's "temperatures," and to smell and taste "their scents."[59] Though his synesthetic sensitivities can leave him feeling "overwhelmed. Overstimulated. Frustrated. Out of control," they also prime him to discern forms of "beauty, order, sense, meaning, joy, and reason" that are imperceptible to most neurotypical people.[60] Prahlad is attuned to modes of relation and communion that resonate with what we've come to call affect, even as they contest the rigidity of an affective syntax predicated on the excision of meaning from nonmeaning, feeling from emotion, and abstract from real.[61]

Through my own experiences of disability, I've found that these uncompromising divisions are further disputed in the context of pleasure. While sensory overload makes it challenging for me to occupy loud, humid, and crowded spaces, I take tremendous gratification in low-stim activities that abled people do not always register, let alone appreciate, as activities. Receiving a kiss on the forehead and tracing the wet impression it leaves on my skin. Tilting my pelvis back and forth on the exercise ball I use as a desk chair. Hearing the sound of my own baritone voice as I sing the theme song to *Golden Girls* each night before bed. These small delights and joyful rituals are rendered meaningful by my disabilities, which have trained my bodymind to take in more of the world at a time, to feel more of its pressure and smell more of its breath, to notice how the tones from my throat or weight of my muscles soothe the cacophonic vibrations rolling across our dying planet. What I'm describing is a (neuro)queercrip affectivity hinged on discursive hypersaturation. So much meaning all at once that none of it makes sense. So much meaning that it hurts. So much meaning that nonmeaning comes to mean "a good feeling."[62] So much meaning that is the ground rhetorical energy marks beyond affect. Rhetorical energy as a universe of significations—so much meaning—freed from their signs.

As Prahlad's, my own, and many disabled people's experiences testify, the breadth of rhetorical energy reaches past humans, encompassing all matter, living or not. My approach to rhetorical energy correlates with much of the recent scholarship on the rhetoricity of nonhuman animals and inanimate objects. Scholars such as George Kennedy, Diane Davis, and Debra Hawhee all write about the rhetorical capacities of nonhuman animals, theorizing them both in relation to and as distinct from histories of human rhetoric. Kennedy's engagement with nonhuman animals comes alongside his own theory of rhetorical energy that he explains as "the energy inherent in communication."[63] Kennedy reasons that since "there is no room for doubt" that nonhuman animals communicate with one another, it behooves rhetoric scholars to conceive of nonhuman meaning making as rhetorical, even if humans are not able to comprehend the messages being sent and received.[64] He goes on to argue that if we can acknowledge nonhuman animal rhetorics, then we should also recognize that there is an array of "physical actions, facial expressions, gestures, and signs" that constitute human rhetoric beyond verbal language.[65] These multiple modalities, taken together, make up Kennedy's rhetorical energy, which shares features with my own understanding of the phrase but also differs at some critical junctures.

With regard to similarities, both Kennedy and I distinguish rhetorical energy from verbal—what Murray calls discursive—rhetoric. We agree that rhetorical energy constitutes a rhetorical field that has yet to receive nearly the attention it deserves from rhetorical studies, and we agree that nonhuman animals, insofar as they have the capacity to signify, are implicated by rhetorical energy. However, Kennedy and I disagree on the purpose of rhetoric itself, whether it "secures or benefits the human individual every day" or whether its effects are less predictable.[66] Kennedy argues that speech (and it's not clear whether he means "speech" as verbal communication or signification more generally) "is prior in biological evolution and prior psychologically in any specific instance," meaning that rhetors have survived to the extent that they have used rhetoric well.[67] In fact, he claims outright that "the function of rhetoric is the survival of the fittest."[68] My use of rhetorical energy and my understanding of rhetoric more generally is less confident in the innate good nature of signification.

While I admit that rhetoric has historically been used in democratic contexts to gain or maintain power, and though I appreciate the value of including rhetoric as part of a robust education, I am not convinced that the "fittest," contra Kennedy, are always the savviest rhetors or that rhetoric always serves the fitness of rhetors. There are many routes to survival that do not include rhetoric or Aristotle's "artistic" means of persuasion. War, rape, genocide, colonialism, enslavement, and violence at all scales can be incredibly effective tools to demonstrate one's supposed superiority, despite that none of them is particularly "artistic."[69] For me, rhetorical energy precedes signification and thus does not indicate fitness or dominance but gestures to a more complicated rubric of political, social, cultural, and geographic contexts.

I take issue with Kennedy's assumption that rhetoric and, by extension, rhetorical energy necessarily enhance one's quality of life, that they are "powerful force[s] for the . . . well-being of the individual."[70] For queer people, neither rhetoric nor rhetorical energy is always in our favor. Transphobia, racism, homophobia, ableism, and ageism, among any number of systemic modes of oppression, can all factor into one's rhetorical energy, depending on who, where, and when you are. As a result, many people spend their lives fighting their own energies, pushing back against the intensities and ephemeral significations that crowd their being in the world. Kennedy claims that rhetoric "has secured and benefited culture generally . . . throughout the history of the evolution of social animals and human society."[71] Following the lead of feminist rhetoricians, though, I contend that rhetoric's role throughout history depends largely on whose history is being told. To paraphrase Karlyn Kohrs Campbell, normative folks have one hell of a recorded rhetorical history, but the documented histories for queer people are often meager, fraught, or outright nonexistent.[72]

As I show in the chapters to follow, some queer people do successfully manage their significations, at least temporarily. They learn how to wield their rhetorical energies to their own benefit, harness their own affective potential, and build kinship networks that help them to survive. But to link these acts of survival to rhetorical skill would be to condescend the lengths people must go to in order to fend off poverty, state-sanctioned violence, or death. It is to miss the point that people's efforts to stay alive are born out of necessity; they are not playing a game or solving a puzzle. I acknowledge that the work of queer folks in this project is rhetorical. Queer silence, after all, is intended to reveal and elucidate the rhetorical efforts of people who have heretofore flown beneath the radar of queer politics. I argue only that rhetoric is more complicated and less altruistic than Kennedy's rhetorical energy would have us believe.

This point notwithstanding, the work that Kennedy began on nonhuman rhetorics is indispensable to my own understanding of rhetorical energy. Hawhee's "Toward a Bestial Rhetoric" picks up on Kennedy's primary argument "that animals—not just human ones—practice rhetoric."[73] She acknowledges that at the time of its initial publication, rhetoric scholars were not enthusiastic about Kennedy's thesis; they worried that he was "going off some deep end and taking the discipline with him."[74] But in the eighteen years between Kennedy's provocation and Hawhee's response, the field changed dramatically, allowing Hawhee to ask again whether "rhetorical energy resides in places where human animals may not even tread."[75] My interest in rhetorical energy stems from this question not so much because I am concerned with nonhuman animals (though I appreciate others' work on the subject!) but because I am suspicious of the subject/object distinction that rhetorical theory seems to assume. Thomas Rickert shares this concern in *Ambient Rhetoric: The Attunements of Rhetorical Being,* where he argues that rhetoric "must be grounded in the material relations from which it springs."[76] These material relations—those that contextualize rhetoric—refer to what he calls "ambience" or the idea that "rhetoricity is the always ongoing disclosure of the world shifting our manner of being in that world."[77] Rhetoric for Rickert is neither a distinctly human art nor one free of human intervention. Ambient rhetoric is on the brink of "what is (privileged) human doing and what is passively material."[78] Much like how I describe rhetorical energy as a form of signification that exceeds human bodyminds, Rickert's theory posits "an originary affectability or conditionality and a notion of persuadability that has a material dimension."[79] This material dimension is decidedly not living, but it is also not nonliving. It has "animacy," as Mel Y. Chen explains, which is to say that objects can be charged with signification and can carry "*affective* invest[ments]."[80] Building on Jane Bennett's approach to affect in *Vibrant Matter: A Political Ecology of Things,* Chen argues that animacy is not only "part and parcel . . . of bodies' materiality" but also a "specific kind of affective and material construct" that "is shaped by race and sexuality."[81] Rhetorical energy, echoing elements of both ambient rhetoric and animacy, captures the interanimation and cross contamination of discourses, signifiers, and signs that vibrate through people, nonhuman animals, and objects. That is, rhetorical energy exists not only in the bodyminds of humans but in all animate matter.

Neither rhetorical energy nor rhetoric more generally can be easily divided between subjects and objects; they dissolve the distinctions between these categories, flowing freely between me, you, her lizard, and their flowerpot on the floor.

This dissolution of categorical difference, however, should not be mistaken for a flattening of material difference, which would risk repeating the errors of affect theory by invisibilizing the networks of power that inform and constrain rhetorical energy. As Chen makes clear, the value of animacy—and, I would add, rhetorical energy as well—lies in its "consideration of affect in its queered and raced formations."[82] These formations are both abstract and real: they are virtual, "pressing [themselves] into linguistic materiality."[83] My understanding of rhetorical energy is attuned to the conditions that produce it, the technologies that surveil it, the institutions that discipline it, and the sensoria that perceive it. Rhetorical energy, for me, shapes how people experience their bodyminds and move about their worlds precisely because of the interplay between their queer significations and the material realities that they must live in, under, and through.

Rhetorical energy can be imagined as a rain cloud in the middle of summer, a cumulonimbus, filled with water, dirt, pollutants, toxins, and whatever else the sky manages to soak up off the ground. When it rains, and it will rain, all of that stuff—what we might think of as affective condensations—will come pouring down not as a light breeze or sticky air or a sprinkle of dew but as a warm, heavy shower that drenches everyone and everything in its path. Those who can stay inside, do; others, maybe children, run out into the storm with their arms outstretched. And still others, those with nowhere to run or hide, hunch their shoulders and feel themselves soak. When the rain stops, everyone pauses a moment to collect themselves: to stare out the window or to look down at their dripping clothes. They all realize, in a shudder, that things are different than they were before. The dry folks see themselves; the wet folks feel their wetness. And from their windows, the dry see the wet on the street. From the street, the wet see the dry at their windows. Then suddenly, just as the people caught outside start to dry themselves off, the sun breaks out from behind the clouds and absorbs the wetness all again. New particles floating up into the atmosphere, rearranged and reassembled but ultimately still glued together into raindrops, to come thundering down elsewhere at another time.

In this metaphor, the people caught out in the rain are the queer folks whose rhetorical energies present as many constraints as they do resources.[84] And while I won't go so far as to argue that queer people are more marginalized, more signified, or in this case more wet than any other vulnerable group, queers' uniquely abject position allows their wetness to penetrate deeper, linger on the skin longer, and leave a more noticeable residue. The discourses surrounding *queer* are so fraught with inconsistencies, contradictions, and outright misrepresentations of queer lives—not to mention enmeshed with convoluted ideologies of race, gender, disability, and age—that I would be remiss not to emphasize queer people's particular experiences. In other words, rhetorical energy is not itself an exclusive concept for queers, but it is informed by the rhetorical work of deviants who have to continuously adjust and reregulate our energies each time we leave our house, step onto a train, turn a corner, or enter a room. We are always getting wet in a new rain shower and, realizing there is no use in drying off, have to decide what to do with all of the water, all of the affect, all of the ambience, all of the animacy, all of the energy dripping off our skirts, pooling on the floor around our feet, and catching the eye of everyone in the room.

From Energies to Bodies

Before I progress further, I want to pull back to summarize what I've said thus far concerning the rhetorical matrix and rhetorical energy. While the two concepts are interrelated, they are not interchangeable, and a concise distinction between them will help to explain how the following chapters build on the theoretical work spelled out here. In short, the rhetorical matrix is a visual framework, a model, for understanding the conditions that produce signification. Rhetorical energy is a concept to explain how rhetoric functions in our lives. One of the key distinctions between the matrix and energy lies in the difference between *signification* and *rhetoric,* two words that I have not bothered to separate until now. In this project, *signification* refers to the state of having meaning, whereas *rhetoric* refers to the situation of that meaning in context—what traditional rhetoric scholars would call an audience. So while the rhetorical matrix helps us to understand meaning (signification), rhetorical energy helps us to understand meaning in relation (rhetoric). The various expressions of signification that make up the matrix—such as verbal, visual, material, and embodyminded—can all be distilled from rhetorical energy. Indeed, all forms of signification feed rhetorical energy because signification relies on its affectivity to be perceived. Without rhetorical energy, no one would doomscroll on social media, read a news article, or watch a performative art installation. The collision of two or more rhetorical energies sparks the first brush of intensity that triggers a more engaged interaction with specific signifiers. The rhetorical matrix provides a way to understand these signifiers, the array of modes to signify, and the ways that various silences signify as well.

The relationship between silence and rhetorical energy is particularly relevant because of the paradoxical position that many queer people hold, one where we are both silenced by political, cultural, and religious institutions and heavily signified, our rhetorical energies beaming. At once, poor, disabled, trans, old, Indigenous, Black, and brown queer voices are drowned out or dismissed by legislators and religious leaders, even as our bodies, fashions, cultural practices, and dialects are misappropriated by white, nondisabled, cisheteropatriarchal communities and corporations. The steady rise of homonormative and homonationalist discourses, which exceptionalize the experiences of white, abled, middle-class gay and lesbian colonizers, further marginalizes the most vulnerable queer populations. Those left at the margins of the margins find themselves ever more silenced, lacking agential representation yet feeling their bodyminds signifying more intensely.

Trans, queer of color, queer Indigenous, and queer disability scholars have long been aware of this uneven institutionalization of queer politics, and it is such unevenness that makes the project of *Queer Silence* as challenging as it is necessary. Attending to both formalized silences and weighty significations, this book intervenes in the conversations in trans studies and disability studies about the experience of working with and against discourses that claim to represent trans and disabled people in ways that do not align with how these communities understand themselves. Their rhetorical energies are inundated by significations that often work against them rather than for them. Yet, despite the violence of these significations, these communities sometimes latch onto their queer rhetorical energies as a powerful resource. Queer silence is both a condition of oppression and a key to its undoing. The contradictory nature of queer silence—at once oppressive and potentially liberatory—illuminates how I understand *queer* more generally. It bears repeating that the subjects who populate this book are queer less because of their identities than because of their "*nonnormative* and *marginal*" relationship to state and institutional power.[85] Identity is important to this project, to be sure, but it does not by itself render a person queer. Instead, I follow Jean Bessette in thinking *queer* rhetorically or "*in situ*."[86] *Queer* is not a description of who a person is but a space a person occupies that shifts according to audience, time, place, and occasion. "*Queer to whom? When? Where, and how?*" Bessette asks, "*Normative to whom? When? Where, and how?*"[87] By thinking *queer* rhetorically, I hope to localize it, to reveal its contingencies, and to situate it as a material-discursive effect produced by our bodyminds in relation rather than as an entirely internal and individuated characteristic.

While calls for situatedness are common in queer studies, my attention to rhetorical energy demands a degree of contextualized specificity that remains largely unusual, even in rhetorical circles. I argue that *queer* be situated not only from culture to culture, decade to decade, nation-state to nation-state but also from person to person, minute to minute, room to room. Who occupies the category of "queer" can change with the turn of a doorknob, and how a person's queerness signifies can alter with a single breath. This kind of hyperlocalization reveals both the infinite configurations of power that organize marginalized people and the equally infinite coalitional possibilities among them. *Queer* in situ mobilizes what Karma R. Chávez calls "radical interactionality," which "holds in tension both the predictable ways oppression and power manifest in relation to and upon particular bodies while also carrying possibilities for creative and complicated responses to oppression."[88] *Queer* does not collapse the differences among racialized, disabled, and gender nonconforming people, or among any combinations thereof, but it does hold space for all those bodymind configurations that fall outside of white, abled, cisheteronormativity. This space cultivates coalitions that may relate to sexual nonnormativity proper but not necessarily. Instead, queer coalitions erupt from Brennan's "axis of the heart": our energies spilling out sideways from our variously queered bodies to loop us together into one big mess of rhetorical abjection.[89] Chávez refers to this looped mess as a "coalitional moment" or when people who don't seem to belong together nevertheless find their way into the same fight.[90] Different queers who have been differently queered all queering shit up together.

What I find most compelling about Chávez's approach to cross-movement work is her insistence that the present we are in and the future we are working toward are intimately intertwined: "Coalitional subjects believe in the vitality of broadening imaginaries that will open possibilities for livable life."[91] Chávez avoids both naive utopianism and complacent liberalism, focusing instead on "expanding the very limits of the practicable."[92] By looking ahead at the world we want, she argues, coalitional moments can begin to reshape the world we have. Queer silence produces the energetic conditions that underlie these moments. Silence is the transformation of individuated queerness into a collective resistance, the renegotiation of one person's rhetorical energy into a coalitional rhetorical response. While not every instance of queer silence is coalitional, many of them are, and these instances remind us that queer silence is ultimately a political praxis, a way of joining my silence with yours to make it through another day.[93]

I should clarify that while the politics of queer silence can be liberatory insofar as they offer marginalized subjects a strategy to resist dominant discourses, the everyday practice of queer silence itself is not necessarily "progressive" or even ethical. Similar to the way I would not claim that queer politics are always already "good" or that all queer people are "good" people, I am hesitant to position queer silence as a virtue of queer martyrdom. Rather, I follow Kadji Amin's desire in *Disturbing Attachments: Genet, Modern Pederasty, and Queer History* to "deexceptionalize" queerness and to thereby acknowledge that queer people are only human, that politicizing any given person's deviance does not guarantee the sudden formation of a transformatively deviant politics.[94] Amin proposes "deidealization" as a way of distinguishing *queer* from that which allegedly marks the furthest reach of any leftist agenda. As he puts it, "Deidealization is not the wholesale destruction of cherished ideals, but a form of the reparative that acknowledges messiness and damage, refuses the repudiating operations of idealization, and acknowledges the ways in which complicity is sometimes necessary for survival."[95] Queer people fuck up and do fucked up things for a lot of different reasons, and *queer* itself is not an indicator of righteousness, even if experiences of queerness can foster empathy and a desire for justice. Queer people do their best, but many of us aren't exactly provided the conditions to support our best all of the time.

For this reason, I want to deidealize queer silence from the beginning of this project, to acknowledge from the outset the messiness "of living with damage in a damaged world."[96] This messiness presumes nothing, except that people do what they feel they have to do in order to survive. Sometimes survival involves the large-scale structural critiques that queer studies and rhetorical studies scholars applaud; sometimes it doesn't. Sometimes queer silence looks a hell of a lot like shame (chapter 2), like complicity (chapter 3), like lying (chapter 4), like giving up or giving in (chapter 5). But as Amin reminds us, these things are "sometimes necessary."

With the intention of extending the same kind of political generosity that Amin proposes with deidealization, I turn to trans studies and disability studies as two fields that consistently honor the political complexity of wielding queer bodyminds in violently queerphobic spaces. While there are important tensions between trans and disability politics, especially with regard to how they view people's relationships with medical-juridical institutions, I will save that discussion for chapter 4, where I deal with them at length. Here, I want to focus on the ways both fields nuance notions of embodymindedness by attending to how discourse interacts with matter. This work goes beyond acknowledging that bodyminds signify to examine the processes by which flesh is imbued with signification. Much like how rhetorical energy bridges discourse's virtuality and bodies' materiality, so too do trans studies and disability studies regard bodyminds as both discursive products and material entities: as stuff that receives injections, endures surgeries, is named and renamed, classified and diagnosed, treated, cured, and readmitted, pathologized, institutionalized, released, arrested, dressed up, stripped down, processed, and spit out, but remains stuff all the same.

Within trans studies, embodied material discursivity takes on a relational edge, whereby the heavy condensation of signifiers that attend trans being-in-the-world says less about the "meaning" of transness than about the location of a given trans person, their situatedness. Susan Stryker refers to this situatedness as "a *poesis* (an act of artistic creation) that collapses the boundary between the embodied self, its world and others, allowing one to interpenetrate the others and thereby constitute a specific place."[97] In "Dungeon Intimacies: The Poetics of Transsexual Sadomasochism," Stryker presents BDSM as an example of how trans people's bodyminds undergo constant modification through the discursive (re)productions that interpellate us as trans. "Transsexual sadomasochism" becomes not only the literal participation of trans people in BDSM erotics but also a stylization of trans life. Stryker explains, "I envision my body as a meeting point, a node, where external lines of force and social determination thicken into meat and circulate as movement back into the world."[98] This image of discourse thickening and thinning captures the affective interplay between rhetorical energy and queer bodyminds. At no point does rhetorical energy overcome the body, dissolving it into oblivion, but it is always oscillating between thick and thin, contracting and expanding, moving closer and further away. Trans studies offers the tools to unpack how people's bodyminds come to mean in relation, what happens when people's energies collide. The field is attuned to the discursive movement between and among bodies, revealing how a person is transformed by every energetic interaction. It follows the sadomasochistic pulses, tracing the ebbs and flows of power, violence, and resistance as they pump in and out.

While these particular sadomasochistic pulses are typically linked to issues surrounding gender and sex, they can also be useful for theorizing other axes of discursive materiality. "Trans* life," Stryker argues, "demonstrates the fraught viability of enlivening movements across the hierarchized categories of being. It bears witness that . . . the flesh can, at times, come to signify anew."[99] Over the next four chapters of *Queer Silence,* this "fraught viability" is readily apparent across identities, lines of difference, and positionalities. Grindr users, ex-gays, trans elders, and neuroqueers all engage their rhetorical energies to manipulate or reshape how their bodyminds are read and received by others. The metaphors that Stryker offers—poesis, sadomasochism, thickening, nodes—all assist us in visualizing embodyminded signification at work. The concepts open themselves up "across the hierarchized categories of being" to serve as reminders of how discourse materializes and how material produces discourse: ongoing processes of resignification bound up with flesh.[100] In Stryker's words, they "demonstrat[e] how body modification can become a site of social transformation."[101]

Disability studies, another important interlocutor in this project, is similarly invested in the emergence and circulation of embodyminded significations, but the field more acutely articulates its suspicions about how these significations are used to amplify or diminish people's agency. Histories of disability demonstrate that processes of identification, which themselves are a kind of emerging signification, are routinely used to maintain hierarchies of human life that almost always relegate disabled people to the bottom rung. Ellen Samuels uses the phrase "fantasies of identification" to illuminate how contemporary identity politics "are haunted by disability even when disabled bodies are not their immediate focus."[102] That is, disability becomes the well of sociality through and against which all other identities draw their particularities. As Samuels points out, "The fantasy of identification . . . is always far less concerned with individual identity than with placing that individual within a legible group."[103] Echoing Foucault, disability studies reveals that the formalization of signifiers into identities is not an accurate, precise, or, to an even lesser extent, natural process. Rather, identification is about establishing order and maintaining control—typically by way of insulating white cisheteronormativity against the threat of disability.

Nevertheless, identities cannot always be easily avoided or eschewed. For many disabled people, identity is stamped on in response to our perceived appearance, affectivity, or rhetorical energy by a person or institution with more cultural capital, making it difficult if not impossible for them to escape the identification. When identified this way—by mandate rather than self-naming—it becomes all the more difficult to advocate for oneself, especially when many marginalized identities are definitionally hinged on a reduced agential capacity. Catherine Prendergast proposes "rhetoricability" to describe the inverse relationship between disability and agency, whereby the more disabled a person is perceived to be, the less agency and autonomy they are allowed.[104] Doctors, though ostensibly charged with helping their patients feel better, often act as "unimaginative literary critics" who are solely invested in locating symptoms (i.e., significations) and formalizing them into diagnoses (i.e., identifications).[105] These newly minted diagnoses are then amplified to overwrite any other identity that a patient holds; thus, a patient "can only be seen as arhetorical, the test, the record of symptoms, Exhibit A."[106] It's worth noting that as a person's rhetoricability diminishes, their rhetorical energy tends to signify more intensely—an effect of liberalism's drive to shore up white cisheteroableism. The more a person's bodymind comes to signify for them, the less likely that person's actual voice will be heard or their subjectivity acknowledged.

The capacity for whiteness and heterosexuality—among other normative states—to remain simultaneously pervasive and culturally invisible depends on the stigmatization and signification of aberrance and nonconformance. The many and conflicting significations that attend disabled people, for instance, are not only substituted as evidence for our diminished rhetorical capacity but also inverted to guarantee the untainted rhetoricability of nondisabled others. Variously labeled evil, saintly, deviant, sick, ill, inspiring, hysterical, possessed, adorable, immoral, shifty, suspicious, cute, contagious, and corruptible, the rhetorical energy surrounding disability is full of contradictions, illustrating not a coherent framework for understanding disability experience but instead "the dominant power structure's deep and abiding desire for such a fantastical solution."[107] The solution, in this case, refers to the elimination of disabled people's agency to preserve the value-neutral objectivity and unmitigated autonomy of abledness.

As they pertain to this project, disability studies and rhetoricability speak to the conditions under which many people engage queer silence. Even as some LGBTQ people have managed to secure their own rhetoricability—often by throwing mental disability under the bus to claim their own sanity—many queers continue to find themselves navigating the carceral violences of medicine and the criminal justice system. I understand this navigation as an effect of "subjection," the term Dean Spade proposes to explain trans people's interactions with state authority. Subjection "indicates that power relations impact how we know ourselves as subjects through these systems of meaning and control—the ways we understand our own bodies."[108] Even if the naturalization of LGBTQ identities has secured resources for some homonormative and transnormative folks, it nevertheless puts other queer people, especially those who experience multiple vectors of marginalization, at risk for further harm. For those people who are not wealthy, white, or nondisabled, the significations that attend sexual and gender deviance continue to delimit their rhetoricability. Disability studies, attentive as it is to the effects of institutionally driven processes of identification, urges queer studies to move past its political skepticism of identity politics to engage more deeply with the rhetorical implications of identification as they are bound up with embodyminded significations that people do not choose for themselves. Identity is not always something that can be resisted, at times because it is necessary to secure lifesaving resources (e.g., health care) and at times because a person's rhetorical energy is hailed into an identity without their consent (e.g., my femme ass is clocked every time I walk out the door). Neither an uncritical identity politics nor a purely anti-identitarian position is useful in this case. Subjection begets identification, which in turn begets "a counter-trend of segregation."[109] For those whose identities are unchosen, their rhetorical energy can be self-destructive, and their rhetoricability is constricted.

As the following chapters demonstrate, queer silence is most often deployed in segregated spaces. The significations layered on and flowing through queer people come to bear most heavily on those bodyminds who do not have access to the "*formal* integration" offered to homonormative and transnormative people.[110] These multiply marginalized folks are left to refigure their own invisibility—their enforced silence—as an opportunity to renegotiate their rhetorical energy, to turn their significations on their heads. While this strategy is not always successful and often entails intimidating risks of embarrassment, ostracization, violence, or even death, it is also among a select few options for many of the folks who use it. Queer silence becomes the way out, the way to represent, the way to exist in a world where, in the words of C. Riley Snorton and Jin Haritaworn, their lives are "barely conceivable."[111] The rhetorical matrix gives us a lens that conceives, a lens that can diffract the various forms of signification at play. The matrix model makes room for silence as the condition of emergence for signification, and rhetorical energy names the birth and rebirth of each signification as it traverses modalities, bodies, and technologies. Queer silence, bringing both concepts together, provides a route into queer life that too often goes unnoticed. Queer silence latches onto the minute, watches for tiny, inching movements, hears the thrum of affect pulsating through the air, and smells the rain as it beats against our heads.

The theoretical work in this chapter builds the foundation for the more analytic and populated chapters to come. Each chapter brings something new to queer silence, but the terms *rhetorical matrix* and *rhetorical energy* both appear throughout, like two cords winding around each other, meandering through the fields, forests, and dense urbanscapes that hold queer lives. It is my intention that the concepts introduced in *Queer Silence* maintain relevance elsewhere. Certainly, I should hope that the queer voices who are central to this work should be echoed in future applications as well, and I have tried to emphasize throughout this chapter that "queer" is an inherently racialized, gendered, and disabled space that exceeds any neat identity category. Throughout the remainder of this book, I highlight such moments of excess—racism and transphobia on Grindr, the ableism that hinges religion and science, ageism within popular trans discourse, settler colonialism in disability rights activism—but I am also eager to see where others find rhetorical energy useful, to know how the rhetorical matrix works alongside or in tension with conversations that I do not consider here, to hear of more, different, and new queer silences. That is to say, I intend this project to remain open to applications, reevaluations, and materializations that exceed what I have written. Just as Glenn was careful to qualify *Unspoken* as "a rhetoric of silence," a singular one among many, I too hope that the queer silences identified in this book will soon be accompanied by many others. My goal is neither comprehensive nor representational but directional. I want to point queer studies toward silence, toward the rhetorical, resistive, political, and survivalist efforts of folks who may not signify like a typical queer subject, toward the ones who queer studies may not have realized could signify at all.

2

White Squares to Black Boxes

With a lazy thumb, I scroll through Grindr, the self-described "world's #1 FREE mobile social networking app for gay, bi, trans, and queer people to connect."[1] The app's interface allows me to see dozens of profiles at a time, each one occupying a tiny square on my phone's screen. I have had the app off-and-on for over a decade now and have used it in towns and cities across the country, chatting and meeting up with an incredibly diverse group of people. It was through Grindr that I received my first kiss, had sex for the first time, and met my first long-term partner. The app has been an extension of my sense of queer identity and community from the beginning. I downloaded it long before I officially "came out," first as gay and then as trans, and have often relied on it to connect with other queer and trans people. But when I moved to a rural college town for graduate school, I noticed a rather abrupt change in my experience of the app.

Grindr itself did not change; it still relied on geolocation technology to show me all of the other users who were in my vicinity. I could still tap a user's profile, send them a message, and—if I were so inclined—set up a time and place to meet for talking, drinking, dancing, or fucking. Just as when I used the app in Pittsburgh, New York, Portland, and other major cities, the app presented me with the same "social networking" opportunities. My change in interaction, then, was not a result of Grindr so much as it was with the users who happened to be around me. For the first time, I found my digital profile surrounded by profiles of other users who I could not recognize.

When users first create their Grindr accounts, they are prompted with an option to upload a profile picture—similar to the ones you might encounter on other social networking apps, like Facebook, Twitter, or Instagram. The difference is that, unlike most other social networks, Grindr's most well-known purpose is to allow users an easy way to find partners for sex. So while some users—myself included—upload pictures of their faces to their profiles, other users upload pictures of their exposed chests and abdomens, still others use images of their legs or flexed biceps or taut back muscles, and yet others choose not to upload pictures at all—empty black boxes in a sea of bodies. The variety of images is not particularly remarkable, but in the town where I attended graduate school, the proportion of profiles with identifiable faces was strikingly smaller than the number of profiles with nonfacial body parts or without pictures at all. Whenever I opened the app, I was greeted mostly with bodies or blank boxes that I didn't and couldn't associate with any given person. Indeed, the only way for me to reliably recognize one such profile was if I either struck up a conversation with a user via the private chat function or met with someone in person. Otherwise, no amount of passing familiarity with someone's profile would allow me to identify them based on a set of washboard abs. I was interacting with a digital world that both acknowledged the presence of a queer community and simultaneously concealed the identities of its members.

This peculiar situation—one where I was aware of queer people but not of the particularity of many queer individuals—left me wondering about the rhetorical strategies people use to navigate their queerness. I was then and currently remain curious about the ways that Grindr profiles can be used to regulate users' participation in and identification with a given community. Certainly, some users may choose to feature their abs or hamstrings because they believe those parts are their most attractive features, the features most likely to attract someone for a quick hookup. However, I am inclined to believe that there's something more interesting going on, rhetorically speaking. For many of the users who do not upload face pics, there is also a level of restraint or moderation that flows beneath their participation in the app's erotic energy. They perform a kind of partial self-silencing, what I call "quieting," that reveals some aspects of their queerness but withholds others.

Quieting, here, should not be confused with *quietness,* which could be taken to mean "passivity" or "low volume." My use of *quieting* refers only to how queer people can and do oscillate the intensities of their embodyminded significations across rhetorical media (e.g., verbal, visual, embodyminded, etc.) to regulate how they signify in different ways at different times in different spaces for different reasons. *Quieting* also points to the convergences among sexual minorities, trans and gender nonconforming folks, Black and brown people, Indigenous people, disabled people, and other populations living on the margins, given the ways we all routinely navigate unchosen and unwanted significations attached to our bodyminds. In this sense, quieting provides an opportunity to analyze the queer rhetorical effects of interlocking systems of oppression, as well as the differential manifestations of those effects on particular communities in their local contexts.

Quieting animates the rhetorical matrix, effectively bringing queer silence to life through the fluctuations of energy across various modalities in a given rhetorical situation. Much like a machine operator can pull one lever down while she pushes another up, *quieting* refers to the dynamism of the rhetorical matrix, the way one rhetorical medium might be sublimated so that another might signify more intensely. Sometimes, as I explain below, this dynamism is intentionally activated: Grindr users can choose whether they want to upload profile pictures and what kind of picture(s) they want others to see. For those users who opt out of uploading a photo, they too exert a kind of agency by quieting their own visual signification. Of the users who do choose to upload pictures, factors such as racism, cissexism, and ableism may affect how their images are perceived by others, thus influencing the amount or quality of their online interactions. In these cases, quieting is not purely chosen or entirely enforced but is a tactical strategy in response to violent or hostile conditions.[2] These users redirect their rhetorical energy from one medium to another, quieting themselves as a way to "refuse the silence imposed upon them."[3] Quieting is thus not exclusively a sign of liberation or an indication of oppression; it is the rhetorical matrix in motion, willed into existence because it's wanted or needed or both. Quieting is a thing that helps, even if it hurts. Rhetorically, it is neither only a resource nor only a constraint. It's a resourceful constraint. A constrictive resource.

In this chapter, I explore the constrictive resourcefulness of quieting on Grindr, particularly with regard to users' profile pictures. I am primarily interested in the resistant and subversive potentials of quieting, in the ways users can re/mis/appropriate Grindr's dependence on visuality to engage a queer community without fully exposing their identities. This balancing act between disclosure and withholding shifts the focus of the conversation from determining whether or why a person is "out" about their queerness to what it means to be or come out in the first place. As I note in chapter 1, queer rhetorics helpfully document the rhetorical action of queer activists and queer historical figures, but there has been less attention paid to the rhetorics of contemporary nonactivists, to everyday queers, to layqueers, to those persons whose online claim to queerness is limited to a square of pectoral flesh.

While many queer studies scholars since Eve Kosofsky Sedgwick and her formative *Epistemology of the Closet* explore the experiences of queer people who are not out, they do so primarily through metaphors of or relating to "the closet," a concept that I am wary of using in this chapter. Marlon B. Ross and Vikki Fraser both point out the limitations of closet-related discourse because of its tendency to become a "master paradigm"[4] that catalyzes "a sense of moralizing toward and privileging of the out subject as the only authentic queer subject."[5] Davin Allen Grindstaff goes further to note that "coming out requires a rhetorical abstraction" where the process of disclosure is ultimately a process of normalization that elides "its social conditions."[6] Were I to presume the outness or closetedness of Grindr users based on the appearance of their profiles, I would be purporting to know their desires, intentions, circumstances, and experiences—when, in fact, I know none of these things.

Thus, I choose to forgo further consideration of the closet in this chapter, opting instead for a theorization of quieting that acknowledges a multiplicity of queer representations, positionalities, and potentialities in public and private. This theorization takes up Michael J. Faris's call for a "queer turn" in rhetorical studies that pivots away from questions of identity toward "how relations are created through affective intensities and the circulation of desires online."[7] By exploring quieting on Grindr, I position quieting not merely as in "a reciprocal" relationship with speech, as Cheryl Glenn positions silence, but also as in constant negotiation with other forms of signification that reveal the queer rhetor as one whose queerness is contingent on their relations.[8] Quieting, in this way, does not replace the closet as a narratorial apparatus for identifying or manufacturing queer persons so much as it brings to light how queer subjects are produced and structured by their rhetorical performances of silence.

To understand silence on Grindr, we must expand our sensoria, dilating out from the verbal to include the visual. Much of what makes Grindr a prime space for queer silence is its dependence on visuality, or what rhetorical scholars call visual rhetoric. Defined by Lester C. Olson, Cara A. Finnegan, and Diane S. Hope as "those symbolic actions enacted primarily through visual means . . . endeavoring to influence diverse publics," visual rhetoric is a broad category that contains both "the cultural practices of seeing and looking, as well as the artifacts produced in diverse communicative forms and media."[9] As it pertains to this chapter, *visual* refers to both the act of seeing and the artifacts that are seen, considering that users on Grindr are both witness to others' profiles and the objects of others' gazes. Visual rhetoric directs us to the signifying power of this interaction between the viewer and the viewed. It is not only that the images depicting queer bodyminds signify but that their signification is made possible through the viewing of other users.

As the first point of contact that users have with one another, images are among the few available resources that can persuade someone into starting a conversation. Moreover, profile pictures occupy the vast majority of the space on Grindr's main feed. Visual rhetoric, in this context, is tremendously powerful, undoubtedly carrying the potential "to influence diverse publics," per Olson, Finnegan, and Hope's definition. Indeed, choosing not to post a picture might seem counterproductive: why use an app that is primarily visual if you're not going to let yourself be seen? Yet, as I argue in chapter 1, the rhetorical energy of queer bodyminds often exceeds the constraints of a single medium, spilling into other signifying outlets. When users choose not to upload pictures, they are not so much cutting off their rhetoricity as they are hacking into the range of media within the rhetorical matrix, quieting the visual, and sabotaging the app's interface to their own designs.

To best explain this subversive process, I divide the chapter into four sections. First, I offer an overview of visual rhetorics, paying particular attention to their intersections with digital and material rhetorics. Second, I turn toward queer digital media studies, especially to those conversations that attend to issues of community building, communication, and intimacy. In this section, I also explore how interactions on queer digital media, including Grindr, are informed by race, gender, and disability in ways that often coerce the quieting of users of color, trans and gender nonconforming users, and disabled users. While I am optimistic about digital media as a space for queer intimacies, that optimism is delimited by a racist cisableism that infiltrates online communication. Together, these first two sections lay the foundation for Grindr as my case study. In the third section, I turn to the app itself, providing a context for the theoretical work by examining the rhetorical effects of various kinds of profile pictures, including "blank" profiles. While I refer to Grindr and profile pictures throughout the chapter, the final section grounds the broader discussion in specific examples. I conclude with the implications of my analysis, remarking on both its relevance to queer people and its more scholarly intervention in queer studies.

Visual Matters

> It was a strange image. Just this uneven patchwork of white squares, each with handwritten names, some in script and some in block letters, all individual. We stared and read the names, recognizing too many. Staring upward, people remarked: "I went to school with him" . . . "I didn't know he was dead" . . . "I used to dance with him every Sunday at the I-Beam" . . . "We're from the same hometown" . . . "Is that our Bob?"[10]

In this passage, Cleve Jones is recalling the moment that first inspired him to start the NAMES Project, which since the late 1970s has invited people to donate handmade quilts that memorialize loved ones who have died from AIDS-related complications. The quilt, though perhaps one of the most famous forms of protest from the Gay Liberation era, is one of many demonstrations that calls attention to queer people by emphasizing the presence of the queer bodymind. The visual image of the quilt, spanning thousands of square feet, acts as a spatial and material metaphor for queer embodiment.

Among the most important features of visual rhetoric is that its focus is never only visual or contained by a single sense; rather, visual rhetoric is a way of approaching rhetorical artifacts with a fine-grain attunement to the visual. As Finnegan puts it, visual rhetoric is "a mode of inquiry . . . that makes issues of visuality relevant to Rhetorical Theory."[11] In this way, visual rhetoric is less about isolating visual phenomena than it is about emphasizing the visuality of existing rhetorical artifacts and "encourag[ing] us to (re)consider aspects of Rhetorical Theory in light of the persistent problem of the image."[12] A visual rhetorical approach to the NAMES quilt does not establish it as a signifying artifact but rather invites us to include the quilt's visual dimension, alongside its material, spatial, and textual dimensions, in our analyses of it.

Amy D. Propen refers to this model of visual rhetoric as a "visual-material spectrum" in order to emphasize that "material and multimodal rhetorical artifacts are also implicated in the projects of visual rhetoric."[13] Using the NAMES quilt as an example, a visual-material spectrum invites us to examine how the image of the quilt is inseparable from what it's made out of, how much space it occupies, and what words and symbols have been threaded into the patchwork. As Brett Ommen suggests, "audiences encounter visual images as material surfaces."[14] Thus, the quilt becomes not only an artifact to see but also one to touch, stand beside, and carry. To see the quilt is inextricably bound to what the quilt feels like. Much like the bodyminds that the quilt is meant to represent, it is at once something visually glimpsed and sensuously felt.

Propen's notion of a visual-material spectrum is particularly useful in digital contexts where visual technologies are imbricated with users' material bodyminds. Using GPS devices as an illustration, Propen argues that their "use of visual and audio cues . . . elicits interaction and bodily engagement," revealing a "posthuman, mediated body."[15] In this context, "posthuman" draws on John Muckelbauer and Debra Hawhee's definition of "posthumanism as an attempt to engage humans as distributed processes," which can themselves be understood as mediations—some visual, some material, some verbal or textual—that, together, define subjectivity.[16] Posthumanism acknowledges that people come to be agents only by way of the discursive forces that flow through and around them. The visual-material spectrum helps elucidate a component of this subjectification process, highlighting the sheer proportion of modern life that is mediated by digital technologies and how these technologies not only interact with but also produce subjects.

From GPS devices to televisions to computers to phones to new "smart" refrigerators, our daily, mundane activities are filtered through digital screens, which have not only visual interfaces but also material heft and girth. Combined, the visual materiality of these images mitigates our existence in the world. As Propen puts it, digital technologies do "not constitute a kind of prosthetic extension of the body that transcends materiality" but instead "serve as a rhetorical artifact that engages the body."[17] The touch screen attached to the fridge is more than a fun accessory; it reestablishes how you interact with the fridge, how you define the fridge, and, ultimately, how you define yourself in relation to the fridge. "The digital is not only irreducible to what we see," write Casey Boyle, James J. Brown Jr., and Steph Ceraso, "it also exceeds that which we feel—in any traditional sense—and extends far out to what helps organize our collective bodies."[18] Herein lies the value of visual rhetoric for this chapter, as well as for the field of queer studies: the Grindr app is not simply enhancing queer life but rebuilding it from the ground up, crafting identities, interactions, and intimacies that would not have existed otherwise. The visual rhetorical appeal of Grindr is not that you can see profiles of other queer people but that you can come to understand yourself among them. To use Grindr is to constitute a queer self through the app's visual materiality.

Missing from this equation, of course, is consideration of the other users who populate Grindr's feed. The profiles that fill the screen are—much like the quilts from the NAMES Project—meant to be representative of real bodyminds. Indeed, the rhetorical force of profile pictures is in their connection to the users who operate the accounts. To see and interact with a Grindr profile offers the sense that one is seeing and interacting with a living, breathing person. However, as Roland Barthes points out, photographs purport "an illogical conjunction between the *here-now* and the *there-then,*" where what we see in pictures is not the thing itself but a past version of that thing, some "evidence of *this is how it was.*"[19] Though profile pictures on social media and dating apps are hypothetically meant to represent their respective users in the present, the "temporal equilibrium" of photography instantiates an immediate disjuncture between what is seen and what is.[20] Even in digital contexts, where recency and timeliness are expected (if not assumed), pictures can never be authentic copies of the thing; they will always be behind. The face you see is only an illusion of the "*real unreality* of the photograph."[21] This illusion notwithstanding, Barthes argues that photography's value is in the ability of images to capture one's attention, regardless of the accuracy or authenticity of their representations.

In *Camera Lucida: Reflections on Photography,* Barthes introduces the "*studium*" and "*punctum*" to explain the interplay between viewers and images. Whereas the studium is what the viewer brings to a photograph—"for it is culturally . . . that I participate in the figures, the faces, the gestures, the settings, the actions"—the punctum is "that accident which pricks me," the characteristic of a photo that commands you to view it.[22] The studium, Barthes suggests, is interpretable and "coded" insofar as we can name the identities, relationships, experiences, and cultural forces that affect our reading of a photo. For a Grindr profile picture, the studium might be white teeth in a wide smile, the size of a pectoral muscle, or the density of a pair of eyebrows. These are features of a picture that users are trained to look for, that they are meant to find appealing or at least to notice. The punctum, however, is more or less "a 'detail,' i.e., a partial object."[23] The punctum is the dirty mirror behind the person, the clutter of lotions and shampoos on the bathroom counter, or a tattoo of a heart with a woman's name in it. These details are not meant to be the focus of the picture, nor are we viewers necessarily invited to pay attention to them; yet, we do. They have "a power of expansion," suddenly becoming the only thing in the photo that we care about.[24]

For Barthes, as for me, the punctum is where images store their signifying power. For the punctum, the unnamable detail that pricks us, gestures to a rhetorical landscape outside the discursivity of the studium, it "is a kind of subtle *beyond*—as if the image launche[s] desire beyond what it permits us to see."[25] On social media and dating apps, that desire is synonymous with the illusion mentioned above: that there is a real body behind the picture. The punctum on Grindr is that every profile is more than a profile, that it's a person who I might like, who might like me, who might be like me. The punctum becomes a puncture through which technology is meant to connect people; we approach profiles as if they were glass windows with users clearly on the other side. However, as the variety of profiles on Grindr illustrates, where not all users upload pictures, digital technology disrupts the relationship between the punctum and the image. Blank profiles raise the question of whether there can be a punctum without an image. Or put rhetorically, can visual rhetoric exist without a visual?

Quieting and the rhetorical matrix play important roles in answering these questions because if we can situate visual rhetoric within a broader framework of signifying media, where both presence and absence (speech and silence) signify, then perhaps we can imagine visual absences just as we might verbal silences. Quieting, despite its implicit connection to sound, can also name the process by which visual signification can be sublimated, even within a visual medium like Grindr, by emphasizing an artifact's material rhetoricity. Similar to Propen's visual-material spectrum, quieting captures the oscillation of signification across rhetorics, illuminating the range of media and modes within the rhetorical matrix. Suddenly, contra Barthes, the punctum is not restrained by the presence of an image but depends only on the force of signification through a visual medium. Blank profiles, as I show below, "prick" their viewers, despite not having a picture at all. I argue, in fact, that the punctum of these profiles is defined by their visual absence, that their relative invisibility—their quieting—only draws attention to their material presence. In this sense, the punctum's prick is not momentarily affective, what Barthes calls the "floating flash," but more densely and powerfully embodyminded.[26] Grindr users' bodyminds prick one another through the digital medium. Much like Glenn explains silence, quieted blank profiles "can be equated with a kind of emptiness," even as they signify.[27] Users' rhetorical energies gush forth, puncturing the digital screen.

To experience this puncture is to encounter another's rhetorical energy, effectively becoming tethered to another user's bodymind through Grindr's digital interface. This tethering reveals what Joe Edward Hatfield calls "an embodied process of networked intimacy formation," wherein "human bodies collaborate with the ambient materiality of digital technologies and media."[28] When a Grindr user is grabbed by a profile, blank or otherwise, they are dealing with an "excess" of energy—perhaps an erotic one, perhaps not—"that seeps through" the app's attempts to structure, contain, and regulate it.[29] This excessive energy shocks users, pricks them, like a string of staccato bodies. As I explain in chapter 1, rhetorical energy is affective because it is at once embodyminded and impossible to materialize. Always changing, rhetorical energy cannot be made legible beyond its mere intensity. It can be experienced, even if it can't necessarily come to mean anything in particular. Yet, when manifesting as the punctum of an image, rhetorical energy reveals its fundamental difference from affect: its compounded discursivity. Rhetorical energy carries residual traces of the bodyminds through which it flows, along with the significations attached to those bodyminds. So when a user is drawn to a profile, pricked by its image, they are struck by a wave of intensity that, though affectively indeterminable, is nevertheless packed with meaning. To have your Grindr screen punctured is to be pierced by the residue of another user's lively materiality.

In the previous chapter, I discussed the embodymindedness of rhetorical energy through disability studies, mad studies, and queer of color critiques of affect theory, which problematize the assumption that the material body distracts from the "autonomy of affect."[30] On Grindr, one cannot help but wrestle with the bodyminds of the users, both individually and collectively, who are not only operating the accounts but visibly plastered all over the screen. Sara Ahmed's approach to affect in *The Cultural Politics of Emotion* and *The Promise of Happiness* is useful here as she proposes a relational model to reestablish affect's intimacy with emotion, with "bodily processes of affecting and being affected."[31] While affect theory tends to be critical of emotion as "something that happens inside," as opposed to affect's exterior virtuality, Ahmed uses *emotion* to refer to an embodyminded instantiation of affect.[32] What we feel as emotion, she suggests, is the "stickiness" of affect as it is passed from one person or object to another.[33] She writes, "Affect is what sticks, or what sustains or preserves the connection between ideas, values, and objects."[34] Like Teresa Brennan (see chapter 1), Ahmed notes the physical and material effects of affect, but she goes further than Brennan to argue that affect's effects continuously reorient us to the world in new ways. "Before we are affected," Ahmed writes, "before something happens that creates an impression on the skin, things are already in place that incline us to be affected in some ways more than others."[35] Affect's effects affect future affects. The effects of affect are deeply affective.

Likewise, each exchange of rhetorical energy alters us and our relations forever. Each time a user on Grindr views someone else's profile, not only does the other user's bodymind come to matter but the viewer is irreversibly affected by this sudden mattering. The viewer has been impressed upon. They've been left sticky with rhetorical excess. And this excess, while decidedly indeterminable, is heavy with material and embodyminded signifying potential. I'm talking about a kind of virtual weight that not only reorients us to the world, vis-à-vis Ahmed, but also reorients the world to us. Rhetorical energy as the prick that pricks back, the impression that presses back, a kind of sticky that sticks back, the potential to mean that changes every other meaning potential. Rhetorical energy as what could come to mean but doesn't because the user kept scrolling, because his roommate walked in, because a siren went off outside, because Netflix asked if he was still watching, because her dick itched, because their battery was about to die. Affect's effects affect future affects. Rhetorical energy as what meaning is and could be and can be and won't but should be and would never be, even if we wanted it to be. Rhetorical energy as *I feel different today* and knowing deep down that it's true: that you are different, that you feel different in the world, and that the world feels you differently too.

Digital Intimacies

For many queer folks, opportunities for feeling different have been made possible by digital technologies, where we have in recent decades turned to find one another, build social networks, and educate ourselves on issues affecting our communities. John Edward Campbell documents the popularity of Internet Relay Chat (IRC) communities in the mid- to late 1990s among gay and bisexual men. He writes that even in those early years of the internet, people used the technology "for the discussion, exploration, and eroticism of the male body."[36] "Cyberspace" quickly grew to "function as the locus for queer community formation," where users could help "construct a safe and affirming space for the exploration of erotic practices and desirable bodies."[37] Notably, the embodyminded or physical dimensions of online communication have been a consistent focus of queer digital media studies, as well as queer studies more generally. Campbell speaks back to what he calls "the online disembodiment thesis," which assumes that "there is an absolute demarcation between the real and the virtual, and therefore a radical disjuncture between experiences in cyberspace and those in the physical world."[38] Though he acknowledges that there can be meaningful differences between online and off-line interactions, he resists the idea that digitally mediated communication is somehow "less real or meaningful than experiences offline."[39] He is instead more interested in how queer internet users "are complicating normative understandings of the body and transfiguring themselves, even if only momentarily, into freaks and cyborg subjects."[40]

Admittedly, the language of freaks and cyborgs recalls the participation of disabled users, who are more likely to be shamed for their apparently freakish bodyminds and made to feel guilty for using particular technologies to survive than they are to be praised for either.[41] I will speak more to the specific experiences of disabled Grindr users below, but it's worth emphasizing here that the hybridization of queer people and technology is not reducible to a single meaning or interpretation. In many ways, the image of a cyborg is helpful, some fifteen years after Campbell's work was first published, given the mobility of the internet through smartphones and other smart technologies. As the convenience of digital communication increases, making it easier to travel and be online, so too does the posthuman, digitally mediated cyborg become a more appropriate metaphor for some queer people. Yet, Alison Kafer is right to caution "against easy celebrations of the technological fix," noting that not all technologies are affordable, useful, or wanted and that many technologies are produced in exploitative conditions that are unsustainable for the environment and debilitating for the workers who build them.[42] Thus, the integration of mobile tech into queer life is uneven at best, illuminating both the inaccessibility of apps like Grindr for multiply marginalized queer populations and the varying quality of experiences that users have on such apps. The queer cyborg, as I'll argue, is almost always white, cis, and nondisabled. That said, unlike when Campbell was writing in 2004, and even less so than when he was researching in 1996, few people wait until they're home to chat online. More of us are doing it anywhere and everywhere, at any and all times.

More recent work on queer digital media elaborates on this transition, emphasizing the disappearing boundary between online and off-line environments. In *Gaydar Culture: Gay Men, Technology, and Embodiment in the Digital Age,* Sharif Mowlabocus argues that gay spaces are "now *both* digitally and physically manifested, and that these multiple manifestations occur simultaneously and shape one another continuously."[43] One helpful example is the gay bar, which Campbell introduces in comparison with online chat sites, calling the latter "virtual gay bars": "Like physical-world gay bars, these particular IRC channels function as safe spaces for queer-identified individuals to congregate, fashion friendships, affirm their sexual identities, locate (cyber)sexual partners, and build supportive communities."[44] Mowlabocus points out that Grindr, which uses technology that was not available when Campbell was writing, "may well be accessed by a man while in a bar, in order to assess the compatibility of other gay men nearby."[45] Thus, the distinction between online and off-line gay bars is no longer clear. The virtual gay bar is embedded in the physical gay bar, and the physical gay bar is remapped by the virtual one.[46] As one Grindr user told Courtney Blackwell, Jeremy Birnholtz, and Charles Abbott, "What I like about Grindr is that it makes every space a potentially gay space. . . . Grindr gives me the chance to pull out my phone and have a gay bar in my pocket."[47]

Nevertheless, Mowlabocus agrees with Campbell's primary thesis that digital culture cannot be separated from the material bodyminds of queer users. Offering the term *cybercarnality,* Mowlabocus suggests that "practices of embodiment [are] central to gay men's investment in digital communications," and he goes on to argue that regardless of the internet's liberatory potential, the internet has also occasioned "*new techniques of (self)surveillance*" among its users.[48] Specifically with regard to profile pictures and "stats"—the numerical data users can provide about their height, weight, penis size, serostatus, and age—cybercarnality helps us understand how digital technology "provides the means for watching [queer bodyminds], in multiple ways and with multiple consequences."[49] This is not to say that digital culture or the internet is decidedly bad for queer people, just that it is not a utopia either. "Given the attendant history of surveillance that runs throughout the history of gay male culture in the West," Mowlabocus explains, it is unsurprising that "the gay man is continually involved in a process of surveying, regulating and controlling both his own identity, and those other identities that he comes across in [a digital] environment."[50] The purpose of cybercarnality is to track the implications of this surveillance, especially as it pertains to users' interactions with one another.

Of particular interest to Mowlabocus and me are profile pictures. These images take center stage on Grindr, occupying the vast majority of screen space on both the main feed and individual profiles. Of the three most common varieties of profile pictures (i.e., face pics, body pics, and blank profiles), Mowlabocus insists that face pics on queer digital networks are the most valuable, acting "as a form of currency" that "demonstrates an investment in space that resonates with the argument regarding visibility in gay space . . . and your willingness to openly identify as gay or bisexual."[51] Since faces are often the most distinguishable part of a body, face pictures allow for easy differentiation among users. If you are looking at a grid of profiles, all with body pics or no images, it can be challenging to tell them apart. Face pictures, however, are identifiable and, Mowlabocus argues, "articulate[] issues of self-identification, honesty and integrity."[52] Users who do not upload face pics are regarded with suspicion, according to Mowlabocus, because "being *seen* as an out gay man is an important facet" of queer digital culture, whereas to withhold one's identity "serves to dislocate the individual from this circuit of trust and place him in a zone of ambivalence."[53] This perspective appears to be shared by Grindr, which in its most recent app update allows users the options to filter out blank profiles and exclusively view profiles with face pics.

I do not disagree that faceless profile pictures are less identifiable or that some users find the accompanying profiles frustrating. A friend of mine once told me, "If the profile is blank, it's getting blocked!" This friend found blank profiles so troublesome that he did not even allow them on his main feed. Nevertheless, I am less confident than Mowlabocus about the all-or-nothing value of face pics. Recalling the function of quieting, I contend there is equal, albeit different, signifying potential held in body pics and blank profiles. Especially for multiply marginalized users, opting out of face pics can serve as an important mechanism for self-protection. Shaka McGlotten reflects in their research on queer virtual intimacies that "for [them] and some of [their] informants . . . the particularities of [their] racial enfleshments have operated as obvious and not so obvious drags on [their] erotic or romantic possibilities."[54] Race on Grindr not only echoes the systemic racism of white supremacy but also "perhaps even heighten[s] forms of racial injury."[55] These forms often include the reduction of racialized users to fetishistic stereotypes, where erotic interest from other, usually white, users is based not in a desire to connect but in a fantasy to dominate, submit to, or otherwise engage the illusion of racial difference. For *Mic,* Mathew Rodriguez writes that "perhaps the most casual and most common place minority gays experience racism is in interactions on apps like Grindr" where users "brandish their racial dating preferences with the same unapologetic bravado that straight men reserve for their favorite baseball team."[56] The phrase "racial dating preferences" is a euphemism for unacknowledged racism because the "preferences" typically analog the wholesale rejection of nonwhite people. Owen Jones's title for his article in the *Guardian* puts it most pointedly: "No Asians, No Black People: Why Do Gay People Tolerate Blatant Racism?"[57] The answer, in part, is that racism in queer digital culture is commonly entangled with users' sexuality and thereby legitimized by its eroticization.

Fetishization and exclusionary preferences go unchecked precisely because they are coded as erotic, hence what Sharon P. Holland calls the "erotic life" of racism.[58] Holland positions the erotic "at the threshold of ideas about quotidian racist practice," and she argues that "quotidian racism can seem rather *unremarkable*" in much the same way that some white Grindr users see no problem with including race as a dating preference.[59] Yet, as Holland points out, even when eroticized, racism continues "to police the imaginary boundary between blood (us) and strangers (them)," perpetuating false, phrenological ideas about the biology of race and its phenotypical characteristics.[60] Anthony Lorenzo contextualizes Holland's work within his own experiences as a Black man on Grindr, concluding:

> Predictably, racism is as rife here as it is anywhere else. . . . Where do you turn? The outright rejection of you based on your race is tempered not by more understanding men, but by attraction to you based on your race, or more specifically, based on pre-conceived notions of what your race has to offer: Big cocks, thug-like masculinity, animalistic lust.[61]

His question, "Where do you turn?," resonates with the anxiety C. Riley Snorton builds into his metaphor of the "glass closet" that "demonstrate[s] how blackness transforms the closet from a space of concealment—however partial or contingent—to a site of confinement and display."[62] According to Snorton, many of the tropes and narratives associated with queerness (e.g., the closet) are irreconcilable with Blackness, "where darkness does not reflect a place from which to escape but a condition of existence."[63]

So, too, on apps like Grindr, the illusion of an inclusive queer space is dissolved by sexual racism, suggesting to users of color, and Black users in particular, that "there can be no elsewhere when darkness is everywhere."[64] In McGlotten's words, "racialized microaggressions," such as receiving fetishizing messages from other users, "produce powerful speculative fears about the effects racial difference can have not only on one's chances for getting laid but for more ontologically essential longings such as being wanted or loved."[65] If uploading a face pic carries such great personal risk, it makes sense that some users might not want to be immediately identified. "'Race' traps the body in real life," as Andil Gosine puts it: revealing one's racial identity as a person of color thrusts users back into the racist discourses of the non–digitally mediated world.[66] By withholding one's racial identity, users secure a level of control over how and when their bodyminds signify online.

Many trans users, too, are hesitant to upload pictures of themselves for fear of limiting potential engagement with other, predominantly cis, users or inadvertently making themselves vulnerable to targeted, transphobic harassment. In an interview with Arisce Wanzer for *Into,* an online magazine catering to queer and trans readers, Black trans user Jace Every admits that "at least twice a day" he receives messages on Grindr that attempt to undermine his legibility as a trans man.[67] He recounts, "I've gotten everything from 'Men don't have pussies' [to] 'You're an abomination.' . . . The amount of hate that is received outweighs the positivity nine times out of ten." Unlike some trans users, Every does have a visible face pic on his profile and explains in a provided "About Me" space that he is trans. He acknowledges, though, that this decision reduces the number of enjoyable interactions he has on the app: "The guys that approach me are the ones that fetish (*sic*) us, and they immediately are like, 'I've always wanted to try an FTM [female-to-male transgender person].'" Morgan Potts, another trans user, echoes Every's experiences when he laments that on the app, "femininity is punished, or fetishized (another punishment)."[68] Despite identifying as a "trans boy," he frequently encounters "disbelief" about his masculinity. "Lots of guys, thinking I'm a trans woman, neg me to be more femme. . . . As a trans 'man,' I'm constantly told that I'm undesirable." Many trans users are thus caught in a space between illegibility and undesirability: they are either misrecognized for a gender they aren't or unwanted for the gender they are.

Disabled users find themselves in a similarly impossible position where they are either denied the agency to be sexual or hypersexualized into a fetish object. Reflecting on the ableism he experiences on Grindr for being deaf, Hayden Smith said in an interview that "disabled people are never just people; we're either objects of pity or objects of fascination and inspiration."[69] Abled users can't help but to make a big deal out of others' disabilities. A user's disabilities become the sum total of their identity on the app; they become the only conversation anyone wants to have, and not typically in a supportive, let alone erotic, way. "If you're disabled, people think it's their right to know how you're disabled, why, or how it happened: 'What's wrong with you?'" Charlie Willis told Patrick Strudwick for BuzzFeed.[70] Yet, if a disabled user does not disclose their disabilities upfront, abled users might later accuse them of lying or being deceptive about their bodyminds. When asked why he felt the need to disclose his own disabilities on Grindr, Josh Galassi said, "I suppose I thought it was the respectful thing to do, I would never want someone to think I was catfishing them or hiding something."[71] Like trans users, disabled users must weigh the risks of coming out, which might lay the groundwork for microaggressions and invasive questions, against the risks of trying to pass as nondisabled, which is not always possible and sometimes leads to an even greater risk of violence later on.

Potts, the trans boy cited above, frequently encounters this dilemma when chatting with other users. He says:

> [T]he first thing you're expected to supply in conversation after "hey" is a dick pic. . . . I often have to tell potential hookups that, no, I don't have a dick—at least not one which is attached to my body. They'll reply, "whatever you want to call it, [I] don't care," thinking that I'm a dysphoric trans woman. No, I mean I don't have a penis, I don't have testicles; I have a vagina. It feels like an apology.[72]

The emotional labor required by this conversation—where disclosure "feels like an apology"—is often too much for users to bear. In "How to Scruff a Trans Guy," Nic Cameron recalls that he used to keep his trans identity a secret "until decent conversation and compatibility . . . developed" but had "rather dismal success. I've been blocked, harassed, and ignored. . . . It became too painful for me to cruise this way, so I've gone back to plastering 'trans' all over my profiles."[73] For many marginalized users, profile pictures are a catch-22: either they reveal their marginalized identities up front and suffer random abuse from other users or try to pass and risk having to apologize for their bodyminds later on.

While I want to be careful not to collapse the experiences of differently marginalized users, it is worth noting the ways race, gender, and disability are triangulated on Grindr. It is not only that white, cis, abled users construct their own sense of belongingness against racialized, trans and gender nonconforming, and disabled bodyminds but also that the "currency" of face pics, per Mowlabocus, is mobilized as a surveillance tactic to police visibly deviant bodies. Eric Darnell Pritchard, writing specifically about Black queer digital spaces, suggests that it is the "recursive use of print and image [that] creates a Black queer world where rigid and constraining beauty and body politics are reinforced constantly."[74] While the "recursive use" of face pics might indeed produce a kind of currency, offering some users a buy-in to queer community, it is a currency structured by a deeply racist, cisableist economy wherein only a slim margin of homonormative users are paid full price for their identifiability. For those many users who fall outside of this slim margin, face pics offer a much lower rate of return, rendering marginalized users simultaneously "hypervisible as they are . . . grouped into neoliberal status categories" and "invisible as individuals."[75] The initial promise of visibility on Grindr reveals itself to be an identitarian ploy, subsuming the unique experiences and bodyminds of multiply marginalized persons within a monolithic classification system structured by homonormativity. Far from securing users entrance to a safe and uplifting digital space, visibility on Grindr often leads to heightened vulnerability to racist, transphobic, and ableist violence.

The concerns over visibility notwithstanding, McGlotten urges marginalized users on Grindr not to dismiss the app entirely. "I also suggest that optimism and one of its attendant iterations, hope, offer up distinct but in some ways equally speculative orientations toward social worlds," they write.[76] Borrowing Michael Snediker's definition of *queer optimism,* McGlotten rejects the temptation of "a promissory future" in exchange for an "immanent present [that] might be *interesting.*"[77] Optimism, thus, is not necessarily tied to positive affect or even affect that is temporally displaced into the future; it is simply a resistance to foreclosing the potential of the present and an insistence that "we nonetheless creatively live lives that push inward and outward, that exceed the constraints of life as we know it."[78] For McGlotten, the promise of queer optimism is that things might turn out differently than they are right now. In *Rhetorical Feminism and This Thing Called Hope,* Glenn also refers to this potential as "hope," as that which "keeps us alive and keeps us working. Even as we move, on a daily basis, toward our inevitable death, most of us create possibilities, embrace hope."[79] Similar to McGlotten's optimism, Glenn's hope is not naive; neither of them are idealists. But they both lean into the unknown, choosing to embrace "the possibilities of struggling together toward something more beautiful, more humane."[80]

On Grindr, this struggle is for connection and intimacy in a world that often makes no room for bodyminds that look, move, or love differently than white, cis, abled men. While the social terrain online is far from utopian for marginalized users, it "hasn't . . . yet settled into cold facticity" but bubbles with anticipation for something otherwise.[81] As McGlotten puts it, "feeling black and gay online . . . continues to shimmer with the right to refuse the certainty of no future, as an interesting interest in the present."[82] So, too, for non-Black users of color, as well as trans and disabled users, we would be remiss to ignore Grindr's potential, that it might yet become interesting. Indeed, Josh Hepple, a disabled user, recalls that before downloading the app he had "never even had an encounter with a man. . . . Since getting Grindr, I have met around 60 men and have found the experience unbelievably rewarding and liberating."[83] I am certainly not trying to dismiss the real and pressing concerns that marginalized users have about Grindr's safety or to suggest that we all simply be patient for the app to become safer. Rather, I am pivoting attention from what the app fails to offer to what it is offering nevertheless.

Profile pictures, despite the pain they can potentially cause, reveal the insuppressible rhetoricity of queer bodyminds. The "immanent present" that McGlotten and Snediker direct us toward is embedded in these images and, even more radically, in the absence of these images. What McGlotten calls "virtuality"—"the incipient social and affective worlds . . . that queer publics create, nourish, and sustain"—I link to rhetorical energy, which shares and mobilizes the "immanence, capacity, and potentiality" of virtuality by traversing across bodies.[84] That is, if "intimacy is already virtual in the ways it is made manifest through affective experience," *rhetorical energy* names the happening of that experience.[85] Rhetorical energy is virtual intimacy unfolding.

Much like quieting animates the rhetorical matrix, rhetorical energy shuttles affect through and across bodyminds. And the digital rendering of queer bodyminds on Grindr serves as an example of how these encounters occur, regardless of the presence or absence of a delineated sign or signification. Rhetorical energy never says anything in particular, but it persistently makes its presence known. As I show below, Grindr is a medium for this energy, allowing virtual intimacies to flourish and actualizing hope for a today worth living.

Imaging Absence

Since I first downloaded Grindr, I have always used a picture of some kind. Mostly, I have used face pics—something smiley and usually casual (see Figure 3). One of my more recent images, and the one I've included in this chapter, is of me sitting on some concrete steps at a pumpkin festival. I appear as a white person with brown facial hair. I am wearing black skinny jeans, a low-cut tan shirt, and a denim jacket. I have on white shoes and a gold necklace. I'm smiling and wearing light makeup. From a visual rhetorical perspective, the message of the image is clear: it says, "Hi, I'm friendly! Come talk to me!" Barthes might add that, excepting the keys awkwardly placed between my legs, the picture is all studium, no punctum. What you see is what you get. With my face visible, I can be identified both within and outside of the app; I am recognizable as a unique individual. If a person were to spot me somewhere—not at a pumpkin festival but, say, at the grocery—they would still be able to match me up with my profile. In this sense, my rhetorical energy is very matter-of-fact. When a user encounters my profile on Grindr, I am immediately identified as a queer person. And not just any queer person but a particular one; I become *that* queer person. It's all simple, really: Grindr is a social networking app for queer folks. My face is clearly visible on the app, so when people see my face, I am read queerly. Since faces are generally distinguishable from one another, the queerness bestowed upon me by the app will transfer outside of it. Grindr users who have seen my profile can now recognize me as a queer anywhere at all.

For many users, this queer legibility is desirable. As several individuals explained to Mowlabocus about their decision to upload face

FIGURE 3. My most recent profile picture on Grindr, circa 2017. Photograph by J. Logan Smilges.

pics, "[I] am proud of who I am, get appreciation, let other users see me," "[I choose to include a face pic] in the interests of my own integrity. A photo implies that I am open and honest about who I am," and "Allowing people to see how I look makes them more comfortable—I am not afraid to be seen."[86] However, the confidence these users have in their images and in how their rhetorical energies will be received should not be taken as generalizable evidence of how all users feel about face pics. The value and possibility of queer legibility is contingent on both my own and other users' proximity to whiteness, adherence to masculine gender norms, and perceived abledness. Though I am transfeminine and disabled, it is no secret that my body is often read as a nondisabled, cis man. And on Grindr, this reading carries tremendous privilege, even if it does often lead to me being misgendered and having to come out to others as disabled later on. My picture, appearing as it does, comfortably fits within Barthes's studium: "that very wide field of unconcerned desire, of various interest, of inconsequential taste."[87] It's not that I am inconsequential but that my image is: it's a nice picture, one that makes me look—if we're being very honest with each other—like a basic white gay. It's a picture made possible by the combination of my race, gender expression, and invisible disabilities. That other users would be "unconcerned" by my picture, that it would appear "inconsequential," is an effect of my combined white, masculine, and nondisabled presentation.

While I agree with Mowlabocus that face pics can occasionally "provoke *punctum*" because of "their relative amateurism," I am more inclined to side with Kathryn Bond Stockton, who argues that the punctum is fundamentally contingent on cultural context.[88] "Politics . . . can be tied, in highly sophisticated ways," she writes, "to the art of the detail—are themselves an art of the detail, in many circumstances."[89] Though the punctum is meant to be purely affective, Stockton points out that even Barthes himself "uses *studium* . . . to draw out *punctum*."[90] In other words, the viewer is just as responsible for eliciting an image's punctum as is the image itself. The punctum is at once "unlocatable," vis-à-vis Barthes, and predetermined.[91] With regard to my profile picture and face pics of other apparently basic white gays, the possibility of there being a punctum is limited by the normativity of the image. The punctum is much stronger, I argue, when this normativity is disrupted, such as with images of racialized users, gender nonconforming users, and users with visible disabilities. In these cases, the studium of white, cis, nondisabled users, who are perhaps more likely to fetishize and harass others, is pricked by the presence of bodyminds that are different from their own. Stockton paraphrases Barthes to suggest that the punctum "is diverting" in that "it draws inordinate attention to itself, diverting attention away from the *studium.*"[92] We can take this to mean that perceived difference, whether racial, gendered, disabled, or otherwise, distracts normative users, captivating them and forcing a confrontation with their own bodies. Even and perhaps especially with blank profiles, the absence of an image fractures the visual-material layout of the app, drawing users' eyes toward its invisibility and highlighting the viewer's own fleshy presence.

Consider, for instance, one of the stock photos Grindr has available in the Apple App Store, where iPhone users can download the app to their phone. In this image, which unfortunately Grindr has refused my request for permission to reproduce, the main feed of the app appears as a multiracial and gender expansive rainbow of faces, with the users representing a range of colors, sizes, genders, and stages of undress. Every single profile prominently features the user's face. I have to laugh at this portrayal of the app, which any quick Google search will quickly dispute. Never once have I used Grindr without the seamless collage of bodies being broken by body pics and blank profiles, by absences. For me, these absences become the punctum of the screen; they prick me, grab my attention. Even if users are not interested in chatting with faceless profiles, they are nevertheless forced to navigate them: to scroll past them, to block them, or to grumble about their existence. Blank profiles thus participate in McGlotten's virtual intimacies insofar as their invisibility harkens toward their materiality. This materiality refers not only to the digitally rendered material (i.e., the black box) but also to the embodyminded material of the attendant user. The embodyminded rhetorical energy of the user radiates through the digital material, manifesting as a visual absence. It is a "hyperrhetorical" string of maneuvers and transversals tantamount to quieting, where rhetorical media are manipulated to suit a given situation.[93]

The role of quieting is all the more obvious if you select one of the blank profiles, so that the app zooms in to fill your screen with a genderless figure's silhouette couched inside a black box. In this image (nonimage?), there is no visual information available about the user. In the bottom corner of the profile, you are sometimes shown the user's name, which can be as nondescript as "dude," sometimes their age, and occasionally an indication of whether they are "online now." Aside from these details, all that remains is the outline of a human head and upper body. At first glance, the image is pure studium; there's nothing exciting about it. However, the outline of a figure is a reminder of the picture that should be there and, conversely, the one that isn't there. The picture's absence is thus the punctum. But how can an absence prick? How can it captivate? How can nothing do something?

Herein lies the trick of quieting, which disguises rhetorical energy beneath layers of remediation. For most Grindr users, the discursive charge attached to queer people (embodyminded rhetoric) is digitized as a profile (material rhetoric) and subsequently visualized in a picture (visual rhetoric). When users opt out of profile pictures, their rhetorical energy remains at the level of digital material. The profile's spatial dimension is a reminder that a user does exist, even if they are not visible.[94] When viewers encounter a blank profile, then, they are faced not with pure studium but with pure punctum. The absence is nothing but a prick. In Barthes's words, the blank profile "is sharp and yet lands in a vague zone of myself; it is acute yet muffled, it cries out in silence."[95] The notion that an image might "cr[y] out in silence" is fitting for the rhetorical matrix, where we might regard visual absence as a variation of queer silence. When a medium is effectively erased, such as the case with the absent visuality of blank profiles, quieting becomes silence. When the signifying potential of a given mode of expression has been completely extinguished, it has been quieted, and it is silent.

There are of course instances of quieting that do not result in silence. It bears repeating that quieting refers to the regulation of signifying intensity, not to any particular end or destination. So while quieting can lead to silence, it does not have to. A perfect example on Grindr is body pics or those images that are faceless but nevertheless show some of a user's body, such as their chests, abs, quads, or calves (see Figure 4). In the provided image, a shirtless Black person wears green briefs that spell "THURSDAY" backward across the waistband. They are using one arm to take the picture, and their face is outside the shot. Profiles such as this still carry visual signification like face pics, but there is something lost in their identifiability. Even if the picture contains a body part that is awesome in its magnitude, strength, or appeal—biceps bigger than my thighs—the image is unique only to

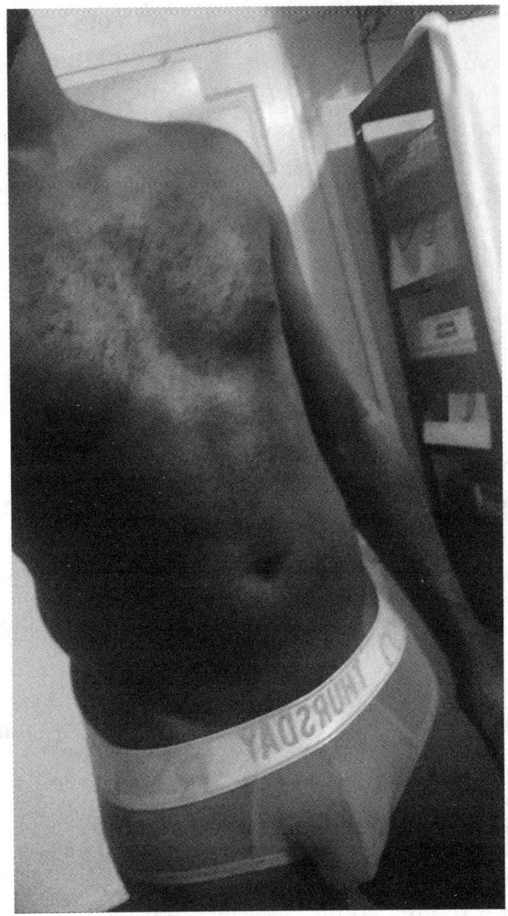

FIGURE 4. Grindr profile picture with a body pic, or image of the user's faceless body. Photograph courtesy of the author's friend.

the digital interface, while it is surrounded by other images. As soon as users leave the app, the chance of noticing that same body part on a stranger diminishes considerably. Body pics, then, limit their rhetoricity to the digital space of the app, where users are encouraged to recognize each image as synecdochic for a queer person. Outside the app, the body parts may lose some of their discursive power as they lose their connection to the queer significations on Grindr that lent them meaning to begin with. In other words, body pics are regulated visual artifacts that constrain what information is offered to other users. Unlike face pics and blank profiles, both of which immediately remind viewers of the queer subjects operating the accounts, body pics restrict their queerness to a single patch of flesh.

Ironically, body pics can sometimes withhold even more than blank profiles because their punctums are more variable. While the totalizing present absence of blank profiles is sure to prick users in an app designed to facilitate visibility, naked bodies take on a greater range of (non)meanings. Sometimes, the image of a body that deviates from homonormative beauty ideals—such as gender nonconforming, fat, Black and brown, and disabled bodies—can elicit attention because of their perceptible difference from the viewer's own body or from the bodies the viewer is accustomed to seeing.[96] In these cases, the naked body itself can be a punctum, an epidermal jolt that fissures a viewer's expectations for masculinity, thinness, whiteness, and abledness that tend to define the genre of body pics. But for those users whose bodies conform to normative expectations, the punctums of their body pics are less clear. It's these such pictures that sometimes leave me wanting more (because I'm horny) but don't typically prompt my engagement. Barthes feels similarly, writing that "there is no *punctum* in the pornographic image; at most it amuses me (and even then, boredom follows quickly)."[97]

This is not to say that anyone's body pics are bad or useless. Far from it, full and partial nudity are indispensable to cultivating the erotic intimacies that sustain queer sexual cultures. Mowlabocus, in fact, reinstates the punctum in pornography, arguing that it "can be as present within the pornographic image as it is in other less explicit photos."[98] In body pics, this detail may be separate from the body (e.g., Mowlabocus writes at length about refrigerator magnets) or it may be part of the body. In Figure 4, which was generously supplied by a friend who uses the picture on Grindr, I am struck by how the light catches curls of hair sprouting across their chest and by the way their dick is folded over to the side rather than tucked straight down, as if pulled toward the same unknown gravity that tilts the photo. Compared to my friend's toned frame, and in contrast with the deep ravines lining their pelvis, the curls of hair and shape of their dick makes their body seem more relaxed and vulnerable, like pieces of themself that escaped their control. For me, these details are interesting and attractive, but their punctal capacity is less certain. Read contextually, vis-à-vis Stockton, I can imagine viewers for whom my friend's Blackness may itself be a punctum or may influence what other details they perceive as punctal. Given how often Black men are fetishized, it is not unthinkable that some viewers would exploit my friend's Blackness as a backdrop onto which they could project their own racial fantasies. These fantasies may very well transform the hair on his chest or the appearance of his dick into punctums that feed on the charge of erotic racism. In another context, such as the one I am writing from, the picture can be situated within a sexual culture dominated by thinness, muscularity, and abledness, which all index my friend's body within the realm of normativity. As such, the details I notice aren't enough to prick me. Neither forms a punctum like a blank profile; neither generates an interruption. I might be turned on because my friend is beautiful, but I am not shaken to the core.

Like face pics, then, body pics can also appear as studium: composites of features that people either like or don't like because they adhere or depart from what we come to expect from them. "The *studium* is of the order of *liking,*" Barthes declares, "not of *loving*; it mobilizes a half desire, a demi-volition; it is the same sort of vague, slippery, irresponsible interest one takes in the people, the entertainments, the books, the clothes one finds 'all right.'"[99] "All right" seems appropriate for images that have been quieted but not silenced, neither visual enough for identification nor absent enough for a material mirage. Body pics occupy the hazy middle ground of multiple signifying media. They are the collision of visual, material, and embodyminded modalities—each of the three struggling for a predominance it will not receive. The resulting effect of the photo can be muted, much like the picture itself is cropped: there's something missing, despite there being so much going on.

Quieting is complicated and contradictory in this way. On the one hand, it reveals the interplay among media within the rhetorical matrix. It captures the fluctuations and regulations of signification as people try to navigate the discourses that signify their bodyminds. According to Jana Sawicki's reading of Foucault, the power of discourse lies in its equal potential for attachment "to strategies of domination as well as those of resistance."[100] With regard to domination, sometimes people are quieted without their consent. When Cameron, one of the trans Grindr users I cite above, recalled his initial resistance to disclosing his transness online, it was because he feared retribution. He had been harassed into invisibility. Other times, quieting is an intentional act of subversion, a mode of resistance, against the compulsion to signify in a particular way (see chapter 3). More commonly, though, quieting is an effect of both domination and resistance. Without the threat of domination, what is there to resist? Without resistance, how can we name what domination threatens? McGlotten's call for optimism and Glenn's turn toward hope urge us to engage these questions with the trust that there is room for change, that at any time, perhaps even now, things might be different enough to keep going, albeit in a new direction or in a new way. Quieting is that different going, that going different, that reconfigures how we signify, so our rhetorical energy might radiate a little longer.

One question that I've returned to frequently since I began thinking critically about digital media and Grindr is how I can hold myself accountable to my online queer communities, especially to those folks whose headless torsos and blank profiles initially sparked my interest in the subject. How do I honor the people who live in that rural college town where I attended graduate school—the farmers, local shop owners, and café servers alongside the other faculty, students, and staff who work for the university? What does the language of quieting and the framework of the rhetorical matrix do for them? In line with my commitments to transfeminism and disability justice, it is important to me that my work enrich the lives of the subjects who populate it; otherwise, I don't believe it's worth doing.[101]

My hope is that quieting provides a tool with which folks online might extend one another a little more generosity, find for themselves a little more self-reflexivity, and share with the world a little more insight about the range of "embodied possibilities" that inform our collective definition of *queer*.[102] Attending to the partially visible and invisible bodies of Grindr users, quieting and the rhetorical matrix acknowledge profiles as sites dense with rhetorical energy. This acknowledgment is especially pertinent to those users whose relationship to queerness is not exclusively or at all identitarian. While queer rhetorics have largely neglected the experiences of people who choose to remain discreet with their sexual and gender identities, and though queer studies has depended on a limited range of spoken, visible, or otherwise legible rhetorical acts to mark objects as queer, the rhetorical matrix insists that *queer*'s rhetoricity is excessive, persistent, and not always intelligible or self-evident in the way we want it to be. The matrix extends *queer*'s rhetoricity to a broader network of people, honoring what Faris calls "desire's and sexuality's free-flowing natures."[103] Likewise, quieting grants recognition to those users who navigate digital spaces, like Grindr, as havens, as sources for community building, and as a means for socialization. Together, the rhetorical matrix and quieting recover those users and their unruly queer bodyminds, saying, "I hear you, and I see you—to the degree that you want to be heard and hope to be seen."

In rural spaces, this recovery is part of an active and necessary project of "queer antiurbanism" that works to transform the spaces, politics, and aesthetics that come to mind when we think *queer.*[104] Coined by Scott Herring, queer antiurbanism redesignates rural locales as potentially "supreme site[s] of queer critique given that stereotypical images of the region or the rural can be used for unexpected ends."[105] The frequency of body pics and blank profiles in the town where I attended graduate school is a reminder of the "stereotypical images" that typically accompany rurality, suggesting widespread closetedness, internalized homophobia, and the precarity facing those who are found out. But as quieting demonstrates, these images can indeed "be used for unexpected ends," as they invigorate (rather than sublimate) the rhetoricity of the queer bodymind. Blank profiles bring to light both the possibility and concentration of queer life where it might otherwise go unnoticed. Body pics similarly capture the queer erotic charge bound up in the arms, chests, and bellies of the people we pass on the street or see across the hall.[106] While perhaps not an exclusively "non-urbanized queer stylistics," quieting nevertheless puts pressure on "the standardizing function of metronormative habitus," proffering ways of being and doing *queer* that butt up against modes of visibility and desirability (or visibility as desirability) that have come to play central roles in urban queer sociality.[107]

The rhetorical matrix also offers queer studies a methodology for examining knots of visual, material, and embodyminded silences. Beyond acknowledging that queer silence exists, the matrix asks us to consider the modality of silence, the way it interacts with its attendant significations, and its particular purpose in a given situation. It avoids concluding that either silence or signification ever exists independently of the other, even in the same moment. It also encourages a reflexive praxis, urging us to consider the applicability of verbal metaphors, like quieting, for other types of signification. Amy Vidali suggests that the value of sensory metaphors, such as how I use silence, lies in the tensions and limits they generate.[108] I believe that queer silence is worth naming as a kind of silence because it turns the conventionally ableist connotations of silence inside out. What was once marked as passivity and weakness might be reclaimed as tactical and resilient. While there is no question that terms like *quieting* and *silence* can limit the imagination, so too do all terms chart their own courses for where our thoughts are and are not meant to travel. I believe this is what Kenneth Burke meant when he said, "Even if any given terminology is a *reflection* of reality, by its very nature as a terminology it must be a *selection* of reality; and to this extent it must function also as a *deflection* of reality."[109] Though the rhetorical matrix helps us to understand some queer rhetorical work, it cannot help us to understand all queer rhetorical work, or at least not all queer rhetorical work perfectly well. There is undoubtedly something lost when we map verbal terminology onto nonverbal action, though what that something is I cannot say. I suppose that the difficulty I have naming what is lost is precisely why the terminology is limited. If I knew its limits from the beginning, I'd write a different beginning.

And yet, I'm not really starting at the beginning. The language of silence has a long history in queer studies and gay activism in which this book attempts to intervene. This chapter in particular takes up silence's cousin, quietness, to wonder about how a silent bodymind or a quieted image might help us to read the subtleties of signification that lie in the folds of elbows and corners of screens. It asks, what do we learn from the verbal register that is restricted not to orality but to the words associated with it? What would remain unspoken if we were to no longer speak of silence? Whose bodies would decompose? Whose images would fade to black—and not the black of blank profiles but the black as in gone forever? Whose speech would go unheard? If we stopped talking about silence, who would be forgotten?

Perhaps one way of approaching these questions is to start listening, looking, feeling, or otherwise sensing out what is hidden. As with many of the users on Grindr, queer rhetoricity too often goes unnoticed because it is quiet, not because it is weak or ineffective. By paying attention to the subtle, maybe queer studies can begin to discover the significance of silence. The rhetorical matrix and quieting offer the field a way to acknowledge the contributions of queers who have heretofore remained unnoticed. It recognizes their presence not simply as an anonymous or empty existence but as a substantive and penetrating resilience. Just as the power of the bodyminds who died from AIDS pushed past the quilts that memorialized them to cover all us queers with meaning, so too do the faceless and blank profiles on Grindr make known that we are here: loud, meaty, and right in front of your eyes.

3

Queer(crip) Masquerading

Two apparently heterosexual, married couples sit at a table in a French restaurant. The server comes to take their orders, and after he walks away, one of the women asks the two men, "So did you guys notice anything?"

Her husband responds sheepishly, "He was a very good looking guy. Yeah, *that* is a beautiful man."

The other woman's husband counters, "I'd say he needs a little more of the masculine butch, a little more of the all-American guy."

"So that's your type?" the first woman asks.

"Well, yeah, sure," he responds.

The above scene is from TLC's *My Husband's Not Gay,* which aired as an hour-long special in 2015 and followed the lives of several ex-gay men and their families.[1] *Ex-gay* refers to those people who experience homoerotic desire or same-gender attraction but choose to pursue a heterosexual marriage and lifestyle. Supported primarily by conservative evangelical and fundamentalist Christian denominations, the ex-gay movement has been steadily gaining popularity over the past two decades as an alternative to conversion therapy, which attempts to alter a person's sexual orientation. The label, though sometimes contested, is mostly a welcome alternative for those Christians who are not comfortable identifying as lesbian, gay, or bisexual because it acknowledges their homoerotic desire even as it rejects what they refer to as the "gay lifestyle."[2]

Responses to the ex-gay movement from LGB-affirming organizations have been overwhelmingly negative. Prior to the *My Husband's Not Gay* premiere, GLAAD (Gay and Lesbian Alliance Against

Defamation) issued an official complaint against TLC, citing both a Change.org petition with over seventy thousand signatures and Sarah Kate Ellis, GLAAD president and CEO, who said that the "show is downright irresponsible. No one can change who they love, and, more importantly, no one should have to."[3] Likewise, Wayne Besen, the executive director for Truth Wins Out, an organization devoted to delegitimizing the ex-gay movement, said that "it's highly irresponsible to propagate the false notion that people can and should choose between their sexuality and their faith. . . . For [TLC] to air this infomercial for junk science is unconscionable."[4] In both GLAAD's and Truth Wins Out's statements, the focus of concern was primarily linked to the "irresponsibility" of claiming that sexuality is a choice, that a person can choose whether to be gay. For several decades, the Left's response to religiously motivated homophobia has been that gay and lesbian people are "born that way." The logic follows that if same-gender desire is biologically innate, then it must be ordained by God and thus spared from religious condemnation. To some degree, this train of thought and the critiques born out of it are useful. As Besen mentions elsewhere in his statement, "impressionable, scared teenagers in conservative religious homes might be watching. Rejection by religious parents leads to depression and oftentimes suicide for LGBT youths."[5] The risk that parents might use *My Husband's Not Gay* to shame their queer children's sexuality justifies a measure of concern over the documentary.

However, what I find strange about the accusations against *My Husband's Not Gay* is that none of them take seriously the lived experiences of the men featured on the show. These ex-gays are fully aware of their homoerotic desires and typically acknowledge that "change" in their sexual orientation is not something they expect to occur. As Alan Chambers, former president of the once-largest ex-gay organization in the world, frequently told members, "the opposite of homosexuality isn't heterosexuality; it's *holiness*."[6] This explicitly religious worldview is obviously at odds with the perspectives of GLAAD and Truth Wins Out, but it is also full of nuance that is effectively flattened by most secular critiques. While I do not contest that evangelical discourse is steeped in heterosexism, or that the ex-gay movement is motivated in part by homophobia, I do think queer scholars and activists should be careful to distinguish between ex-gays themselves and the particular religiocultural conditions that make ex-gay life appealing. The ex-gay identity, despite being informed by antiqueer discourses, nevertheless offers some people a vocabulary to articulate their queerness, social networks through which they can build relationships with other queers, and the space to establish a measured degree of harmony between their sexuality and the rest of their lives. John Fletcher puts it thus: ex-gay "ministries end up producing an essentially novel sexual identity, one that oddly resembles the fluid, binary-challenging identity modes called for by queer theory."[7] Ex-gays are at once not gay and not straight; they inhabit a liminal space that can only be reliably called queer. Ironically, then, the gay-affirmative organizations that derided TLC's documentary cast themselves in the very role they accuse ex-gays of playing: that of being "irresponsible" with representations of queerness. The fury and concern that stem from watching an ex-gay person live in a way we typically associate with straight people—in a heterosexual marriage—inverts what Eve Kosofsky Sedgwick calls "homosexual panic."[8] In this case, rather than the panic explaining antigay violence, it reifies a particular discourse and set of social constructs surrounding what it means to be gay.

The impulse to characterize and typologize queerness is certainly not a new one, and queer studies scholars, such as David Halperin, have written at length on variations of homoeroticism.[9] However, *My Husband's Not Gay* and the ex-gay movement merit further consideration not only because they offer an alternative representation of queerness but also because this representation involves multiple layers of resignification, a process I call *queer masquerading.* This phrase refers to the particular ways that queer people, including ex-gays, can manipulate their rhetorical energy not across modalities or media as with the Grindr users in chapter 2 but within the fleshy constraints of their own bounded bodyminds. In order to resignify their queerness, ex-gays engage what Tobin Siebers calls the "masquerade" or "an alternative method of managing social stigma through disguise."[10] The ex-gay disguise is a disability one, for ex-gays understand their homoerotic desire, in part, as a mental illness. In this chapter I argue that ex-gays seek not to eliminate their queerness but to silence it, harnessing the signifying potential of their queer rhetorical energy to recode and retool it as disability.

Given that many readers will be unfamiliar with ex-gay life, I divide this chapter into three sections, the first of which historicizes the ex-gay movement within the medical and religious contexts from which it stems. The second explains the ex-gay claim to disability through Siebers's masquerade. While Siebers was a literary and cultural scholar of disability, I present him additionally as a rhetorician. His theory of the disability masquerade can be understood not only as a performance (his metaphor) but also as an embodyminded rhetorical act that requires a person to reconfigure their rhetorical energy. In this section, I adopt *Coming Out Straight: Understanding and Healing Homosexuality* by Richard A. Cohen, a famous advocate for the ex-gay movement, as a case study for the variation of queer silence that ex-gays employ to gain control over their rhetorical energy. Then in the third section, I speak to the implications of ex-gay masquerading for both queer studies and disability studies scholars, many of whom are invested in queercrip cross-identifications. To conclude, I return to *My Husband's Not Gay,* asking what those of us invested in embodyminded rhetorics and queer politics might learn from the ex-gay masquerade.

A Queercrip History of Ex-Gays

The term *ex-gay* has multiple meanings. Within so-called reparative therapy, which was a psychotherapeutic variation of conversion therapy popularized in the 1990s, *ex-gay* referred to those people who used to experience homoerotic desire but no longer do. The founder of reparative therapy, Joseph Nicolosi, argues that ex-gays have "taken a different developmental route" from mainstream LGB people to uncover their natural heterosexuality.[11] The prefix *ex-* in this instance is synonymous with *post-* or *former,* indicating that the individual used to identify as gay but no longer does because the characteristic associated with gayness (i.e., homoerotic desire) has been allegedly replaced by pure, unadulterated heterosexual desire. For at least a decade, this definition was by far the most common, reflecting reparative therapy's insistence that total conversion from homosexuality into heterosexuality was possible. Indeed, the motto for the now defunct—but once largest—umbrella organization for reparative therapy, Exodus

International, was "Change is possible."[12] The emphasis on change helped to frame the ex-gay identity as a kind of transitional stage, an indication that the client was on their way out of homosexuality and into heterosexuality, pursuing "the common human task of growing toward wholeness."[13] In fact, reparative therapists encouraged their clients to identify as heterosexual as quickly as possible, even if the clients still experienced exclusively homoerotic desire. Nicolosi suggests that since "an identification deficit lies behind . . . homoerotic attractions," clients should adopt a heterosexual identity as a rhetorical motivation for cultivating heteroeroticism.[14] The term *ex-gay,* then, was not so much a desired state as a clinical one, a symptomatic moment in the process of becoming.

Much of the ideology behind Nicolosi's work stems from the psychiatric and psychoanalytic theories of the mid-twentieth century, when homosexuality was formally and institutionally pathologized. In its first edition of the *Diagnostic and Statistical Manual of Mental Disorders* (*DSM-I*), the American Psychiatric Association defined *homosexuality* as a "sexual deviation" along with "transvestism, pedophilia, fetishism and sexual sadism (including rape, sexual assault, mutilation)" within its list of sociopathic personality disturbances.[15] This framing encouraged a variation of cisheterosexism that relied on disability prejudice, where gender-normative heterosexuality is idealized by way of presumed abledness.[16] Psychiatrists devoted extraordinary energy to developing supposed cures and treatments for homoerotic desire, typically using religiously inflected motivations to justify poor interpretations of Freudian psychoanalysis.[17] These practices mostly tapered off by 1973, when homosexuality was removed from the *DSM-II.* However, some conservative religious groups continued to promote variations of conversion therapy, including the pseudoscientific reparative therapy, through the turn of the century for men "dealing with 'sexual brokenness.'"[18] In fact, it has only been within the last decade that the largest reparative therapy organization in the United States began to reconcile with the inefficacy of its own practices.

In January 2012, the Board of Directors for the Alliance for Therapeutic Choice and Scientific Integrity acknowledged "the expressed pessimism regarding sexual orientation change" in a public statement.[19] Initially, the organization tried to dismiss the severity of people's concerns, claiming that the problem was not one of clinical efficacy but of clients' unwarranted expectations. Too often, the statement suggested, did clients "intentionally or inadvertently" take on "a categorical conceptualization of change" when they should have "conceptualized such change as occurring on a continuum."[20] "Change" in this case refers to the previous pledge that sexual orientation change is possible, that gays can be made straight. By pivoting from a dimorphic to a spectral model of sexual desire, Alliance hoped to foster more "realistic expectancies" among ex-gays that protected the clinical reputation of reparative therapy, even as it continued to promise "sustained shifts in the direction and intensity of [clients'] sexual attractions, fantasy, and arousal."[21] It was a way of saving face without folding entirely.

By May 2016, however, Alliance admitted that conversion from homosexuality to heterosexuality is not "scientifically or politically tenable."[22] In another public statement, the board of directors announced that terms such as *reparative therapy, conversion therapy,* and *sexual orientation change efforts* would no longer be used by the organization.[23] Instead, Alliance adopted the new term "Sexual Attraction Fluidity Exploration in Therapy" (hilariously referred to as "SAFE-T"), which more explicitly avoids suggesting "that categorical change is the goal and in so doing creat[ing] unrealistic expectations."[24] SAFE-T is meant to emphasize the inherent malleability of sexual attraction while simultaneously avoiding associations with words like *orientation* and *identity.* The benefit of using *attraction* in tandem with a word like *fluidity* is that neither can be quantified, making it nearly impossible to collect data that reliably evaluates the effectiveness of the practice. While phrases like *sexual orientation* and *sexual identity* connote a kind of permanence, or at least stasis, *sexual attraction* is ambiguously dynamic. That is to say, I *have* a sexual orientation and a sexual identity; they are ontological characteristics that help constitute my self-concept. However, I *feel* a sexual attraction; I experience it phenomenologically as it passes through, over, and around me.

From the perspective of SAFE-T practitioners, this distinction between *having* and *feeling,* being and experiencing, is helpful because it allows them to downplay the relevance of a person's stated sexual orientation in exchange for an exclusive focus on their attraction and desire. In its 2016 statement, Alliance praises SAFE-T because "it avoids the implicit assertion that orientation changes or that orientation as an immutable reality even exists."[25] And in their most recent "Guidelines for the Practice of Sexual Attraction Fluidity Exploration in Therapy" (2018), the organization is careful to use the language of "developing heterosexual potential," rather than that of conversion or reparation to a fully-fledged heterosexual identity.[26] By rejecting orientation and identity politics entirely, SAFE-T practitioners are able to frame sexual desire as entirely fluid, thereby obviating labels of attraction or desire.[27] To identify as gay or straight within the SAFE-T framework is nonsense, like trying to name water at different places in a stream. It's all water; it's all sexual attraction; it's all heterosexual potential.

By disassociating experience from identity, SAFE-T clients invoke the term *ex-gay* in an entirely new way from its previous usage to describe a temporary layover between binary sexualities. Rather than denoting the embodyminded experience of transitioning from homoerotic into heteroerotic desire, *ex-gay* now names a political identity, one that simultaneously derives from and staunchly rejects the LGB community. Quoting from an ex-gay therapist who is himself ex-gay, ethnographer Tanya Erzen recounts the words of Frank Worthen: "We recognize that [ex-gay] is an artificial label and it is a humiliation to all of us. But it is our witness to the world, in terms that the world can understand. It proclaims that change is possible. It is a light, shining in the darkness of deception."[28] This excerpt captures much of the nuance and, ultimately, the paradoxical nature of the ex-gay identity. On one hand, it is artificial insofar as it does not describe the lived experience of the subject who uses it because the majority of (if not all) people who identify as ex-gay still experience homoerotic desire. There is nothing "ex-" about their gayness. And it is the very artificiality of this prefix that makes the label "a humiliation," a reminder of the heterosexual they have not become. On the other hand, aside from this personal indictment, the term also functions as a "witness," a proclamation, "a light" by which a subject is transformed from a poor soul plagued with homoerotic desire to an evangelist preaching the possibility of spiritual change. Embedded in this transformation are traces of moralizing sentiments, residue from the influence of evangelical Christian traditions.[29]

Other scholars who work on ex-gay themes note the inherent queerness of ex-gay life. Erzen likens ex-gayness to a "queer conversion."[30] Lynne Gerber calls it "queerish."[31] W. C. Harris argues that it "could breed a queer(ed) fraternity."[32] In all of these cases, the ex-gay identity is understood not only as a rejection of secular LGB identifications but also an embrace of an alternative form of *queer,* one that falls more in line with how queer studies intends the term to function: as that which cannot "signify monolithically"[33] and that "*resists calculation.*"[34] *Queer* has always been at its most powerful when it is not owned but cast, not taken on as a self-identification but pointed elsewhere. As Butler puts it, "The expectation of self-determination that self-naming arouses is paradoxically contested by the historicity of the name itself."[35] To call oneself "queer" in an effort to align oneself with other queers is to immediately reduce the rhetorical power of the word, which is predicated on "self-determination." With regard to its potential to subvert normativity, *queer* is most useful when it remains something of a surprise. Ex-gays embody this subversive surprise because, as Erzen attests, "their narratives of testimonial sexuality are performances that, while sincere, point to the instability and changeability of their own identities rather than serve as a testament to heterosexuality."[36] The queerness of ex-gays refers not to their affiliation with LGB people but to their position contra evangelical Christianity and mainstream LGB discourse. Ex-gays are not closeted or hiding their supposedly true sexuality; rather, they openly occupy an identity category that is irreconcilable with Western, secular models of homoeroticism. They are queer but adamantly not queer-identified: queer but not Queer.

In addition to its engagement with and against secular LGB identity politics, what ex-gays call the "Gay Explanatory Framework," the ex-gay identity also plays into broader cultural narratives surrounding medicalization and disability.[37] In *Cultural Locations of Disability,* Sharon L. Snyder and David T. Mitchell introduce the "cultural model" of disability as a way to acknowledge that "environment and bodily variation (particularly those traits experienced as socially stigmatized differences) inevitably impinge upon each other" and that any "definition of disability must incorporate both the outer and inner reaches of culture and experience as a combination of profoundly social and biological forces."[38] This is to say that disability is never entirely biological or entirely social, that it appears to different degrees and in different variations depending on how particular bodyminds interact with particular spaces at particular times. In short, disability is contingent. Historically, however, disability—much like queerness—has been read through either religious or medical lenses.

According to the moral model, disability is accorded spiritual value, indicating either God's wrath or salvation. Nancy Eiesland, a theologian, explains that in the Christian tradition, a disabled person is "either divinely blessed or damned: the defiled evil doer or the spiritual superhero."[39] To live as disabled is to practice "virtuous suffering," where the plight of moving through a world that is hostile to disabled bodyminds is understood "as means of purification and of gaining spiritual merit" and of giving in to "social barriers as a sign of obedience to God."[40] In this sense, disability takes on a "moral weight," in the words of Deborah Beth Creamer, which invites pity and sympathy rather than drives social or political action.[41]

The medical model of disability, which largely superseded the moral model during the Industrial Revolution, regards disability as a clinical defect, one that must be quickly fixed, treated, cured, or otherwise remedied. Sayantani DasGupta adds, in her short essay titled "Medicalization," that the medical model is linked to capitalism, where "those bodies perceived to be unproductive and/or nonnormative [are] sequestered, controlled, diagnosed, and otherwise administered to by the growing medical profession."[42] For ex-gays, the moral and medical models play off each other: ex-gays pathologize their queerness (medical model) to signify as disabled within their religious communities (moral model). Though the moral model is imbued with ableist, disability-phobic rhetoric, it is tame compared to the homophobia and heterosexism that ex-gays risk facing should they take on the "Gay Explanatory Framework." While evangelicals pity and objectify disability, they rarely tolerate LGB identities and routinely excommunicate or reject gay-identified members from their congregations. By coding themselves as disabled, ex-gays secure a position within evangelical spaces while maintaining a level of openness about their homoerotic desire.

In order to successfully pass as disabled, ex-gays must navigate a complicated rhetorical terrain, one that Gerber refers to as "an appeal to creation."[43] "In the context of homosexuality, with both science and LGBTQIA rights activists routinely poised to challenge normative Christian claims about sexuality through an appeal to nature," she writes, "ex-gay ministries need a way both to fix the essentialism of sex and gender and to undermine claims that homosexuality itself may be essential, determined by nature, and therefore immutable."[44] The resulting "appeal to creation" draws on psychoanalytic theories from the early and mid-twentieth century while belying the religious motivations behind them. Organizations like Alliance medicalize ex-gays as having a psychiatric disability, whereby homoerotic desire can be understood as an unfortunate, albeit static, condition.[45] Though homosexuality was removed from the *DSM-II* nearly fifty years ago, most ex-gays are skeptical of secular medicine, especially of mental health organizations like the American Psychiatric Association, for being biased against Christians and political conservatives. Thus, they typically seek out explicitly religious therapists or pastoral counselors, many of whom are unlicensed, to make sense of their homoeroticism.

While outsiders may doubt the efficacy of these openly religious and often unlicensed practitioners, Tom Waidzunas reminds us that there is a "field of therapeutics" that "cuts across the institutions of medicine, mental health . . . , and theology."[46] This field is defined by competing claims to expertise, allowing that "someone on the fringe of science may still find credibility within religious institutions."[47] As Gerber puts it, "Ex-gay ministries want to retain access to nature and science as authoritative discourses. But they are well aware that locating their project in either of those domains may render it vulnerable if and when they can no longer contain rival claims within those discursive terms."[48] Organizations like Alliance and their associated evangelical practitioners act as a middle ground between secular science and religious orthodoxy, insisting on a "dialogue between religion and psychology"[49] that ultimately filters what information from "nature and science" meshes with Christian morality.[50] In true conservative fashion, Alliance justifies this gatekeeping as a check on the unmetered progressivism of the American Psychiatric Association (APA). Among Alliance's "Three Guiding Principles" is a commitment to "Reliable Research and Viewpoint Diversity" in order to "appropriately serve and appreciate clients with differing, yet equally healthy needs."[51] By filtering through only those medical theories that confirm evangelical cisheterosexism (i.e., homosexuality as a gender deficit), SAFE-T practitioners develop a rapport with their clients as both clinically competent and religiously righteous. Indeed, for many of their clients, it's their evangelical ethos that gives credence to their medical knowledge.

Notably, not all ex-gays are religious. Though a minority, secular ex-gays do exist and often occupy the same therapeutic spaces as evangelical ex-gays. One of Alliance's primary arguments is that homoerotic desire—when expressed through the "gay lifestyle"—entails a host of health-related dangers that are independent of the eschatological concerns that homosexuality raises. In a report written by SAFE-T practitioners James E. Phelan, Neil Whitehead, and Philip M. Sutton, being gay maintains not only a correlative but also a causal relationship with all sorts of disabilities, illnesses, and diseases. "In fact," they write, "it is difficult to find another group in society with such high risks for experiencing such a wide range of medical, psychological, and relational dysfunctions."[52] These dysfunctions include alcoholism and substance use, risk of contracting HIV, risk of other STIs, suicide, maladjustment, and a host of mental disorders, such as anxiety, depression, disordered eating, bipolar disorder, agoraphobia, obsessive-compulsive disorder, panic disorder, and psychosis. Phelan, Whitehead, and Sutton are also quick to suggest that "people who are homosexually-oriented" are more likely to cheat on their partners, be "wildly promiscuous," develop sex addictions, rape and molest people, be "generally more violent and criminal," and participate in presumably evil sex practices, such as water sports and fisting.[53] Within the context of SAFE-T, this assortment of comorbidities is explained causally, with homoerotic desire positioned as the gateway to a life of pain and godlessness. While it is true that sexual minorities are more likely to experience some mental disabilities, ex-gay proponents jump at the opportunity to stigmatize these conditions and to blame sexual minorities themselves for the correlations.

Michael Hobbes, author of the well-circulated *Huffington Post* article "Together Alone: The Epidemic of Gay Loneliness," acknowledges that there are rising rates of anxiety, depression, substance use, and suicide among gay men in the United States. He gives example after example of gay people he knows who are, for lack of a better word, "struggling":

> There's Malcolm, who barely leaves the house except for work because his anxiety is so bad. There's Jared, whose depression and body dysmorphia have steadily shrunk his social life down to me, the gym and internet hookups. And there was Christian, the second guy I ever kissed, who killed himself at 32, two weeks after his boyfriend broke up with him. Christian went to a party store, rented a helium tank, started inhaling it, then texted his ex and told him to come over, to make sure he'd find the body.[54]

Hobbes also includes quantitative research, citing study after study indicating that gay men are more likely to be sad, unsatisfied with their relationships, lonely, and more insecure than their straight peers. With an almost audible sigh, Hobbes writes, "All of these unbearable statistics lead to the same conclusion: It is still dangerously alienating to go through life as a man attracted to other men."[55]

Ex-gay advocates, in turn, use these "unbearable statistics" as evidence for the supposed disabling nature of homoerotic desire. For example, Michael Brown, an ex-gay proponent, misappropriates Hobbes's article to reinforce a heterosexist perspective on marriage and human relationality. Though most responses to Hobbes's article cite social stigma and homophobia, especially among queer youth, poor and working-class queer people, and queer people of color, as responsible for the dismaying statistics, Brown blames the inadequacy of same-gender relationships: "Could it be that, generally speaking, there's something intrinsically unfulfilling about homosexual relationships? Could it be that, by divine intent, ultimate relational fulfillment for human beings can be found only in heterosexual marriage?"[56] It is these sorts of rhetorical questions and their implied answers that encourage ex-gays, both religious and secular, to embrace a model of queerness that promises a future of health and happiness, even if that model necessitates self-pathologizing and the conflation of heterosexuality with abledness.

Additionally, the notion that unmedicalized queerness is "intrinsically unfulfilling" helps situate the ex-gay lifestyle as more than a personal choice, boosting it to an evangelical opportunity. Ex-gays argue that the pain attached to being gay is a call from God to repent, and they see themselves as models for the "hope" God offers through salvation. Ironically, this mode of evangelizing through visibility bears stark resemblances to mainstream LGBTQIA rights activism, where representations of sexual and gender diversity are a top priority. In fact, Fletcher argues that "evangelicals . . . operate via a sophisticated technology of activist outreach."[57] Though he acknowledges that evangelizing has often taken (and still takes) shape as colonial violence, he also insists that "evangelicals have the most venerable, most searching, and most comprehensive discourse about how to proclaim messages and persuade audiences."[58] Christian evangelism can be likened to a kind of consciousness raising that aims to bring awareness to what Christians understand as a broken world. The comparison to activism is useful for Fletcher and for me because it allows us to appropriate the critical discourse we typically reserve for "*left-progressive performance activism*" to understand social change efforts more broadly.[59]

Specific to ex-gays, Fletcher suggests that the lens of activism reveals "how exquisitely aware they are of their dubious reputation in non-evangelical culture and their status as abusive agents in many LGBT contexts."[60] It is not that ex-gays are ignorant of how others perceive them; they readily acknowledge their own marginalization both from mainstream LGB folks and within their own religious communities. Nevertheless, ex-gays embrace their ostracization as a symbol of martyrdom, believing that their sacrifice is for all of humanity. In Fletcher's words, the ex-gay lifestyle "resituates [ex-gays] into a grander context of Christian living within a fallen world. Same-gender attractions figure as persistent temptations, tendencies of thought and behavior that it is a Christian's duty to resist."[61] As performance activism, we can understand ex-gays as mobilizing their lifestyle—complete with pathologization—toward "the advancement of broader social or political agendas."[62] Thus, the ex-gay claim to disability is not only about self-protection or survival but also about social transformation. Ex-gays pursue a cultural queer conversion.

The Ex-Gay Masquerade

I understand this evangelical model of conversion as a uniquely ex-gay instantiation of the queer masquerade introduced above. In "Disability as Masquerade," Siebers addresses the ways and reasons that some disabled people (mis)represent their disabilities in order to make their lives easier or more manageable. He argues, via Erving Goffman, that since disability is often stigmatized, it typically befalls disabled people to either pass or cover their disabilities. In *Stigma,* Goffman associates *passing* with those whom he calls "the discreditable": those persons who recognize that they have the potential to become stigmatized if others find out about a particular aspect of their identity (e.g., a person with light skin who hides their Black ancestry to pass as white).[63] *Covering,* by contrast, refers to efforts by already-discredited people to minimize the effects or legibility of the stigmas that mark them (e.g., a blind person who wears sunglasses to "spare" sighted people from seeing their eyes). That is, covering is for those who cannot pass, for those whose stigmatized characteristics cannot be hidden. For Goffman, covering is meant "to withdraw covert attention from the stigma," focusing others' attention on another aspect of one's identity.[64] Covering is diminishing, managing, distracting.

Siebers, though, worries that this definition of *covering* is too narrow to encompass all stigmas, including those associated with many disabilities. While he acknowledges that passing is not the only way to reframe one's identity, he is unsatisfied with covering as the only alternative. He wonders specifically about people who "disguise one kind of disability with another or display their disability by exaggerating it."[65] The intention here is neither to pass as nondisabled nor to diminish the visibility of one's disabilities but to "[claim] disability as a version of itself,"[66] effectively—per Krista Kennedy—"writing a life beyond the one society proscribes."[67] This writing is what Siebers calls "masquerading," which is not merely to claim one's stigmatized identity but to reclaim it, to perform it otherwise.

The purpose of masquerading, for Siebers, is twofold. First, it avoids the precarity of passing, the ongoing possibility that one's stigma could be revealed or recognized. Second, it allows people "to develop new narratives of the self and new political forms."[68] That is, masquerading holds the potential to transform a negatively charged political identity into a positively charged one. By offering the discredited, as Goffman would label them, the opportunity to reinscribe their bodyminds with alternative identities, masquerading can be profoundly liberating. Siebers recounts a variety of examples, including one anecdote about his own tendency to exaggerate his limp at the airport. He does so to avoid scrutiny and interrogation by airline employees, who often refuse to acknowledge his disability "unless [his] status [is] validated by a highly visible prop like a wheelchair."[69] By performing his disability otherwise, he "resists the prejudices of society," taking control over the narrative that is told about his body.[70] He enacts disability as a kind of subversion, "seizing control of stereotypes . . . to explore alternative narratives."[71]

I take Siebers's project to be distinctly rhetorical because he attempts to regulate how his bodymind is read by those around him. In *Embodied Rhetorics: Disability in Language and Culture,* James C. Wilson and Cynthia Lewiecki-Wilson point out that "one link that emerges [between disability and rhetoric] is disability's relation to rhetoric through the mediating term of the body."[72] Similar to the way it can swarm sexual minorities in some spaces, the rhetorical energy hovering around disabled bodyminds is particularly strong in contexts where their disabilities are stigmatized. And Siebers's masquerade offers a way to lean into that signifying potential, to perform variations of it that capitalize on others' preconceptions. As Jay Dolmage and Lewiecki-Wilson write, "Rhetors make use of disability as rhetorical power" when the "'abnormal' body and voice" are put to "generative rhetorical effect."[73] While all bodyminds are surrounded by rhetorical energy, masquerading names the intentional manipulation of that energy for a specific purpose. In his own example, Siebers uses a limp to elucidate a particular response from the employee; he consciously deploys his energy through an embodyminded performance that produces a rhetorical effect.

Near the end of his essay, Siebers expands his discussion to include not only reclaimed stigmas or exaggerated disabilities but also "feigned disabilities," which he argues "serve as small conspiracies against oppression and inequality."[74] Here, Siebers—however unintentionally—makes room for ex-gays, whose self-pathologization can be taken as a queer masquerade. Although he is critical of nondisabled people outright faking disability, a discussion that I return to below, Siebers's theory nevertheless offers a helpful analytic for understanding how ex-gays operate. I argue that the masquerade models how rhetorical energy offers not only signifying potential but also *re*signifying potential. Ex-gays certainly harness their queer rhetorical energy, but they also refashion that energy to signify differently within their communities, thus drawing on a variation of queer silence that hinges on their ability to rewrite their embodyminded significations. In short, ex-gays enact queer silence by claiming that their queer bodyminds are, in fact, disabled bodyminds. Unlike the users on Grindr from chapter 2, who negotiate silence across various signifying media, ex-gays navigate their silence primarily on the surface of their own bodies. Jack Selzer reminds us: "Language and rhetoric have a persistent material aspect that demands acknowledgement, and material realities often (if not always) contain a rhetorical dimension that deserves attention."[75] In this case, the ex-gay bodymind has a queer rhetorical dimension that is distinctively disabled. Indeed, what is most queer about the ex-gay masquerade is not homoerotic desire but performed mental illness.

The rhetorical maneuvers required to approximate mental illness are made clear in ex-gay propaganda, such as the manuals, workbooks, and testimonies that are recommended reading for ex-gays. One such text is Richard Cohen's *Coming Out Straight: Understanding and Healing Homosexuality,* which was once a prominent piece of ex-gay literature. While Cohen himself has been ousted from most ex-gay circles for his support of "holding therapy"—which is just as creepy and abusive as it sounds—his book still serves as a useful example of how evangelicals distill multiple, complex discourses on queerness and disability into a single rhetorical performance.[76] *Coming Out Straight* synthesizes the medical perspectives of early reparative therapists, such as Elizabeth Moberly, Charles W. Socarides, and Joseph Nicolosi, with the religious motivations of most contemporary ex-gays. It is truly a remarkable text that underscores the flexibility and intensity of queer rhetorical energy.

Like most ex-gay proponents, Cohen makes an explicit distinction between gay identity and homoerotic desire; he chooses to label the latter "Same-Sex Attachment Disorder" (SSAD).[77] His reliance on a pseudo-medical diagnosis replaces the assumed "frustration and pain" of being gay with a form of mental illness that is "the result of unresolved childhood trauma."[78] The clinical tone and structure of this formulation is characteristic of Cohen's book and in fact sets it apart from other, exclusively theological works that make claims about the etiology and nature of homoerotic desire. Despite the fact that the book's contents have been rejected by the American Psychological Association and that Cohen himself has been permanently expelled from the American Counseling Association, *Coming Out Straight* nevertheless maintains the air of a professional discussion about a legitimate psychiatric disability.[79] When blended with his religiosity, which Cohen makes explicit by dedicating the book "To God," the clinical tone functions like a credential, making him seem both educated and spiritually sound.

Perhaps even more important than his learned expertise is Cohen's autobiographical perspective. Erzen points out that the most effective ethical appeal among ex-gay practitioners is testimony. She writes, "Personal experience is the prerequisite for a position of authority," that "their skill resides primarily in their experience of the same sexual conflict."[80] Fittingly, the first chapter of Cohen's book is titled "My Story: Coming Out Straight," where Cohen offers his own personal narrative about addressing "the homo-emotional wounds of [his] past."[81] "In childhood and adolescence," he begins, "I remember my father screaming at us and my mother clinging to me. I was quite distant from him and too close to her."[82] After years of temptation, sin, struggle, and healing, Cohen emerged as "a Wounded Healer"—his euphemism for an ex-gay poised to profit off others suffering from SSAD.[83] Once he establishes this highly personal, deeply religious reputation, Cohen transitions to his medical expertise.

The book's second chapter, "Definitions and Causes of Same-Sex Attraction," offers a visual diagram that unpacks the medical framework used by ex-gays to understand their homoerotic desires. The diagram lists three bulleted points that together explain the diagnosis of SSAD. The first, "Homosexuality is a symptom," suggests that "homosexual feelings, thoughts, and desires are symptoms of underlying issues."[84] These "issues" range from poor parent-child relationships, to previous sexual abuse, to a failure to identify with one's gender at birth.[85] The second point, "Homosexuality is an emotionally based condition," specifies the diagnosis as a mental one, locating the "problem" of homoerotic desire not in the body but in an "unconscious drive buried deep in the psyche."[86] This decision to classify SSAD as a mental illness certainly recalls previous diagnoses issued by the APA to pathologize homosexuality, but it also works to reinforce a division between mind and body. By locating erotic desire solely in the mind, ex-gays are more easily able to distinguish between sexual attraction and sexual behavior, a split that undergirds the foundation of ex-gay life. The final bullet point in the diagram provides the official name for the diagnosis: "Homosexuality is a Same-Sex Attachment Disorder." Thus is homoerotic desire concretized as a pathological condition.

In contrast with previous pathologizations of queerness, such as the versions used historically by the APA, SSAD is not a condition to be remedied or cured. Although the subtitle for both the first and second editions of *Coming Out Straight* is *Understanding and Healing Homosexuality,* all three published editions of the book echo Alliance's commitment to changing sexual identity (i.e., SAFE-T) rather than converting homoerotic desires into heteroerotic ones. Ex-gays acknowledge their attraction to the same gender and reject acting on that desire, but they do not predict a recovery from it, such as might be expected in reparative therapy. As Brothers on a Road Less Traveled, an ex-gay organization, clarifies in a self-published anthology of ex-gay testimonies, "For most people who seek change [in their homoerotic desire], heterosexuality is not actually the ultimate goal—happiness and peace are."[87] Unlike most medical diagnoses, which are meant to identify a condition so a clinician can recommend a course of treatment or care, SSAD is both the condition and the treatment. To be pathologized as an ex-gay is to take on the identity of psychiatric disability and the corresponding narrative that it is an unalterable, intrinsic condition. Rhetorically, this diagnostic step works to unmoor ex-gays' rhetorical energy from secular queer discourses, where their bodyminds are coded and read within a sexually minoritizing framework. By introducing a new discourse via medicine, Cohen and other ex-gay practitioners can rewrite queerness as a disability, effectively resignifying queer bodyminds as disabled ones.

Being ex-gay involves more than just taking on a personal identity, however. *Coming Out Straight* includes six ex-gay testimonies—short autobiographies from people who have received the SSAD diagnosis—that speak to the social and cultural dimensions of ex-gay life. According to sociologist Christy M. Ponticelli, who has done extensive field work in ex-gay spaces, these testimonies are essential to securing the disability narrative. The testimonies offer "an interactional group process" where ex-gays can take on "a new universe of discourse and biographical reconstruction."[88] Ex-gay testimonies offer a sense of community and support for people to affirm and validate one another's newly minted diagnoses. It is a way of making their queer disability legible both to others and, more importantly, to themselves. By sharing their personal testimonies with one another, ex-gays construct a form of relationality around their mutual queer silence. Unlike people who embrace the "Gay Explanatory Framework" and who bond over their shared stakes in LGB identification, ex-gays relate to one another through their shared rejection of LGB identity in favor of a disabled one. The testimonies thus act as a membership card, both offering an explanation for an individual's history of queer embodyminded significations and situating them within a community of others who are committed to signifying differently.

Ponticelli writes that these testimonies are typically made up of four constitutive stages: innocence, suffering, epiphany, and transformation.[89] The ex-gay begins by recalling their prepubescent childhood, a period before the woes of sexual maturity. Christian, one of Cohen's ex-gay exemplars, reminisces: "My childhood, in my eyes, had been perfect. My parents had provided me with a beautiful home, clothes, food, and social and travel experiences."[90] The second stage transitions to an acknowledgment of what Ponticelli calls "the initial 'virus,'" which is often a tragic event or series of events that eventually manifest SSAD.[91] Christian admits: "[I] left myself wide open for inappropriate touch by one relative and sexual abuse by teenage boys who would baby-sit and take me on outings. This helped to peel away more layers of what had felt like, 'I'm gay.'"[92] Afterward, the speaker moves to the third stage, epiphany, when they recognize that their homoerotic desire is "unhealthy," a realization that leads them to transform themselves, the fourth stage, into a happy ex-gay.[93] Christian's tipping point was when his wife gave him "the best ultimatum of [his] life: 'Go see Richard [Cohen], or move out and get a divorce.'"[94] Though he had his doubts initially, Christian began therapy, where "it became apparent that [he] was living a wonderful, productive life with [his] wife, children, and friends."[95] The progression from purity to tragedy to awakening to fulfillment adds depth to the ex-gay identity, providing an alternative "coming out" story that coheres with evangelical righteousness.

It's worth noting that since Ponticelli published her research in 1999, the final stage of ex-gay testimony, "Transformation," has evolved. Ponticelli suggests that "by giving testimony, the [ex-gay] demonstrates that she has accepted the role of 'healed.'"[96] The use of past tense here aligns the ex-gay identity with the reparative therapy movement, in which clients are expected to experience heterosexual desire. But the premise of the ex-gay movement is that, as Cohen writes, "*healing is a journey, not a destination.*"[97] To be ex-gay is not to be healed but to be healing; it is not a static identity but one necessarily in flux, reflecting the ongoing tension between erotic desire and religious commitment. It is this tension that legitimizes the rhetorical performance of the ex-gay masquerade. While secular outsiders might be quick to dismiss the claim to disability as "a joke," evangelicals and ex-gays themselves understand it as a scripturally based gesture of righteousness born out of the inevitable conflict between a fallen world and a holy god.[98] In other words, by embracing a pathologized identity, ex-gays ensure their own protection from religious ostracization: the medical diagnosis shields them from accusations that they are unrepentant. Disability thus functions as a relational catalyst, a mechanism through which ex-gays can align themselves with a particular group. As we see in *My Husband's Not Gay,* ex-gays envision their identities as a means to community membership and fraternity. It just so happens that their means entail the rhetorical construction of a pathologized identity and a disability community.

Of course, the move to take on a disability identity for the purposes of forming solidarity or building relationships with other disabled people was not invented by ex-gays. Disabled people have written extensively about the importance of reclaiming *disability* as a term of empowerment. Simi Linton, for instance, writes:

> When disability is redefined as a social/political category, people with a variety of conditions are identified as *people with disabilities* or *disabled people,* a group bound by common social and political experiences. These designations, as reclaimed by the community, are used to identify us as a constituency, to serve our needs for unity and identity, and to function as a basis for political activism.[99]

Here Linton eloquently frames the political nature of disability. To claim disability is to engage in a speech act that is distinct from any diagnosis or medical opinion. It is an act of resistance and pride; it is a way to "assert our right to name experience."[100] Other scholar-activists, like Eli Clare, draw parallels between the reclamation of disability and other stigmatized identities. In *Exile and Pride,* Clare writes that "*Queer* and *cripple* are cousins: words to shock, words to infuse with pride and self-love, words to resist internalized hatred, words to help forge a politics. They have been gladly chosen."[101] His pairing of *cripple* with *queer* asserts a kind of similarity in the ways that both words have been taken up by their respective populations and used to push back against dominant discourses.

It is because of this drive to reclaim identities rather than to create new ones that Siebers's concept of masquerade can be enacted so successfully. Reclaimed identities presuppose a recognition that identities are always already political, shaping the material world in which they exist. As Siebers puts it, identities "are narrative responses to and creations of social reality, aiding cooperation between people, representing significant theories about the construction of the real, and containing useful information about how human beings should make their appearance in the world."[102] To reclaim a disability identity, then, is not simply to adopt an optimistic perspective toward disability but to align oneself with an alternative definition of what disability is and how it affects one's engagement with the world. Masquerading can be understood as a form of this reclamation process, a way "to explore alternative narratives."[103] To masquerade is to respond to Linton's call for disability "as a social/political category," to take on a disability identity not because its symptoms are self-apparent but because it is "a basis for political activism."

The ex-gay masquerade throws Siebers's and Linton's works into crisis. While masquerading is undoubtedly a political act, ex-gays remind us that not every political act is guaranteed to be liberatory. In his essay, Siebers admits to the possibility that nondisabled people might co-opt masquerading to their own, ableist ends. One such end is what Siebers terms "disability drag," or when a nondisabled person pretends to be disabled. Siebers ties this possibility to entertainment, recalling that "when actors play disabled in one film and able-bodied in the next, the evolution of the roles presents them as cured of a previous disease or condition."[104] For Siebers, then, disability drag is a kind of temporary performance, where "disability appears as a facade overlaying abledness."[105] What Siebers did not predict was the possibility that people might take up disability not as a single, contained performance but as an ongoing, constitutive component of their identities.[106]

Enter ex-gays. As Cohen's *Coming Out Straight* illustrates, when people take on an ex-gay identity, they masquerade their queerness as a disability, using the medical rhetoric of pathologization as an "alternative narrative." Ex-gays appropriate the disability masquerade not as nondisabled people, contra Siebers, but as people with a rhetorically manufactured disability that they plan to adopt as a permanent characteristic of their identity. Moreover, as Steve, the author of another of Cohen's testimonies, points out, the ex-gay identity is intended to be political, meant to forge community among a group of people who feel marginalized by mainstream society. Steve writes, "For those of us healing homosexuality, we have the added burden of societal pressures. . . . We often get shunned by some for having homosexual feelings and by others for not 'accepting' our sexuality as it is."[107] Steve's comments are striking because they mimic the very motivations that Siebers adduces to justify masquerade as a political act. Ex-gays, like many disabled people, feel as if they are fighting a double standard where they are expected to deny the existence of their homoerotic desire/disability or accept it as a given embodyminded characteristic, existing outside of any symbolic discourse. As both ex-gays and many disabled people know, though, identities are political, and masquerading offers a way for them to take ownership over their identities. Ex-gays successfully masquerade and do so under the arguably legitimate premise that they are fighting for agency over their own bodyminds.

Indeed, it is this premise that captures the significance of ex-gays for the fields of queer studies and disability studies. The ex-gay community not only claims disability through self-selected pathologization but also politicizes the relationship between queerness and disability via the masquerade. It is a multistep process of identity construction that simultaneously draws on the organizing strategies of disability activists even as it rejects the affirmative, liberatory exigencies that drive queer and disability activisms. Ex-gays have managed to align themselves with the rhetorical structure of antiableism, all the while perpetuating cisheteroableist ideologies. This conflict between strategy and objective, between the means and ends, raises a critical question: what are the implications of the ex-gay masquerade for the future of queer and disability activisms, considered both independently and in coalition?

Rhetorics of Queercrip Coalition

We might begin answering this question by turning to Robert McRuer's foundational *Crip Theory: Cultural Signs of Queerness and Disability,* where McRuer advocates a variation of the queer claim to disability that ex-gays espouse. In *Crip Theory,* McRuer builds on Adrienne Rich's "compulsory heterosexuality" to reveal "compulsory able-bodiedness," which he argues is interwoven with Western conceptions of heterosexuality.[108] He goes further to posit that "compulsory heterosexuality is contingent on compulsory able-bodiedness, and vice versa," that the two concepts are mutually dependent.[109] The bulk of *Crip Theory* is McRuer's response to this entanglement of sexuality and dis/ability, for if heterosexuality and abledness constitute each other, so too must queerness and disability.

Crip, a word that McRuer positions as the disability-inflected equivalent of *queer,* is a "critical term" intended to speak "back to both nondisabled and disabled liberalism and, even more important, to nondisabled and disabled neoliberalism."[110] *Crip* and *queer* both reject models of identity politics that are grounded in liberalist condescension (e.g., "people with disabilities as very special people, physically challenged, differently abled, or handicapable")[111] and neoliberal exasperation (e.g., "I just don't know what the right term these days is").[112] For McRuer, queers and crips not only share histories of moral and medical stigmatization but also, echoing Clare, carry the political import to upend dominant discourses linked to the capitalist devaluation of nonconforming bodyminds. Given these twin potentials, he staunchly supports coalition work between queers and crips and, moreover, welcomes the possibility of hybrid "queercrip" identities. Though McRuer is careful to warn that "nondisabled claims to be crip could quite easily function as appropriation," he nevertheless goes on to "argue in favor of unlikely identifications" that include queer claims to disability.[113]

One example of such a cross-identification comes from McRuer himself, who recalls giving a presentation on HIV/AIDS activism in South Africa's Treatment Action Campaign (TAC), during which he "came out as HIV-positive," despite that he was at the time HIV-negative.[114] In the context of this particular queercrip performance—what Fletcher might call performance activism and what Siebers might call a masquerade—McRuer was "coming out crip" to disidentify with "the most familiar kinds of identity politics."[115] Specifically, he was responding to the meeting's theme of "Interiorities" by "draw[ing] attention to the politics of looking into queer and disabled bodies" and simultaneously embodying TAC's activism to espouse a "queer project[] of solidarity and contingent universalization of HIV-positive identity."[116] In other words, McRuer's queer claim to disability was motivated by his desire to resignify both queerness and disability, "to raise questions . . . about what exactly people wanted or expected to see inside disabled and queer bodies."[117] He recognized the meaning-making potential of his queer rhetorical energy and its overlaps with crip significations. By coding his queer bodymind as disabled, he disrupted expectations about whose bodies might inhabit a particular space: a meeting space, an academic space, a space where experiences of marginalization are too often discussed from a spatial, temporal, and material distance. Queercrip activism and crip theory more generally are oriented "to how bodies and spaces are being materialized in the cultures of upward redistribution."[118] For McRuer, to come out crip is to join the ranks of "unlikely identifications" that pursue "yet-to-be-imaged (queer and disabled) cultures of downward redistribution."[119]

As the case of ex-gays makes evident, however, not every claim to solidarity is a claim to mutual liberation, and not every attempt at coalition building constitutes a helpful step toward social equity. While McRuer's own example is perhaps justified by the specificity of HIV/AIDS as a nexus of queer and disabled experience, not all queercrip formations draw from that same historical/cultural juncture. And even those that do situate themselves within the legacy of queer-disability entanglements are still at risk for rehearsing, rather than reconciling with, the ableism that has come to define their mutual history. This ableism, we might recall from the introduction to this book, stems from gay activism's repeated disavowal of disability as a means to depathologize homosexuality and exceptionalize "queer." Occurring first in protest over the APA's medicalization of homosexuality, mental disability was forcibly relinquished to make room for "the homosexual" to emerge as a socially respectable and economically viable identity category. Then, in the context of AIDS, the stigmas attending illness and disease were rejected to isolate homophobia and heterosexism as the sole contributors to gay men's oppression by the medical-industrial complex. In both cases, disability served as the underbelly of *queer*; only by disability's haunting absence could *queer* secure its legibility. *Queer*'s attachment to nonnormativity is thus delimited by its history of dispossession: *queer* is infinitely mobile until it rubs against disability, at which point its political urgency dissolves.

Ex-gays, despite their apparent allegiance to both masquerade as a queer political strategy and to disability as an essential part of their identity, dredge up this history of dispossession not to contest its terms but to reverse its course, turning the liberatory potential of queercrip back on itself. Rather than using the history of pathologized queerness as an exigence to support social, political, and relational models of disability, ex-gays harness the medical model, recalling and reaffirming decades of unnecessary diagnoses and treatments for all disabled people. Subsequently, they embrace a moral model, reveling in the spiritualization and moralization of their fabricated diagnosis. While ex-gays are enacting a kind of queercrip political action, providing their own narrative for a queer disability, they do so under the assumptions that homoerotic desire is a condition that needs to be tempered and controlled and that conditions like these, which are in need of control, must be pathologized. In this sense, the ex-gay queercrip is a tautological aporia: an identity birthed, bred, killed off, rebirthed, and bred again by its own self-loathing.

Despite the fact that both Siebers's masquerade and McRuer's queercrip are meant to aid disabled people and the goals of disability activism, the existence of the ex-gay movement illustrates the messiness of political action rooted in (re)constructions of identity. Ex-gays, their ability to successfully politicize their disability identities through masquerade notwithstanding, are indeed inimical to the liberatory projects underway in queer and disability movements. Though Siebers rightly acknowledges the potential for the disability masquerade to be misappropriated, it is apparent that there are additional forms of co-optation, including that used by ex-gays, where the masquerading subjects are claiming disability permanently. Also, while McRuer already exhorts nondisabled people to "be wary of identifying as crip," it is worth dwelling in that wariness by considering the historical legacies of medicalized queerness and disavowed disability, as well as the ways these legacies come to bear on contemporary identity and political formations.[120] For ex-gays, these legacies are made current, reinvigorated for the twenty-first century.

Yet, my purpose in this chapter is not simply to shame ex-gays or how they understand themselves, even if I do find their evangelical instincts dangerous. I would be remiss if I did not acknowledge the queercrip potential of ex-gays that, much like the signifying potential of rhetorical energy, is not material or tangible but does hold open a space for potentialities that evangelical Christianity would not make room for otherwise. Gerber admits that ex-gay ideology "allows a degree of flexibility in terms of gendered tastes, practices, and self-presentation."[121] Likewise, Erzen claims that "the ex-gay label provides a hopeful framework because it places sexuality within the realm of the religious and even supernatural," effectively "remov[ing] the bulk of the responsibility from the men themselves."[122] Regarding disability, the ex-gay masquerade rejects the idea of divine healing, that "good" disabled people can expect God to cure them. It also places limits on the medical model, insisting that there are authorities outside of Western medicine that can interpret disability for themselves. Admittedly, none of these queercrip effects are intended, nor are they producing any wildly progressive change for the acceptance of queerness and disability within evangelical spaces. But for ex-gays themselves, the masquerade makes their lives more livable; it grants them "a degree of flexibility" and "provides a hopeful framework"—two things that are not available to queer evangelicals very often. In this context, the queercrip potential, the space for liberatory possibilities, is just that: a little rhetorical room, a little air, a little fissure that lets in a little light.

To end this chapter, I'd like to return to *My Husband's Not Gay* to introduce Tom, one of the featured ex-gay men, as he prepares for a date with a straight woman, Emily, who is unaware of his homoerotic desire. In one of the final scenes, Tom tells her about his "condition," saying, "I deal with something called same-sex attraction. We call it SSA. But I'm attracted to men." Emily's response comes in the form of a question. She asks, "What is it that makes you want to continue on in the way that you've chosen?" The viewer is ostensibly meant to understand this question as a reference to his ex-gay identity because Tom responds, "It's just what I've always wanted the most. You know what I mean?"

"What is it that you've wanted the most?" Emily interjects.

"To be married, have a wife, have kids, have a family. To live the way I think God wants me to live."

To this answer, Emily nods approvingly and almost immediately agrees to go on another date. What is striking about this brief exchange is the ease with which heteronormativity and abledness—as well as queerness and disability—are folded into one another. All of the nuance that goes into ex-gay discourse is boiled down and animated by Tom's queer rhetorical energy, which catalyzes a complete transformation of his identity within just a few lines. Tom makes clear that while his queer disavowal is motivated by heteroreligious obligations, the tool used to fulfill those obligations is disability. Note, first, Tom's phrasing in his disclosure: "I deal with something called same-sex attraction. We call it SSA. But I'm attracted to men." His syntactical structure mirrors that of a diagnosis. First comes the medical terminology, same-sex attraction; then comes the abbreviated version, SSA; this is followed by a description of the symptom, homoerotic desire. Tom masquerades his queerness as a disability, and Emily seems to both acknowledge and accept this framing by referring to his self-pathologization as "the way that you've chosen." While this response lacks the medicalized finesse of Tom's initial declaration, it nevertheless affirms the ex-gay identity as "a way" of life, a mode of being in the world. And as their conversation continues, it becomes all the more evident that this particular mode is propelled by cisheteronormative ideals of entering a monogamous marriage to reproduce. As far as queercrip activism goes, Tom's queer claim to disability contests neither homophobia nor ableism, resulting in a narrative as steeped in heterosexism as it is in compulsory able-bodymindedness. As Tom and Emily share a hug at the end of their date, the viewer is left with the feeling not that the stigmas surrounding queerness or disability have been upended but that perhaps Tom and Emily have a chance at love, at happiness, at heteroability.

Beyond this disappointing message, however, the documentary also reveals the intimate and at times playful relationships that the ex-gay men have with one another. Whether throwing dinner parties with their wives, attending Bible studies, planning weekend retreats, or going shopping, these men have built a community around their queer silence that lets them develop kinship, provide support, and revel in their outsider status. In one scene, two of the ex-gay men, Jeff and Pret, are playing basketball in the park and cannot seem to divert their attention away from the sweaty, muscular bodies of the other men on the court. In a voiceover, Pret says, "When I'm out with the guys, yeah, we'll look at other guys. For sure." Returning to the scene, he asks Jeff, "So what's the danger score?"

The viewer learns that "the danger score" is the ex-gay equivalent of an attractiveness rating, ranked from one to four. Pret explains, "The danger scale is a way to bring out some of the inner feelings, and to figure out 'Oh okay, that is attractive to me, and I didn't even realize it.'" The two go back and forth about the men around them, smiling, laughing, and debating perceived scores. "Two and a half," Jeff says.

"Really? Oh, I'd go higher than that," Pret counters.

Jeff chuckles, "That's some danger."

"That's why basketball's been fun."

These men are having an obviously homoerotic conversation, one that I have had many times with my own friends. Yet, they are filtering it through an ex-gay lens, where homoeroticism is perceived as temptation and, thus, dangerous. As the men's lighthearted attitudes suggest, though, they are not particularly concerned by this danger. In fact, they think it's "fun."

What I take from this exchange is that the ex-gay masquerade, as limiting and constrictive as it may seem according to secular queer standards, is understood quite differently by ex-gays themselves. Certainly, these men cannot pursue the sexual or romantic relationships that we typically associate with men attracted to other men, but it's clear that such pursuits are not the primary concern of these ex-gays. Immediately after Pret and Jeff's conversation, their wives, Megan and Tanya, arrive. The four of them chat for a moment before leaving the park together, smiling. Tom, reflecting on his friends' marriages, says, "They're kind of in a place that I wanna be. I wanna meet a girl and like her and say, 'By the way, I'm attracted to guys.' And that's what my friends have done, and they've made it work." It's a queer confluence of converted crip intimacies. They aren't progressive or Left-leaning or particularly radical, but ultimately, they're queercrip intimacies all the same, creating space for alternative, evangelical ways of being in the world.

There is more that could be said about evangelical Christianity, ex-gays, and their masquerade. As someone who once identified as ex-gay, I know that the complexities of ex-gay life far exceed the parameters of this chapter or this book. The fault lines that the ex-gay movement exposes among religion, science, medicine, neoliberalism, late capitalism, queerness, and disability are deep and, quite frankly, overwhelming. But the exposure of these fault lines also reveals the capacity of queer silence, and rhetorical energy more specifically, to rewrite the surface of bodies, to—in an instant—alter the way a person signifies to those around them. Scholars of embodyminded rhetorics would do well to consider the rhetorical energy of other bodyminds, the ways that flesh comes to signify and, for some us, resignify again and again in new ways, in new spaces, for new audiences. Likewise, queer studies should sit with the discomfort that arises when *queer* attaches itself to "bad" or politically troubling objects, such as ex-gays.[123] Siebers writes, "The world of politics will never be other than a messy place, no matter how much we think we know and how much experience we garner."[124] He is right. Rhetorical energy reveals that no body means just one thing. Rather, the movement of bodyminds entails a movement of discourses that offer new narratives about who we are. Some chosen, some not, these narratives produce subjects (and objects) that are expected to play their parts and their roles. When they don't, such as with queer masquerades, we should pay attention. Because in these moments, the rhetorical landscape is shifting. Energies are flowing. Bodyminds are speaking. And before too long, they'll be saying something else.

4

Disidentifying Silence

I open this chapter with two profiles from Jess T. Dugan and Vanessa Fabbre's photoethnographic project *To Survive on This Shore.* The book captures the experiences of old and aging trans and gender nonconforming people—experiences that often differ dramatically from those we encounter in popular trans narratives.[1] The first profile comes from Mitch, a man with light skin and peppery facial hair, who was fifty-five at the time of his interview and lives in Seattle, Washington (Figure 5). In the image, he looks directly into the camera and wears glasses, a black fedora, a gray blazer, and a striped blue, green, gray, and black button-down shirt. He begins by talking about his father's experience with Alzheimer's disease and the way it affected their relationship. Though his father had been overwhelmingly supportive of Mitch's transition, it became more difficult for him to remember his son's name and pronouns as his memory loss intensified. For Mitch, his father's disease was a frightening experience not only because it made interactions with him painful but also because it raised questions about Mitch's own aging process. I include a few sentences from his interview:

> So I'm looking at my dad and I'm thinking, "What happens when I end up in this situation?" I need to get my papers in order. I need to make sure I have end of life stuff written out. Because by the point at which you are no longer able to make those decisions and you begin forgetting things, what if I forget I'm trans?[2]

FIGURE 5. Mitch, 55. Photograph by Jess T. Dugan, from *To Survive on This Shore: Photographs and Interviews with Transgender and Gender Nonconforming Older Adults.*

This question—"What if I forget I'm trans?"—has haunted me for some time because it unsettles so much of what we trans people take for granted about our genders. For many of us, the painful labor attached to coming out is justified by a desire and promise to live authentically, to be ourselves. Yet, as Mitch's question reminds us, words like *authenticity* are rhetorical, contingent on social, cultural, and material conditions that include our own bodymind's capacity to claim an identity. The question also interrogates the usefulness of words like *authentic* to describe trans people.

FIGURE 6. Bobbi, 83. Photograph by Jess T. Dugan, from *To Survive on This Shore: Photographs and Interviews with Transgender and Gender Nonconforming Older Adults.*

The second profile I open with is Bobbi's, a woman with light skin and blond hair, who is from Detroit, Michigan, and was eighty-three at the time of her interview (Figure 6). In her image, she is looking down at a model airplane in her hands and wearing glasses, red lipstick, a white sweater, and blue pants. Though Bobbi formally began her transition at seventy-one, she resists any hardline distinction between her pretransition and current life. Here is what she says:

> I think people talk in either/or terms, right? Before transition and after. But to me, it's really a development. I'm proud of both lives. I'm proud of both "me"s, if you see what I'm saying. And I feel it has been a remarkable thing to have happened to a person. I'm grateful. You can't just become a woman with a knife or a pill or anything like that. It takes a whole combination in a sequence, in a formation. You've got this time span, it's a learning experience, it's a little bit of everything.[3]

For Bobbi, her relationship to being a woman is not defined by a particular moment of transition, nor is her post-op body a marker of authentic womanhood. Rather, her notion of being a woman is as an ongoing "development," an "experience" that cannot be divided into temporal categories, like "before transition and after." Authenticity is rendered more complicated in this context because Bobbi is "proud" of her multiple forms of expression and identification. Bobbi has always been true to herself; it's just that her conception of "self" has changed over time. Her story testifies to a model of gender that is shifting and dynamic, one that is less concerned with materializing a stable, authentic self than it is with expressing an ever-changing subjectivity.

In this chapter, I want to bring together Mitch's and Bobbi's stories to think about how rhetorical studies can help illuminate the interactions among critical age theory and trans studies. For the purpose of this chapter, I conceive of *trans* broadly, much like Susan Stryker does in *Transgender History,* to refer to any "*movement across a socially imposed boundary away from an unchosen starting place*—rather than any particular destination or mode of transition."[4] Stryker is less interested in the *how* or *where* of gender transition than she is in the *act* of transitioning, the verb. Implied by this definition is an attention to temporality, given that all movement occurs in and through time. While transitioning often entails material changes, such as different clothing, mannerisms, speech patterns, or medical intervention, these changes do not occur all at once, nor do they typically happen simultaneously with a person's self-identification as trans.

To dial in on *trans*'s temporality, I invoke a variation of Jane Gallop's "longitudinal sexuality," which we might modify as longitudinal gender. In *Sexuality, Disability, and Aging,* Gallop uses longitudinal sexuality to "call for reconceptualizing sexuality as developing across the life span," to think of sexuality and, by extension, sexual identity "as radically and diversely temporal."[5] Likewise, in this chapter, I intend to both honor and celebrate the diachronicity of gender as it ebbs and flows throughout a person's life. Importantly, neither Gallop's longitudinal sexuality nor my longitudinal gender is teleological: there is no final stage of sexual or gendered evolution to which we can all aspire. Rather, as with all embodyminded desires, sexuality and gender are unwieldy, frustrating, confusing, sometimes circular in their development, and inevitably bound to surprise us. It's this element of surprise that most excites me when reading trans elders' narratives. It is not a revelatory surprise—a confirmed suspicion—but simply a celebratory surprise that a person is open to change, to newness, to occupying this world and their bodymind differently. By thinking Stryker's definition of *trans* and Gallop's longitudinal model together, I am left with the rather obvious conclusion that being trans and the experience of transitioning look different for everyone. I argue that it is the variability of trans experience and transition that should draw our attention to trans elders since they are so often omitted from popular accounts of trans lives, narratives of transition, and the investments of trans-affirmative organizations—all forms of erasure that I expand on below.

The relative invisibility of trans elders' experiences from trans discourse is linked in part to a particular manifestation of queer silence. This manifestation embraces the potential of nonverbal rhetorics to articulate forms of gender variance that do not necessarily cohere into a single, static gender identity. By using the language of queer silence in the context of trans experience, I am not suggesting that *trans* is simply a variation of *queer*—a theoretical move that would deny the particularity of gender as an embodyminded experience distinct from sexuality. As I write in the Introduction and chapter 1, queer silence is queer because of its opposition to queer studies' dependence on speech as a barometer of political utility. Queer silence can be a trans silence when it is deployed as a form of resistance against speech or when it is engaged by trans or gender nonconforming people at the margins of trans socialization, those whose racial, geographic, class, disability, or age configurations make it difficult to approximate transnormativity. Specific to this chapter and my focus on trans elders, trans silence not only contests the demand that a person embody only one, unwavering gender identity throughout their life span but also shows how this demand is upheld by gendered processes of racialization and debilitation/disablement. In other words, trans silence illuminates forms of trans movement—those material, embodyminded, and extralinguistic forms of trans experience—that reveal the enmeshment of gender with race, age, and disability.

Often trans elders talk about having engaged nonconforming gender expressions long before they identified as trans, and they insist on a coherence between those expressions and their later trans identity so as to maintain a unified, even if dynamic, sense of self across their life span. Trans silence is especially important for those elders who have built families, careers, and lives that they cherish, despite having done so in a gender that did not or no longer suits them. Trans silence is also relevant to trans studies because it emphasizes how age and the discourses that surround aging complicate how we conceive of trans experience and trans identities. By holding up silence as a legitimate and often fulfilling mode of trans being in the world, we can counter an underlying assumption of popular trans discourse: that being trans is a young person's game.

In the next section, I explore this assumption through several high-profile moments of trans discourse over the last few years. Each of these moments shows how neoliberal models of inclusion and diversity valorize white, nondisabled instantiations of youth and youthfulness at the expense of trans elders. Following these examples, I turn to age theory as a necessary intervention in trans studies that draws attention to the temporality of gender and reveals trans silence as the rhetorical product of bringing the two fields together. Throughout the chapter, I rely heavily on queer and trans of color scholars, including Jules Gill-Peterson, C. Riley Snorton, and José Esteban Muñoz, who all identify cisheteronormativity as a weapon of white supremacy, one that has long relied on the temptation of civil inclusion to produce forms of trans/homonormativity that further mitigate the life chances of multiply marginalized queer and trans folks. Following Muñoz's work on disidentification, in particular, I address the challenging relationship between transness and disability, which is necessary in the context of a chapter on age and aging, given that most people will eventually age into a disabled bodymind.[6] In each section, I return to Dugan and Fabbre's *To Survive on This Shore* to introduce additional profiles that showcase trans silence at work and to reground my argument in the lives of trans elders.

The Age of Authenticity

In 2014, the Human Rights Campaign Foundation (HRC) published *Transgender Visibility: A Guide to Being You,* which contains a series of statements on what it means to identify as transgender, why one might choose to identify as transgender, and how one may consider coming out to friends, relatives, and colleagues as transgender. After the title page and before the table of contents, there is a decorative filler page with a single, unattributed quote floating above an image of a person staring off into space, their hands folded beneath their chin. The quote reads, "Every day, I get to experience the joy of living an open, honest life and engaging in relationships as a whole and authentic person."[7] On the surface, this blurb could be taken either as words of trans affirmation or as a debatable but ultimately harmless resurgence of It Gets Better rhetoric, where queer and trans youth are promised a bright, happy, and successful future if they can withstand the trials of their homophobic and transphobic peers.[8]

However, what interests and concerns me about this quote is the way that openness and honesty are paralleled by wholeness and authenticity. Despite that neither *wholeness* nor *authenticity* are particularly meaningful or even helpful terms in a trans context, where transitioning sometimes includes body modification, it is implied that in order for one to be "a whole and authentic person," they must also be "living an open, honest life." Openness and honesty are, of course, referring to being "out" or living as an openly trans person. As a passage a few pages later clarifies, trans people "express . . . openness by being our full and complete selves among our friends, our family, our co-workers and, sometimes, even strangers."[9] This is to say that only open or "out" trans people are whole, authentic, and complete.

By contrast, people who choose not to disclose that they are trans are not only dishonest, as the first quote suggests, but also inauthentic, partial, and incomplete—all of which are unfortunate metaphors, considering the tired accusation that trans bodies are missing parts and are thus "deceptive" or "fake."[10] Embedded in this syllogism is the premise that there is a singular authentic, whole, and complete version of oneself that can be realized. The HRC promises trans people a kind of fulfillment that can only be achieved through self-identification and, by extension, coming out. While others caution that such identity politics ignore the material conditions informing the lives of people of color, disabled people, and sexual minorities, I would like to point out the particular ways that this discourse isolates and excludes trans elders.[11]

Identity, as narrated through fantasies of authenticity and wholeness, depends on the stability of a single trans self over time. This trans self not only must exist but also must have always existed; indeed, this persistent self must be the essence of trans existence. With regard to gender, such a self necessarily implies that each person can only have one true gender, and for trans people, this model assumes that their sex and gender have always been in discord, whether or not they were aware of it. The presumption of a yet-unrealized authenticity thus replaces personal experience and testimony as the most reliable form of self-knowledge. A person is no longer trans because of their desire to occupy their bodymind particularly or to have their bodymind recognized by others in a particular way but because of a thinly veiled biological determinism—what we might call "transnaturalism"—where gender is as innate as sex, grounded in an uncontextualized, individual body rather than in a plurality of bodies that are situated within variegated rhetorical contexts.

Even though it is frequently used in the service of trans affirmation, transnaturalism bares stark resemblances to "gender critical feminist" ideology, where gender transition is tolerated only so long as the biological definition of sex is not eroded.[12] Rather than contesting the biomedicalization of sex, transnaturalism cites a trans person's gender as evidence that their sex is pathological and must be corrected, thereby ignoring the fact that sex, like gender, is a material-discursive product.[13] Transnatural advocates fall into a gender critical trap: their defense of trans authenticity reasserts biomedical authority, which both undermines trans people's embodyminded autonomy and obfuscates the racialized and ableist cissexism embedded in medicine. This cissexism reveals itself in the inequitable distribution of biomedical access, as well as in the presumed outcomes of biomedicalized transition that rest on white, nondisabled standards of dimorphic gender attractiveness. Transnaturalism is thus linked to what Snorton and Jin Haritaworn have called the "transnormative subject," who "largely remains uninterrogated in its complicities and convergences with biomedical, neoliberal, racist, and imperialist projects."[14] Transnaturalism is the rhetoric used to justify the authority of psychopharmacology to pathologize trans as a congenital but ultimately mutable condition through biomedical intervention, regardless of how any given trans person understands themself.

Transnaturalism is especially potent among trans youth, who, as Gill-Peterson argues, have long been "reduced to reservoirs of plasticity, the raw material of phenotype."[15] In *Histories of the Transgender Child,* Gill-Peterson introduces plasticity as an individual's "capacity to take on new form and be transformed by medical scientific intervention early on in life."[16] *Plasticity* both names a characteristic of trans children's bodyminds—their capacity for transnormalization—and adduces their pathological bodyminds to demand the unrestricted authority of biomedicine. This authority is established as early as possible in a trans person's life because plasticity is fixed to childhood, steadily waning after adolescence. Gill-Peterson notes that trans medicine's origins in endocrinology have long "called upon the figure of the developing child to serve as a stabilizing metaphor."[17] Children are thought to be more plastic than adults because plasticity is itself "a capacity to generate and receive imprints of form," much like children are thought to be more impressionable the younger they are.[18] "Something about children's bodies," she writes, "incarnates and takes living form in large part as the personification distilled from an abstract concept. The child, paradoxical as it may sound, is a living figure."[19] In this sense, the trans child is pathology made flesh, is nonconformance materialized into base matter that might yet be saved. As Tey Meadow explains, "Parents and physicians understand the moment of puberty as a determinative bodily shift. Bodies become male and female anew in ways that can only be undone at great cost, if ever. Symbolically, the direction a child takes at that moment is declarative; they 'are' trans, or they 'aren't.'"[20] Once a trans person reaches adulthood, their plasticity is all but dissolved, leaving behind a cemented bodymind that is more difficult to realign with transnormativity. As I explain in the next section, the temporality of plasticity is particularly incompatible with people who transition later in life, for whom it is no longer available.

Even among trans youth, plasticity is unevenly distributed, favoring white trans kids over trans youth of color, who are routinely perceived as "less plastic and therefore less deserving of care."[21] The plasticity of white kids rests on the supposed invisibility of whiteness or, as Toby Beauchamp puts it, on the notion that "certain raced and gendered bodies can serve as normative standards because they are legible and compliant."[22] White trans kids' gender nonconformance puts them at risk of illegibility, but their whiteness matriculates as compliance, as both the plastic condition and potential to have their deviant bodyminds realigned with cisnormativity through early biomedical intervention. The presence of racialized plasticity begets processes of racialized transnormalization, rescuing white trans kids from the horrors of gender illegibility and simultaneously ossifying trans kids of color as always already noncompliant and resistant to "the technician's gaze."[23]

Addressing the ossification of trans kids of color, Kyla Schuller and Gill-Peterson suggest that while their white peers are accorded individual value within a plastic economy, Black, brown, and Indigenous trans youth are "freighted with a different kind of plasticity, one ascribed to the level of the mass."[24] This alternative plasticity, what they call "fungibility," identifies not the capacity of a singular bodymind to be reshaped but the "replaceability" of a bodymind to be swapped out with an indistinguishable other.[25] The relationship between plasticity and fungibility, between an individual's capacity for normalization and a population's expendability, brings into relief the danger of transnaturalism: that it implies only some trans lives are worth defending, let alone caring for. These exceptional trans lives, those of transnormative subjects, ultimately stand in as evidence not of gender diversity but of the power of a racialized medical-industrial complex to eliminate said diversity. "Plasticity," Schuller and Gill-Peterson write, "is the implantation of population-level governance at the dimension of individual organic capacity."[26] Transnaturalism names the discursive product of this implantation, the way it has been strategically reconfigured as a tool of liberal inclusion and progressivism. Transnaturalism is plasticity commodified, nonprofitized, and integrated into mainstream conversations about who trans people are and who trans people are supposed to be. Transnaturalism is the rhetorical process by which plastic trans children are rendered transnormative adults.

For all of those trans people who fall outside of transnormativity, transnaturalism poses a serious problem. A person's lack of plasticity, their fungibility, puts them at odds with a racialized discourse that relies on their potential to be admitted into cisheteronormative whiteness, what Jack Halberstam calls the "new wave of neoliberal incorporation."[27] While it is debatable whether this wave is all that new, it is true that trans people of color, disabled trans people, poor trans people, trans elders, and gender nonconforming folks all encounter transnaturalism as an impossible litmus test of their trans experience. Transnaturalism essentializes biomedical intervention as the definitive mark of trans existence, even as it belies the fact that many trans people do not want medical intervention, few have access to it, and even fewer are able to access the specific interventions they want when they want them. Furthermore, transnaturalism's focus on biomedicalization ignores other, potentially more pressing issues facing trans people at the margins, such as incarceration, police violence, and trans-antagonism in hospitals and nursing homes, and it mistakes the availability of trans biomedicine for its accessibility. As Ann Travers points out, "By enabling some trans kids to reduce their precarity by accessing trans-affirming healthcare, disparities among transgender people are emerging in new and troubling ways."[28] These disparities affect not only less privileged trans youth but also trans adults who have supposedly outgrown the plasticity necessary to transition into an "authentic" life.

It is worth recalling that biomedicine's primary intention with plasticity is to achieve transnormativity, a goal that can only be measured by its approximation of abled, cisheteronormative whiteness. Transnormativity becomes increasingly more difficult to embody as a person ages, as their plasticity—if they were ascribed any to begin with—dissipates with each passing year after puberty. Indeed, if we follow Gill-Peterson's excision of fungibility from plasticity, we might understand trans aging as a fading out of plasticity into fungibility. Trans elders who did not transition when they were young are considered beyond saving, too steeped in their sex assigned at birth to ever realize their "whole" selves, and reduced to sad reminders of why early biomedical intervention is necessary. Omitted from this formulation of course is that, per Beauchamp, "not all gendered bodies and identities are so easily normalized."[29] Even among those who could be rendered normative, many trans people desire variations of trans embodymindedness that are distinctively and visibly nonconforming. Transnaturalism mobilizes racialized plasticity toward only one end—an end that makes no room for nonconformance, whether perceived or chosen.

Claudia Castañeda makes this point clearly, writing that the "transgender childhood constitutes a pathological instance of childhood *and* gender simultaneously—there is 'something wrong' with the child *through* its gender, but early medical interventions can make that gender normal without a trace of its past pathology."[30] She notes that once a trans child's wayward gender has been sufficiently identified, they can be more or less cured of their transness so as to reduce the visibility of their gender nonconformance. Meadow expands on the trajectory of this trans cure, noting that some children who receive early medical interventions may choose never to identify as transgender or gender nonconforming, offering them "wider latitude to misidentify with transgender history and with those who came before them."[31] Thus ironically—though perhaps unsurprisingly—transnaturalism appropriates the liberatory possibilities that medicine might offer trans people and rematerializes them as a form of medicalized trans erasure. Transnaturalism works to obliterate the same trans lives that it claims are so very natural.

We can begin locating this obliteration already in the lives of trans elders. Halberstam warns that as trans youth increasingly receive information about trans experience online and directly from the medical-industrial complex, the amount of contact between trans youth and older generations steadily declines, which sometimes leads to older trans people being "cast as the enemy."[32] "In worst-case scenarios," Halberstam continues, "older generations are seen as potential predators in relation to trans and queer youth and viewed with suspicion."[33] Almost identical to mid-twentieth century fears about predatory homosexuals who hoped to indoctrinate innocent white teens on their way home from school, trans elders are suspected of spoiling youthful gender purity.

A version of this trans elder phobia figured prominently during the 2016 election cycle, when the "bathroom debate" was in full swing. Predictions of men wearing dresses so they could spy on and potentially assault the everyman's wife and daughter flooded conservative media. While these predictions were more explicitly transphobic than the intercommunal, generational tensions that Halberstam reflects on, both discourses rely on the value of youth—and its attendant connotations of innocence and purity—to contrast the ugly perversion of middle and old age. For instance, in one particularly grotesque comic, the artist drew a man (I use this gender marker to reflect the obvious intentions of the artist) with an evil smile and furrowed brow, walking into a women's restroom and holding a camera.[34] He says, "Relax Lady, I'm Transgender," to a horror-stricken woman, who stands at the sink and reaches toward her toddler-sized daughter. Aside from the gross misrepresentation of trans people as innately predatory, the image deploys children as a signifier of desexed innocence and purity: the girl gazes up at the intruding man, her shoulders rounded forward and arms relaxed by her side. If it were not for her world-wise and protective mother—or so the comic implies—the poor girl could be recorded or worse by the menacing "transgender."

Responses by the Left to this comic, along with many others of similar structure and content, tended to focus on the characterization of trans people as criminal or dangerous. The responses attempted to remediate what was taken to be a problem of representation with alternative images of trans people. Among the most widely circulated was a photograph of Corey Maison, a young, trans, white girl with her body faced right, arms crossed, and face staring at the camera. She is wearing makeup and has many traditionally white feminine features: long, curly blond hair, full lips, bright blue eyes, a straight nose, and rounded eyebrows. Her jawline is smooth, her body is lean, and her skin is clear. As far as white femininity is concerned, she is beautiful. The original caption on Facebook explains that "Corey IS TRANSGENDER" and that "for those STILL not able to understand: if this was

YOUR daughter, would you be comfortable sending her into a men's bathroom? Neither would I."[35] The intention behind the photo is to appropriate the symbol of a child to support trans acceptance. The implied argument is that many trans people are themselves children, so if the public wants to protect children, then we need to protect *all* of them, including trans kids.

As Aaron Morrison points out for *Yahoo! News,* however, Corey Maison's image "reinforces the same prejudice it seeks to challenge" by reasserting the value of gender legibility and passibility, not to mention whiteness.[36] Maison's trans identity is revealed in the caption of the photo as a surprise, a deception meant to shock the viewer into facing their own prejudice. *Aha! You didn't even suspect she was trans, did you?* Unfortunately, the photo neglects to acknowledge the range of bodies and gender expressions that the "bathroom debate" affects, nor does it address the fact that trans people of color and gender nonconforming folks are more likely to face violence for using the bathroom.[37] Maison herself certainly is affected by transphobic legislation, such as a bathroom bill, but the overwhelming popularity of her image calls attention to who and what the public is predominately interested in protecting: gender dimorphism and whiteness. Beauchamp suggests that the image of Maison was chosen because "gender-passing white transgender people are far more likely to be interpreted as members of the general public than as the deceptive criminals that bathroom bills conjure."[38] Maison stands in as a good trans kid, a plastic trans kid, a trans kid whom biomedicine is successfully deracializing back into the fold of whiteness, thereby protecting the idea that "gender difference should be obvious and universally recognized."[39]

What tends to be overlooked in conversations about Maison and the bathroom bill debate is how the figure of the child clashes with the very real, material bodies of trans kids. In other words, youthfulness serves a rhetorical purpose beyond its symbolization of innocence and purity, even if—as Lee Edelman famously describes—those connotations help to strengthen the message's appeal. Maison is not merely a "fantasmatic beneficiary" but, indeed, an actual child who has an embodied investment in the politics at stake.[40] I do not mean to deny the interplay between cultural imaginaries and material bodies like Maison's, but I do contend that the rhetorical category of the "transgender child" illuminates the fleshiness of children and draws attention to how young trans people are not protected for their presumed defenselessness but prized for their cultural value.

Youthfulness is a characteristic that, by itself, matters. It is not that we value children because we find their innocence and purity desirable but, conversely, that we value innocence and purity because we desire youth, especially as it is tied to the reproductive capacity of white femininity. Hannah Dyer argues that "children's presumed innocence casts onto them intergenerational debts that relate to the making of race and racism."[41] That is to say, the public's instinct to defend Maison by keeping her out of the men's bathroom was in large part an effect of youth as a harbinger of whiteness. The frantic concern that a men's bathroom might contaminate Maison, that it might sully her prized naivete, can be understood as a rhetorical-meets-eugenic tactic meant to safeguard a future white progenitor from spoiling. Maison's plasticity is on full display here as she comes to serve as a foil for white cis girls, the ones who truly need protection because of their sacred responsibility to materialize white futurity through reproduction. Indeed, Maison's perceived vulnerability is linked not to the real dangers facing transfeminine people in public bathrooms but to the fantasy of white fertility that her plasticity is meant to conjure. Indeed, within the context of her image, Maison's youthful whiteness is the sum total of her worth, for to blemish her purity by sending her into the men's bathroom would be to induct her into adulthood. As an adult, Maison would no longer be plastic; she would no longer remind us of a little white cis girl. We might remember with horror that she's trans.

Margaret Morganroth Gullette links the fear of children aging into adulthood to "age ideology," which rests on the assumption that aging is synonymous with decline.[42] From childhood, we are told that each passing year will incur new challenges, new limitations, new aches and pains, new losses, and new griefs. As we age, we are taught that our only option for maintaining self-worth is to reverse the clock, to invest in making ourselves appear, feel, and function as if we were younger. The master narrative of decline says that *it only gets worse from here,* and the circulation of Maison's image testifies to how our desire for youth, and white youth in particular, can be articulated as altruism. Coming to Maison's defense was at least in part a defense against aging, an attempt to protect not Maison from bad adults but Maison's plasticity from time.

It is necessary to account for the roles of age ideology and ageism because they speak to broader cultural trends, even within the progressive Left. While there is nothing inherently dangerous about cherishing youth and childhood as important stages in one's life, doing so should not come at the expense of devaluing or otherwise caricaturing other life stages. The decline narrative, which creates the conditions for youth's desirability, also produces age categories that are, in turn, pitted against each other as responsible for society's ills. These conflicts are especially harmful to elders, who are represented as "either *feeble, unproductive,* or *demented,* appropriate objects of revulsion, or *politically powerful* Boomer voters whose job security is so unassailable that they do not need a COLA or the heightened scrutiny of constitutional law. The age group can be held responsible for an increasing portion of the national crises (fiscal deficits, high youth unemployment), serving as a scapegoat, a bogeyman, a mass of hysterical projections."[43] Gullette clarifies that old people are victim to both sides of a bad coin, where they are either responsible for the failures of capitalism or the afterthoughts of a neoliberal agenda. They are neither young enough to benefit from institutional diversity and inclusion efforts nor supposedly poor enough (despite rising rates of poverty and unemployment for people who are middle age and older) to receive attention from social services. As Gullette puts it, "'Old,' whatever else it means, means negligible."[44]

For trans elders, this neglect is only exacerbated by conflicting cultural narratives about what it means to be trans. As discussed above, transnaturalism confounds alternative modes of gender variance. Whereas transnaturalism depends on an innate, stable gender throughout a person's lifetime, accounts of gender among trans elders tend to be more fluid, subject to change, and associated more with expression than with identity. As Joe Ippolito and Tarynn M. Witten discuss in *Trans Bodies, Trans Selves,* these accounts are often framed as evidence of trans elders' ignorance: "Many younger trans people feel that trans elders have outdated views or that we are stuck in our ways." They continue, "[Trans elders] can be made to feel invisible, as if our voices do not count."[45]

Recalling Gullette's age ideology, I read this intergenerational tension as a symptom of the decline narrative, where "outdated views" are taken to be a failure to progress, an unforgivable stagnation, a falling away from transnormativity, a decline. The role of ageism becomes even more explicit when we take into consideration the conditions under which many trans elders come to express their gender variance in the first place. As Bobbi, one of the two trans elders we met at the beginning of this chapter, makes clear: the process of transitioning can itself be a pleasurable, rewarding experience. It is a process with its own timeline, including multiple forms of identification, expression, and relation that are all important, beautiful, and worth remembering. A biomedical model of trans experience, according to Beauchamp, presumes "that transgender people will, through the process of [medicalized] transition, eliminate all references to their birth gender and essentially disappear into a normatively gendered world, as if they had never been transgender to begin with."[46] Many trans elders, however, have resisted both normative gender and normative gender development, meaning that they did not grow into a particular gender category but instead have experienced their gender identity and expression change as their sense of self has evolved and shifted over time.

Like Bobbi, these trans elders embrace gender as an ongoing transition, rendering "trans" less an identity category than a description of their gender movement. Similar to how Gullette extricates "age" and "aging" from any "fixed chronology," attaching them instead "to cultural pressures that stabilize age ideology or engineer its novelties," so too do many trans elders disentangle gender from neoliberal authenticity, insisting that it be left open-ended and flexible.[47] Transnaturalism's contingence on gender fixity is driven not only by white cisheteronormativity but also by the exclusion and demonization of elders, whose gender nonconformance denies the ideology of temporary plasticity and threatens the stability of transnormativity. We are thus living in an age of authenticity that refers both to a period of medical-industrial expansion and to the glamorization of youth, to a literal age, to a systematic erasure of "the old."

Identifying Silence

To combat this erasure, I offer a theory of trans onto-phenomenology that seeks to excavate forms of gender nonconformance that do not reach the level of "the authentic" or "whole." That is, I offer a counterresponse to transnaturalism that draws on the model of queer silence I describe throughout this book. Silence here is not to be taken as emptiness but as a signifying absence that often coexists with other forms of meaning-making. In the context of trans experience, *silence* refers not only to the absences of trans people and experiences from archives and public memory but also to the subtleties of gender variance, the ways that nonconforming gender expressions can fly under or around the radar of gender identification.[48] While transnaturalism is organized around a confessional logic, where subjects must align themselves with a particular category (i.e., "I am transgender"), trans silence directs us to alternative modes of being and strategies of relating. Trans silence is a way to conceive of, dig up, unpack, and celebrate gender nonconformance without relying on neoliberal identity politics. For trans elders, silence is particularly important as it makes space for models of gender development that are neither linear nor predictable. Silence, as opposed to identitarian disclosure, remains open to the unbidden, resisting stasis in favor of motion.

What I mean by *motion* is something similar to how Hil Malatino describes "trans lives in interregnum," as "a kind of nowness that shuttles transversally between different imaginaries of pasts and futures and remains malleable and differentially molded by these imaginaries."[49] For Malatino, the interregnum widens the scope of trans temporality to include not only the measured benchmarks of a biomedicalized transition but also those moments in between, outside of, and even in tension with those benchmarks. Even though biomedical markers are incredibly important to some trans people, including many trans elders, transnaturalism stages these markers linearly, as a trajectory from a person's "wrong" body at birth to their "correct" biomedicalized one. Malatino warns that this kind of "teleological account of transition . . . is radically inadequate" because "it doesn't begin to dignify the complexities of trans experiences."[50] These complexities include the circumstances faced by many trans elders, such as those who do not want to medically transition, who choose to medically transition after their plasticity has presumedly expired, or who may have attempted to transition earlier in life but were never perceived as plastic enough to warrant biomedicalized intervention. Each of these groups reveal the racialized exclusivity of "trans" as a liberal subject category, especially as it is defined and cemented by transnaturalism.

The elders who do not or cannot medically transition undergo a process of racialization that exposes a transnormative hierarchy of whiteness. Even among those elders who are white, who may have once been ideal trans children brimming with white plasticity, their advanced age pushes them into an ageist fungibility. Much like how Mia Fischer argues that Chelsea Manning's "inability to 'properly' embody and perform hetero- and homonormativity rendered her as the alien enemy who both betrayed and failed to 'duly' enact whiteness," I contend that there is a similar process of racialization at work against trans elders who have failed to transition in a timely manner.[51] Indeed, the marginalization of trans elders reveals that whiteness has a timeline, that it works according to a calendar that valorizes youth and effaces old age in equal measure. For trans elders of color, this effacement is inevitable: without having been granted plasticity as children, trans people of color can only age further into fungibility. And once a person is fungible, once they are characterized by a bio/necropolitical regime as practically interchangeable, once they are stripped of the autonomy and agency required to desire a trans bodymind in the first place, once they are reduced to their nonconformance and recycled as negative marketing material for trans biomedicine, how should we make sense of them? How do we measure their days? What clock do we use to count their movement, to track their transition in all its complexity, when the only clock made readily available says, simply, *They're too deviant?* or, specific to elders, *They're too late?*

Trans silence is meant to offer a different clock or a thousand clocks or an anticlock that explodes trans temporality beyond the barometers of transition. Trans silence gives us a way to remember the trans child who never was, to imagine into existence the trans child who should have been, or to simply acknowledge the temporal gaps—what Malatino calls "lag"—between when a person wants to transition, when they do transition, and when their transition occasions the kind of gendered recognition they want.[52] Animating trans silence is my belief that trans bodyminds, even and especially the bodyminds of trans elders, are always already transitioning, regardless of a trans identification.

This belief corresponds with the way Karen Barad conceives of "transmaterialities" as "*condensations of responses.*"[53] Barad argues that transness is a material concern because trans bodies, like all bodies, are made up of matter that is, itself, "*a matter of untimely and uncanny intimacy.*"[54] That is to say, matter is neither materially nor temporally fixed; instead, it is always under construction, unfolding. Matter is, in this sense, instinctively trans, echoing the simultaneous deconstruction and reconstruction of gendered embodiment. As Barad puts it, "Nature is agential transmateriality/trans-matter-reality in its ongoing re(con)figuring, where trans is not a matter of changing *in* time, from this to that, but an undoing of 'this' and 'that.'"[55] Transness for Barad is not linear or teleological but indeterminate and dynamic. It allows us to theorize gender in its "radical specificity" rather than relying on grand, overarching frameworks that tend to reassert the authority of biomedicine.[56] Unlike medical or juridical models of gender, transmaterialities work on an individual level, positing a "*self* [that] *is dispersed/diffracted through time and being.*"[57] Such dispersion/diffraction calls attention to the unpredictability of gender, the way trans bodyminds do not evolve into a predestined form but continuously unravel—at once occupying and obfuscating gender norms. Transmaterialities call attention to the movement of gender, filling the space of trans silence not only in theoretical terms but also in deeply embodyminded ones. Gender moves because bodyminds move. Gender is an "ongoing reconfiguring" that exceeds any identification or material makeup, and its motion is silent because it moves too quickly for disclosure.[58] Once labeled, once called into being, it is already too late; the train has left the station, the body has moved on, gender has already unraveled its way past our naming.

To be clear, neither Barad nor I contest the importance of gender identity. The personal, relational, political, and material affordances that a stable identity provides are too great to be discounted, and if transfeminism has taught us anything, it's that our theory cannot outrun or overstep experience. As Barad writes, the purpose of transmaterialities is not "to set trans as an abstraction, to deny it its fleshly lived reality, sacrificing its embodiment in an appropriative embrace of the latest theory trends."[59] Similarly, trans silence is not meant to undercut the existence or value of trans speech: the decades of trans activism that have and continue to experiment with, adopt, debate, and celebrate various configurations of trans identity. At the same time, trans silence and transmaterialities are meant to interrogate the slipperiness between trans identity politics and transnaturalism. Transmaterialities "build on an already existing radical tradition . . . that troubles nature and naturalness 'all the way down.'"[60] In contrast with authenticity discourse, transmaterialities locate identities as necessary constructions, as artificial snapshots of a "being-time" that has already moved on when the camera flashes.[61] Trans silence is a way of accounting for that motion as a complement to the identity-driven snapshots. Whereas focusing on identity, which often takes the form of verbal disclosure, is like combing through photos, attending to silence is like watching home movies, where your interest is not only in who a person is but also in the moment that person occupies: not only what they look like, what they're wearing, and what they're doing but also how they move, who they're with, and where they're going.

Trans silence, much like how I understand queer silence more broadly, is not so much a rejection of speech as it is a redirection of our energies toward other forms of meaning-making. It acknowledges the possibility of trans identification but then looks elsewhere for embodied, material, and extralinguistic moments of gender nonconformance. Rather than flattening out all nontrans identities and expressions as "cisgender," which A. Finn Enke astutely notes "renders 'woman' and 'man' more stable, normative, and ubiquitous than they ever were," trans silence opens up the conversation to include more situated analyses of gender nonconformance.[62] It also foregrounds gender variant subjects who would otherwise be left unaccounted for in trans scholarship. Similar to how, in chapter 2, visual silence makes room for Grindr users who choose not to upload profile pictures, trans silence attends to those manifestations of being-time that sit on the margins—or even outside—of trans identification.

Using trans silence as an analytic is particularly useful when paired with what Gullette calls "age identity." Unlike other forms of identification that Gullette worries are "coming to mean 'me-ness,'" age identity is "an achievement of storytelling about whatever has come to us through aging."[63] It is a narrative technique hinged on how we age, what ages us, and the ways age influences our other identities. Rather than closing in on a single, static identity, age identity turns itself inside out to reveal many pieces of each individual. Gullette calls her age identity "an achieved portmanteau 'me'" that is "made up . . . of all its changeable and continuing selves together—connected in different ways, or intermittently, but sometimes barely at all, to a sensuously material body."[64] Identity, in this image, is both singular and plural, containing many selves that all impinge upon one another in the formation of the Self—the "portmanteau 'me.'"

Age comes into play when considering the temporality of narrative, how all stories take time. As Gullette puts it, "The theory of 'age identity' adds temporality to static identity theory by helping us accept aging as an integral part of our sub-identities."[65] Indeed, age is arguably at the root of all other identities, providing the "spacetimemattering" (to borrow from Barad) in which each identity comes to fruition.[66] Age identity and age theory help to stretch out our understanding of identity across time, working to unmoor identity from moments of disclosure and, instead, focus on trajectories of development. These trajectories, unlike the teleologies of transnaturalism, are retrospective rather than predictive. Age identity looks backward, tracking other identities over time as they appear, change, and fall away; whereas, transnaturalism looks forward, urging bodies into forms of identification that retroactively allege a constant and unchanging self.

Trans silence, attentive as it is to embodied and material change, works alongside age identity to showcase gender nonconformance throughout a person's life. While dominant gender models hinge on gender continuity, age identity invites alternative narratives that do not follow normative plot lines: characters may change names, costumes, or bodily configurations; scenes may suddenly stop halfway through or repeat themselves; the story might even break for a few blank pages while the characters take a moment for themselves. But in any case, age identity takes the whole story into account—at least however much has already happened—even those moments of silence when the characters are finding themselves between lines. For trans elders, age identity and trans silence help to narrativize gender as something greater than identity but still connected to a material body, one that may flicker in and out of various identifications. Next to Malatino's interregnum and Barad's transmaterialities, silence is especially useful for trans elders who have simply had more time to write their gender stories. While age theory can be useful for people of all ages, and trans silence can offer rich accounts of gender diversity among children and young adults, there is something to be said for prioritizing the people who have the most to lose. And as I write above, trans elders increasingly find themselves expunged from a racist and ageist transnormativity and thrust into the precarity of fungibility. Trans silence, inflected by age theory, welcomes these elders back into the fold of trans community, investing in their particularities and listening to their stories.

Disidentifying Silence

I want to offer another profile from *To Survive on This Shore,* the photoethnographic project on trans and gender nonconforming elders. Amy, a woman with light skin, black hair, and glasses, was seventy-seven at the time of her interview and lives in Seattle, Washington (Figure 7). In her image, she is seated on a park bench and wearing a beige skirt, beige shoes, and a black and brown shawl with floral print and tassels. Though Amy knew she wanted to transition by 1980, she was hesitant to pursue it because she feared she would have to divorce her wife, Edith. When Edith passed away in 2008, Amy came out "publicly."[67] She then realized that she "needed to do something" about being alone in her house. As a solution, she began inviting homeless trans women and girls to stay with her. "I'm trying to give people a little bit of safe space and respite from the anxieties of homelessness," she says. By opening up her home to others, Amy created a social support system that is mutually beneficial to both her and to the people who stay with her. "As you grow old, you fear the unknown. You end up needing care." She says, "By inviting people to come stay with me, I have someone to at least look after me on a daily basis and make sure that I'm not falling through the cracks."

FIGURE 7. Amy, 77. Photograph by Jess T. Dugan, from *To Survive on This Shore: Photographs and Interviews with Transgender and Gender Nonconforming Older Adults.*

I propose that Amy's story testifies to the roles that aging and silence play in elder trans people's lives. Her advanced age makes building new support systems more difficult than it typically is for younger people, and her delayed trans identification gestures toward the years of trans silence that filled her life. Amy's story also serves as a reminder that neither silence nor experiences of fungibility are necessarily isolating or reducible to loss. Rather, as Snorton details in *Black on Both Sides: A Racial History of Trans Identity,* it is possible to orient one's fungibility toward resistance—what he calls "fungible fugitivity."[68] Despite the fact that marginalized trans people are not granted plasticity at the individual level, their fungibility en masse can sometimes provide a "capacity to make and remediate personhood through ontological rearrangement."[69] Whereas *plasticity* refers to a person's potential to transform into a different version of themself, *fungibility* concerns the way a person might be swapped out with or for another person entirely. Snorton links his analysis of fungible fugitivity to Black trans people, suggesting that the "ungendering of Blackness" renders it particularly suited to a kind of trans fugitivity contingent on interchangeable Black flesh.[70] If we take the interanimation of race and age seriously, we might consider how Black and non-Black trans elders might experience differential forms of racialization that make variations of fungible fugitivity possible.

These variations do not smooth over the distinct conditions and embodyminded experiences that mark Black trans fungibility specifically, but they do help to explain the queer potential of trans silence for elders, including those who may be non-Black people of color or even white. This queer potential remediates fungibility into a kind of multiracial trans sociability. Indeed, Amy's silence provides the grounds on which she built and maintains her kinship and mutual aid networks with the women and girls who live with her.[71] *Silence,* in this case, refers to the embodied and material consequences of gender nonconformance that exist outside of intentional acts of adornment or embodyminded reconfiguration. Silence is the result of gender nonconformance, the effects of a racialized trans existence. On one hand, these effects may include the loss of family, friends, employment, and housing. Sara Ahmed points out that "an existence can be nullified by the requirement that an existence be evidenced," and within transnaturalism, only evidence of transnormativity is counted as evidence.[72] On the other hand, the effects of trans silence can lay the groundwork for relationships that might not otherwise come to pass. It's these effects—as rare, conditional, and insufficient as they may be—that make Amy's life livable.

Put another way, Amy and the people living with her were both silenced by institutional ageism and transphobia and tactically silent, drawn together by the complementarity of their resources and needs. Amy did not share her house because she is trans, nor did the women and girls elect to take care of Amy because they are trans. Rather, their shared experiences of trans silence—Amy's isolation, the women's and girls' homelessness—created an opportunity for them to support one another, offering what they can, taking what they need. Their bond was fashioned out of what is left over from identity, the stuff that happens before, during, and after coming out. It was a form of relationality conjured out of desperation, even as it opened the possibility for transformative kinship. Trans silence thus operates not only as that which an individual uses to explore gender by themselves but also as something that can be mined for community building.

It is helpful to imagine this communal silence as a form of what José Esteban Muñoz calls "disidentification." In *Disidentifications: Queers of Color and the Performance of Politics, disidentity* is defined as "an *anti-identitarian identity politics*" grounded in "communal structures of feelings."[73] To disidentify is to reject racialized identity categories while simultaneously embracing the affective opportunities afforded by identification with others. It is a way of being oneself, despite refusing to name whom oneself is. Muñoz is clear that disidentification is not so much of a political strategy of representation as it is "about cultural, material, and psychic survival."[74] It is less of an attack on neoliberal multiculturalism than it is "a response to state and global power apparatuses that employ systems of racial, sexual, and national subjugation."[75] Disidentification is a precarious, often injurious, form of resistance used by marginalized populations to stay alive.

One of the examples Muñoz offers is of Ricardo, a Cuban American subject in the documentary *The Transformation* (1996). Ricardo once identified as a trans woman,[76] but after he was diagnosed with AIDS, he realized that he could no longer afford (financially or physically) to continue being homeless, which he had been for quite some time. Ricardo subsequently joined a church, renounced both his trans identity and same-gender desire, married a woman, and began living as a Christian. Muñoz understands Ricardo's decision as a form of disidentification, one where he "worked with and on the ideology of born-again Christianity, attempting to benefit from its rewards (material support, concerned community, companionship) while resisting total cooptation by that discourse."[77] While his disidentity required the loss of "his breasts, his homosexual desire, and his queerness," he nevertheless managed to secure a better end of life than he would have had otherwise. Robert McRuer, in his own analysis of *The Transformation,* allegorizes Ricardo's detransition to a process of cisnormative rehabilitation—one that effectively "depends on the degradation and silencing" of his life as a woman.[78] These are the stakes of disidentification; they are always on the brink of being too high.

Regardless, Muñoz holds out hope that disidentity contains the seeds for "possible future relations of power," where identity will no longer be a criterion to secure representation, support, or access.[79] McRuer agrees, noting that by refusing to reclaim "the degraded other" as a new iteration of the "rehabilitated self," disidentification manages to avoid the circuitous violence of identity politics, wherein "rehabilitated identities . . . are also in some ways normative identities that inevitably incorporate generic sameness *in and through their distinctiveness* and that require and produce degraded others."[80] Disidentity aims to cut off the neoliberal cycle of exclusion-via-exceptionalization, offering in its place "traces of agency, resistance, and hope that are as legible where identity disintegrates as where it comes together."[81] Disidentification's value, then, is less in what it offers now (e.g., Ricardo's end-of-life care) than in what it promises, what forms of queer and unexpected relations it gestures toward. To disidentify is to participate in "the transformative politics" that enable "subjects and groups *to imagine.*"[82] It is to join a movement larger than oneself in pursuit of radically alternative collectivities.

Trans silence can be understood as a trans-specific form of disidentification by the way it resists the tenets of transnormative identity politics, pushing back against the processes of racialized ageism that disqualify trans elders from liberal recognition. While the qualifier *trans* in *trans silence* may seem to be aligned with a particular mode of gendered identification, the function of silence is to undermine the predictability of what a given identity has to offer. As with Amy, her coming out as trans offered her no relief from the demands of her age. In fact, the very real material costs of trans identification are what kept Amy from coming out for over three decades. Her trans silence was informed by identity but ultimately rejected it; silence became a way of navigating gender variability through stealth and thereby outside of any formal category or disclosure.

When Amy did come out as trans, her prolonged silence had already curtailed her possibilities for accessing the care she needed and continues to need. As with the women and girls she houses, Amy's silence is not trans-identified but trans-disidentified, pitted against transnaturalism, where only those who come out white, rich, binary, and on time get the support they need to survive. For many other trans and gender nonconforming folks, including homeless people and elders, silence is all that's left. While perhaps Amy's silence did not incur the same costs as Ricardo's—Amy was able to secure a care network while still living as a woman, after all—it nevertheless did affect the way that her identity functioned in her life. Unlike it did for Corey Maison, trans identification did not immediately garner national public recognition, support, or approval for Amy. Though her profile in *To Survive on This Shore* is striking, with her seated on a park bench, legs crossed at the knee, hands folded over her thighs, and black hair perfectly framing her face, Amy's photo was never shared on Facebook. It wasn't disseminated through LGBTQ media outlets. No one captioned it protectively, "*Amy* IS TRANSGENDER" and that "for those STILL not able to understand: if this was YOUR *grandmother,* would you be comfortable sending her into a men's bathroom? Neither would I."

Amy, like so many trans elders, trans people of color, and poor trans people, among other disenfranchised gender variant communities, was left to fend for herself. Trans silence, expressed through stealth, became her way of getting by, her strategy for being in a world that did not make a space for her. Trans silence was not an excuse for staying quiet but a technique for building, as Muñoz writes, "a version of self that is crafted through something other than rote representational practices."[83] Trans silence was Amy's disidentity and, ultimately, held her "possibility for freedom."[84]

This freedom, though often only glimpsed far off in the distant future, can sometimes be found in the present, offering us little visions of what is to come. One such vision comes from the life of Dee Dee Ngozi, a woman with brown skin and hair, and yet another interviewee of Dugan and Fabbre's, who is from Atlanta, Georgia, and was fifty-five at the time of her interview (Figure 8). In her image, Dee Dee grins toward the camera. She has one hand on her shoulder and another on her stomach. She is wearing a red dress with lace sleeves, a red boa behind her neck, a bracelet with a red stone, as well as red lipstick, blush, and eye shadow. As part of her interview, Dee Dee explains that she previously worked as a sex worker before contracting HIV and securing a job at a local clinic. She also founded a "trans ministry" at her church and serves alongside other women on "the 'mother board,'" despite initially experiencing some resistance. Dee Dee says:

> One day, mother Gladys asked me to come and sit down there with [the mothers]. And after we had our little meeting, after church, Miss Gladys went to do something in the office and then they surrounded me and said, "What gives you the right to be here on this mothers' board? We don't understand it." I said, "Because I'm a mother to the ones you can't love. The ones that you cannot be a mother to, that you throw out on the street every day. Those are my children. The ones you throw away." I said, "That's why I'm here." You could hear a pin drop, nobody said nothing. They went on and accepted me and said, "Come on girl, sit down."[85]

Dee Dee's role in the church and on the mother board is to provide forms of care—what I'm inclined to just call love—to the queer and trans youth who don't receive it from their given families. She is a mother to children whose own parents cannot or will not embrace them, and as one of the few Black interviewees in Dugan and Fabbre's project, her story is all the more important. Unlike Amy, Dee Dee did not age out of her plasticity; she was fungible, even as a trans child, and is giving to her children the kind of affirmation she likely did not receive herself. When the other women on the board attempted to discredit her, Dee Dee defended herself not with identity-based arguments, such as those that rehearse the value of multiculturalism or diversity. Instead, she made her case based on bodily and material need, based on the fact that there are children without the mothering they deserve.

FIGURE 8. Dee Dee Ngozi, 55. Photograph by Jess T. Dugan, from *To Survive on This Shore: Photographs and Interviews with Transgender and Gender Nonconforming Older Adults.*

Dee Dee's place on the mother board is a perfect example of disidentification because she is not a biological mother, but she recognizes the importance of mothering and appropriates the purpose of the mother board to ensure that "the ones you can't love" or "be a mother to" or "throw out on the street every day" are being loved, nurtured, and housed. Her story also demonstrates the power of trans silence because it is due to her experiences of fungibility that she feels compelled to give back in the ways she does. Describing her job at the HIV clinic as having "come full circle," Dee Dee understands her current work as an effect of her previous career in the sex industry. By "push[ing] patients, walk[ing] them to the car, sing[ing] church songs," she is enacting a fungible fugitivity that sutures her traumas with others', knitting together a patchwork of silences into a quilt of radical kinship.[86]

This kinship is radical not only for its persistence in the face of institutional oppression and—in the cases of the other women on the mother board—interpersonal prejudice but also for its intersectional and coalitional potential. Muñoz, while describing intersectionality's role in disidentification, writes that it "is primarily concerned with the *relations* between different minoritarian coordinates."[87] Dee Dee's justification for serving on the mother board echoes this approach to relationality by refusing to disclose her children's names or identities. Her children are known by the simple refrain "the ones," which remediates impersonal fungibility as a deeply intimate openness to difference, to the full breadth of gender and sexual variance occupied by queer and trans youth. Similarly, Dee Dee sees her work at the HIV clinic as a way of giving back to the community of sex workers of which she used to be a part, a community disproportionately filled with women, people of color, and queer and trans folks. Not to mention, the particular kinds of labor that Dee Dee mentions doing at the clinic—helping patients move around and providing emotional support through singing—suggest that she is also assisting disabled people and potentially other elders.

The constellation of individuals that Dee Dee single-handedly brings together goes to show how powerful trans silence can be. Dee Dee is not only resisting the temptation of identity-based activism, nor is she merely theorizing the implications of her own age identity. She is not even limiting herself to helping those people to whom she has easy access. Rather, Dee Dee leverages her own experiences of silence and fungibility to co-opt rhetorics that are not meant for her in the service of people whom she knows only by their need. Dee Dee disidentifies trans silence, harnessing the constraints of a broken system as the tools she uses to fashion a new one.

Transcrip Silence

Until now, my focus in this chapter has primarily been on the interanimation of gender, age, and race. Transnaturalism names a racializing process beholden to a medical-industrial complex that disguises white youthfulness as a baseline impressionability, effectively racializing elder trans folks as fungible monikers of deviant gender nonconformance. I would be remiss, however, if I did not attend to a fourth axis of identity and experience that figures into the lives of many trans elders and serves as the central lynchpin of biomedicine's cultural authority over trans experience: disability. It is not only that many trans elders will eventually age into disability but also that the language of disability (i.e., pathology) is used to explain trans elders' experiences.[88] Though elders presumedly lack the plasticity necessary to achieve the appearance of transnormativity, many still find themselves caught up in transnaturalism as they seek access to biomedical transition technologies. Trans scholars and activists have long lamented the fact that in order to medically transition, trans people must undergo a process of self-pathologization, wherein they align themselves with a dimorphic sex/gender system and affirm the authority of "state science" to facilitate their transition.[89]

Through pathologization, which is thoroughly bound up with a process of racialization predicated on the mutual constitution of whiteness and abledness, trans elders encounter disability as a framework through which they are meant to understand their gender nonconformance. Trans-specific pathologies, including gender identity disorder and gender dysphoria, are the racialized excesses of transnaturalism that, if not cured through biomedical intervention, do little more than "conjur[e] up the specter of gender nonconformance."[90] *Disability* thus comes to name the space of ageist trans fungibility, the realm of old trannies who are as crazy as they are ugly. Disability is at once the gateway to trans medicine's promise of technologically facilitated embodyminded realignment and the scapegoat for when that realignment fails to produce a transnormative subject. It is a trap that disabled people are all too familiar with: medicalized disability renders you either the supercrip who inspires nondisabled people or the pitiable gimp or idiot against which all other tragedies are compared.

And it is this trap, this risk of further disenfranchisement, that makes many disabled people resistant, sometimes even hostile, to medical authority. If submitting to a medical model of disability only makes a person's life worse, why do it?

Because we don't have many other good options, respond trans folks. Herein lies the foremost tension between trans and disability politics, a tension that makes coalitions between the two communities and their respective academic fields challenging. In *Brilliant Imperfection: Grappling with Cure,* trans, disabled activist Eli Clare asks, "How can I reconcile my lifelong struggle to love my disabled self exactly as it is with my use of medical technology to reshape my gendered and sexed body-mind? I'm searching for a messier story."[91] Unfortunately, as each community is increasingly siloed by neoliberalism and as each academic field grows further warehoused as an independent discourse, the margins for messiness between transness and disability become ever slimmer. And as messes are cleaned up, forms of normativity take their place, cleaving trans and disabled people away from each other and into their own, individual, identity-based categories. Jasbir K. Puar, commenting on this process of individuation, calls the subjects of each community "exceptionalized figures."[92] It is not only that each community distinguishes itself from the other but that those distinctions are often framed as oppositional, positioning each as not-X. Halberstam explains that "transgenderism has been excluded from the category of disability both to purge disability of any connection to perverse gendering but also to protect transgenderism from pathologization."[93] I propose, however, that the disidentificatory valence of trans silence may help to draw new lines of communication between the categories. As I explain below and at length in chapter 5, silence can offer ways to acknowledge forms of embodyminded and material meaning-making that exist outside of identity-based politics, and therefore it may also serve to illuminate coalitional opportunities across variously identified and configured bodyminds.

In academia, some scholars have already begun the labor of conjoining the fields of trans studies and disability studies. Perhaps most famously, Puar has proposed "*becoming trans*" as a model of trans assemblage inflected by a disability politic, one that "highlight[s the] impossibility of linearity, permanence, and end points."[94] "Becoming trans" reads Deleuzian assemblage theory alongside disability studies' critiques of independence and autonomy to undercut the notion that anyone can ever "be trans"—that is, "in opposition to the body that is most certainly cisgender."[95] Puar writes, "The question, are you trans? morphs to, how trans are you? . . . Similarly, the question, are you disabled? morphs to, how abled are you? and how disabled are you?"[96] These questions work to "de-exceptionalize" the categories of "trans" and "disability," adopting a series of spectral models for gender nonconformance and debilitation that chart gradations of deviance as they are manufactured within and adjudicated across the austere conditions of global, racial capitalism.[97] Puar seeks to blur the distinguishing features between "trans" and "disability," as well as between "cis" and "trans" and "able" and "disabled," by shifting focus toward "the dissolution" of "qualified difference."[98]

As Clare reminds us, though, Puar's de-exceptionalizing agenda, as intellectually stimulating as it might be, comes at the risk of glossing individual and local lived experiences, especially those of trans disabled people, whose "inexplicable" desires[99] do not always align with what Puar envisions as the "deterritorializing force" of "becoming trans."[100] Some of us feel the urges to, at once, take advantage of medical assistance for a gender transition and resist or even outright decry medical intervention for a disability.[101] These competing desires can carry equal weight for those of us who feel them, and yet only the latter desire seems to fulfill Puar's political project. While Puar does not explicitly denounce medical intervention, she does propose a link between "trans body modification" and "racial recuperation," as well as "constructs of ableism."[102] This link emerges out of the tension Puar establishes between "becoming trans" and what she calls "piecing": the process by which transness is exceptionalized through "the commodification . . . of plasticity."[103] As a neoliberal revision of "passing," piecing works to designate trans subjects "not as gender-normative male or female, but *as trans*," thereby appointing "a new transnormative citizen" that is marked by their visible transness.[104] Puar argues that while piecing "appears transgressive," "becoming trans" more thoroughly rejects the biopolitical maintenance of trans and disabled subjectivity.[105]

By rejecting subjectivity, "becoming trans" pursues an unruly and multiplicative "capacitation of race, of racial ontologies."[106] Building on Amit Rai's "race racing," according to which *race* designates not a limited number of nonwhite ontologies but an "immanent intensive variability," Puar imagines that "becoming trans" might model a proliferation of sex, gender, racial, and dis/ability difference toward a radical project of "speciation."[107] This project would reallocate the racializing significations "that seek to contain and compartmentalize what is raced, what is not raced" in order to explode the legibility or coherence of those significations.[108] Unlike existing iterations of piecing and "being trans" that have supposedly succumbed to the "control economies of bodily inhabitation," "becoming trans" clings to "infinite variation."[109] According to this view, the "becoming trans" subject (and the "becoming trans" disabled subject in particular) comes to figure as a site of ultimate human difference, a species of self-queering queers that runs on "a politics of manifesting beyond what control can control."[110]

What I fear gets lost in this particular critique of trans subjectivity, transnormativity, and transnaturalism, particularly in the formulation of piecing as iterative "of neoliberal market economies," is the fact that neither trans nor disabled people are singularly responsible for the medical-industrial complex, let alone the cisableism that standardizes the white, abled, gender conforming bodymind as normative.[111] I agree with Puar that there is radical queer potential bound up in embodyminded nonconformance, and I agree further that this potential is redoubled when paired with a politics that attends to the raced and racializing dynamics of trans medicine.[112] I do not believe, however, that this potential is reduced or diluted by individual consumer decisions to pursue a gender transition with(in) the medical-industrial complex, even if access to that transition is hinged on the confession of a transnatural testimony.[113] Cisnormativity is not the fault of trans people, so to center the claim that piecing is "a valued asset in control societies" in a critique of trans exceptionalism seems to neglect that trans medicine remains widely inaccessible to most trans people and to forget that many trans people are the victims of gendered biopolitics rather than its primary operants.[114]

To be fair, Puar herself admits that "piecing remains an elusive reality for many"; nevertheless, she argues that the political thrust of "becoming trans" is powered by its wholesale rejection of trans subjectivity: "there is no trans."[115] Piecing thus becomes a synecdoche for all forms of "legal legitimation, state recognition, public accommodation, and resource distribution" that make trans life possible, even if unevenly, in the United States.[116] Piecing is rhetorically fixed as the foil to the more proliferative and deterritorialized agenda of "becoming trans." While there is certainly good reason to critique a trans liberalism that concerns itself only with rights-based arguments—those that actively seek out biopolitical and geopolitical capacitation as thresholds of trans respectability—this critique must be couched in the recognition that sometimes compliance *with* institutions and the state is the most accessible form of protection *from* institutions and the state. That is, sometimes even the most vulnerable trans people will disidentify with a harmful institution (such as the medical-industrial complex) in order to secure relief—however marginal and fleeting—from the conditions produced by that institution. Made in isolation, Puar's argument seems to demand that trans people sacrifice the meager offerings of disidentification at the risk of making their lives even more precarious. Placing the labor of deterritorialization onto trans people neglects, as Carol Riddell points out, to hold cis people—the much larger and more powerful constituency—accountable for their part, effectively "deny[ing] us any element of autonomy."[117] "Us," in this context, refers to the trans and disabled folks who scramble to take advantage of whatever resources we have at our disposal to feel safe, beautiful, and loved. Puar's "becoming trans," committed as it is to perpetual rearrangement, seems disconnected from the conditions that underpin these profoundly quotidian, perhaps even innately human, desires.

Desire, as it turns out, is for me a much more attractive inroad to the trans–disability nexus. On one hand, Puar is right that desire, even the desire to pursue a decidedly queer transition, is never free from the racial capitalist logics that structure trans medicine and aesthetics. These same logics, I add, risk subtending a transnatural model that recalls the contingence of *queer*'s emergence on disability's disavowal: trans medicine as a cure for gender dysphoria and a rehabilitation of the perverse gender deviant into the restored transnormative subject. Though there are important differences between the historical argument to depathologize homosexuality and current efforts to work with(in) the medicalization of gender dysphoria, both revolve around the rhetorical figure of disability—at once distancing themselves from real disabled people and thus shoring up the integrity of medical authority to demarcate the boundaries of abled subjectivity. On the other hand, for many trans and disabled people, the tension between the categories is less historical or political than personal and material. Where should I go to get my hormones? How do I secure reliable access to pain meds? Which doctor is going to sign my permission forms the fastest? Which diagnosis do I need to get insurance to cover my bills? These are questions that smudge the boundary between "trans" and "disability" not through categorical dissolution but through illumination of their mutual contingence. Transness and disability are fueled by desires to occupy our bodyminds particularly and in ways that sometimes require degrees of acquiescence and participation with a medical institution designed to eliminate us. This desire at once "lives publicly in an amorphous tangle called the medical industrial complex and privately in our bedrooms, kitchens, and bathrooms."[118] It is a desire hounded by the same two questions, again and again: what do I want, and what will it take to get it?

Answers to these questions are bound to be as many and varied as the people who confront them. As I've said before, not all trans people want to get doctors involved with their transitions, and not all disabled people are anti-cure. Additionally, not all trans and disabled people have access to biomedicine, even if they want it. It is worth emphasizing that neither pursuing nor rejecting medical intervention is more ethical, progressive, or radical. In fact, as I am trying to argue, the kind of relationship an individual has with medicine is far less important to trans and disability struggles than the much larger question of how do we all live within a culture saturated by the authority of the medical-industrial complex while still retaining a sense of ourselves outside of and beyond it? In what ways might we promote equitable and affordable access to curative technologies without sacrificing the unique and intricate queerness of our desire for the products of those technologies? Cue trans silence.

As Muñoz's disidentity teaches us, the potential to strategically appropriate institutional power for subversive ends is not only a real possibility but already in practice, "called on by minoritarian subjects throughout their everyday life."[119] While a total takeover and dismantling of the medical establishment may not be immediately feasible, there still exists the potential to play into normative expectations of pathology in order to access medical care. It is such play that Tobin Siebers alleges with his disability masquerade in chapter 3. I do not mean to suggest that disidentifying with medical authority is playful in the sense that it is all fun and games; there is no question that such modes of resistance often have painful, dire consequences. But I do argue, along with Paul B. Preciado, that "it [is] our responsibility to remove the code, to open political practices, to multiply possibilities" for a new relationship to cure.[120]

This relationship should neither rely on transnatural glamorizations of biomedical intervention nor rehearse the overly exclusionary politics of the social model of disability, where disability is a product of the built environment rather than an embodyminded reality. Instead, following the guide of trans silence, a relationship with the medical-industrial complex should be premised on the knowledge that people change: our bodyminds change, our names change, our pronouns change, our identities change. And thus, our relationship to the medical-industrial complex must itself be variable and subject to change. Just as trans silence takes many forms over the course of a lifetime, so too do our ties to doctors, medicine, therapies, and cure shift and evolve. Courtney W. Bailey refers to these dynamic relationships as part of "surviving crip stories" that highlight "the process of pursuit rather than the product of cure."[121] Though transnaturalism is bent on the elimination of trans-as-disability, surviving crips recognize that survival never stops; it's never in the past tense. "The term 'surviving,'" writes Bailey, "indicates ongoing, elliptical processes that loop back on (but do not simply repeat) themselves."[122] Surviving crips are not survivors because they *have* survived but because they *continue to* survive.

Sometimes surviving means doing whatever it takes to get your meds, your hormones, or your procedures, including playing into biomedicine's bullshit. Sometimes surviving means saying, *No, I don't need that, doc. You can fuck right off.* It's all survival. Though there are indeed material consequences to submitting to medical authority—occasionally with implications that last (or cost) a lifetime—this is the cost of disidentification. That is to say, disidentifying with cure does not guarantee salvation from the medical model, but it might offer a glimpse into a future where no such model exists—one where, as Clare hopes, "our body-mind desires will spread through us, as vibrant and varied as a tallgrass prairie in midsummer."[123] The potential for transcrip coalitions lies in this glimpsing, for if we can share a glimpse, then perhaps we can share the future.

I end this chapter by returning to *To Survive on This Shore* for one final profile, which helps tie together the potential of a transcrip futurity with age. Danny, a man with light skin who lives in Saint Joseph, Missouri, was sixty-six at the time of his interview (Figure 9). His image shows him sitting in a wheelchair on a patio. His forearms are resting on the armrests of his chair, and he is wearing black tennis shoes, blue jeans, an unbuttoned blue and white striped shirt, and a gray undershirt. His eyes are closed, and his chin is lifted. Behind him is a person leaning over to kiss his forehead. They have brown hair and are wearing a green shirt. Perhaps more than any other profile in Dugan and Fabbre's book, Danny's story demonstrates how interlocking axes of subjection under the medical-industrial complex, such as disability, transness, and age, can fold in on one another. Though Danny is not the oldest participant in the project, he nevertheless experiences his age as a marginalizing factor with material consequences. Danny also recognizes that his transness and disabilities are embodyminded phenomena that both inform and are informed by his social context:

> I started to transition at the age of sixty-four. My cardiologist was reluctant to start me on testosterone because of my age. I was also overweight and my blood pressure was high. I finally went on a half dose, but after three months increased to a full dose. It was great. I was getting facial and body hair really fast and my voice dropped almost immediately. But then I had a stroke, which screwed everything up. The testosterone almost certainly caused my stroke, so I had to stop taking it. All the masculinization that I got, I've lost in the last year and a half without testosterone. I really try not to think about it too much. I had the chance to finally, after sixty-four years,

be happy and be who I was. To look in the mirror and see the guy I should have been all these years. And now it's not going to happen. No chance.

When I had the stroke, the nurses in the hospital treated me badly because I was transgender. They just pretty much ignored me and let me lay for eight hours before they even did a test. The second day, I had another stroke that caused the majority of the damage. But, I have to believe that everything happens exactly the way it is supposed to, so there is some reason I had this stroke. I would like to walk again. I am getting a little stronger every week.

I want to do whatever I can to still be an activist. I want to help younger trans people find themselves and find their answers. I tell them, "Have courage. Keep hanging in there and never give up. You cannot kill yourself, God damn it, because you have to find out what happens next." I have felt like killing myself so many times, but I want to know what happens next.[124]

Danny, like the other elders I cite in this chapter, is nothing if not resilient. His dedication to activism after multiple traumas—experiencing two strokes, receiving inadequate medical attention, and losing corporeal characteristics he had been excited about—is astounding. Yet, again like many elders, Danny's strength is a product of his marginalization. His experiences of silence, whether prior to his transition or when he was neglected by the nurses in the hospital, informed his method of resistance, his refusal to give up, his insistence on "hanging in there . . . to find out what happens next."

While these hopeful sentiments may seem banal, they echo the motivations of other elders, like Amy and Dee Dee, by how they rhetorically transform experiences of pain, isolation, and abuse into fuel for desiring a better tomorrow. Danny's activism may not be directly disidentifying with an existing institution or system of normativity, such as Dee Dee's role on the mother board, but his decision to stay alive is itself a disidentificatory move. To cling to life and to tell other, "younger trans people" to do the same is to reject his own erasure. To

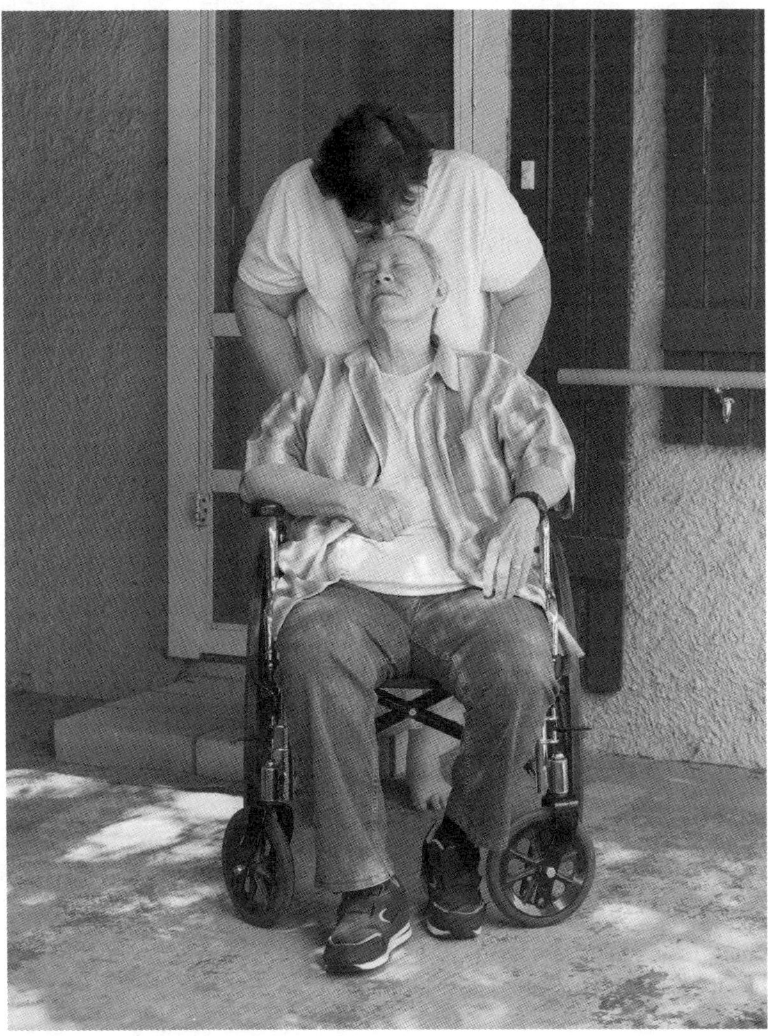

FIGURE 9. Danny, 66. Photograph by Jess T. Dugan, from *To Survive on This Shore: Photographs and Interviews with Transgender and Gender Nonconforming Older Adults.*

insist on “know[ing] what happens next” is to work toward a “next” that is worth knowing, one that includes him and others like him.

Notably, Danny’s politics, conditioned as they are by trans silence, are not restricted to the well-being of trans folks. They also pursue brighter futures for other, new identifications and nonidentificatory ways of being in the world. Encouraging people to "find themselves and find their answers" is the ultimate hope of trans silence because when the world doesn't listen to us, sometimes our best bet is to listen to ourselves and to channel that listening into our dreams. I speak of silence in this way not to overdramatize it or to smooth over the pain that silence often entails but to invigorate our thinking about trans silence as more than emptiness or an indication of victimhood. Trans silence is about recognition, visibility, and acknowledgment outside the parameters of identity, naturalness, or authenticity. For those trans people, many of whom are elders, who find their lives and needs misinterpreted or outright dismissed by neoliberal models of inclusion, trans silence is a way of surviving, making themselves known, and investing in the silenced lives around them. As I say throughout this book, silence can be a way of speaking.

It is this silent speech, this whisper, that offers the most comforting response to Mitch's question from the beginning of this chapter: what if I forget I'm trans? Rather than appearing as a straightforward answer, trans silence hovers around the question, building a warm pool or blanketed basket or just a pair of arms outstretched that are ready to catch him if he falls. If Mitch does forget his trans identity, if his disability recircuits his bodymind so he can no longer occupy the identity he has come to love, and if his age racializes him into fungible obscurity, then silence will be waiting to catch him, to hold him, to keep him in a realm of gender nonconformance that isn't perfect or necessarily what he wants but might be just enough to keep alive, to keep him out of the ground, suspended by a gender that doesn't have a name.

5

Neuroqueer Intimacies

Suspended by a single wire, a dancer hangs high above a stage in his wheelchair (Figure 10). The stage itself is bare, and the background is solid blue, tinted lighter at the top and deepening to darkness as it nears the floor. The dancer appears to be descending through the sky from the sun, or perhaps through water past the sun's reach. The music is somber, even sad, and driven by a single vocalist who chants and sings to a combination of percussive and wind instruments. The dancer moves acrobatically: holding onto the wire with one hand and then the other, reaching far off to one side, letting go entirely to flip upside down again and again. His arms extend away from him, and he moves them up then down from the shoulder, as if he were flapping wings, as if he were trying to fly. Occasionally, he vocalizes, yelling and grunting into the sky or waters. His chair spins. His body seems to tumble in slow motion as the wire inches him closer to the ground. He is falling or sinking, so it seems, but with so much restraint, so much control, that it is difficult to register the descent in real time. When the dancer gets within a few feet of the floor, a spotlight illuminates his face and body, revealing intricate designs painted across his back and the right side of his face; they resemble tattoos. Once his chair touches the ground, the dancer turns his back to the audience, straightens both arms out away from his body, and then lowers them, palms shaking, to his side (Figure 11). The lights dim.

The performance above was part of Sins Invalid's 2008 showcase at Brava Theater in San Francisco. Self-described as "a disability justice based performance project that incubates and celebrates artists with disabilities, centralizing artists of color and LGBTQ/gender-variant

FIGURE 10. Rodney Bell hangs from the ceiling. Still image from Sins Invalid Performance 2008. Courtesy of Sins Invalid.

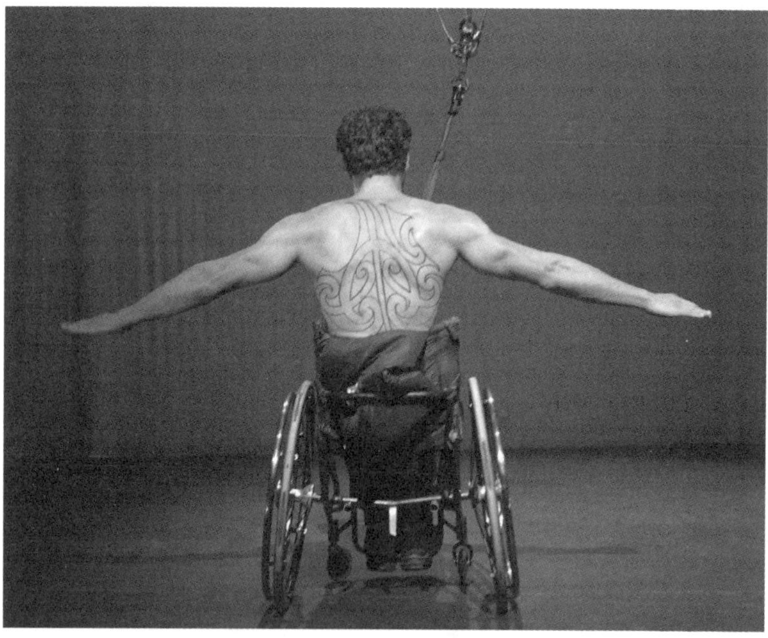

FIGURE 11. Rodney Bell performs on the ground. Still image from Sins Invalid Performance 2008. Courtesy of Sins Invalid.

artists," Sins Invalid has become famous both for the quality of art it produces and for its commitment to an equitable, collective liberation.[1] The dancer from above, Rodney Bell, is an Indigenous performer, choreographer, and activist from the Ngāti Maniapoto tribe in Aotearoa—the unceded land that is commonly called New Zealand—who was at the time working as a principal dancer for AXIS Dance Company in the United States. While I will offer more details about both Sins Invalid and Bell later in this chapter, I want to focus for now on this particular performance.

I want to dial in on the role of suspension, on what it means to be suspended and to be held in suspense. On a literal level, Bell's body is suspended. Even though he descends steadily toward the ground throughout the performance, the wire attached to his chair renders him weightless and his vertical movement perfunctory in the context of the piece. On a similarly literal level, the audience watches in suspense. Regardless of Bell's skill or of the quality of the wire contraption, aerobatic performance seems dangerous. We watch and wait: will he make it to the ground safely? Will the wire snap? Will he fall? Perhaps with disbelief suspended, we think, *Look at him fly.* These reactions and the literal iterations of suspense to which they correspond are relevant and captivating while the performance takes place, but beyond these iterations I am also interested in the figuration of suspense in Bell's piece, the way suspension is performed and functions as a technique of queer silence.

A figurative reading might suggest that Bell's suspended body represents the simultaneous suspension of his marginalized identities as disabled, Indigenous, and, at the time of the performance, an immigrant. This figurative suspension does not erase his identities or experiences of oppression but complicates their relationships to one another, at once emphasizing the intersectional nature of power and subjection and revealing the vulnerability that accompanies intersectional activism, such as that promoted by Sins Invalid. Even as Bell's body comes to represent the material coalescence of disability, Indigeneity, and immigration status, his spatial liminality—hanging between ceiling and floor, sky and earth—throws into relief the instability of individual identity categories and their apparently neat intersections. What does it mean to be both Indigenous and an immigrant?

How do we understand Bell's disability, both in this particular performance and more generally, when disability is contingent on culture and location? How do we pursue Sins Invalid's "collective claim of liberation and beauty," when the very identities we use to organize collectively are murky, conflicting, or ambivalent?[2]

This chapter begins to answer these difficult questions by turning to the cross-movement organizing potential of queer silence. In chapter 1, I hinted at this potential in my discussion of Teresa Brennan's *The Transmission of Affect,* where I noted that the "physiological impact" of rhetorical energy, much like affect, might be put to use not only for individual or intracommunal resistance efforts but also for intercommunal ones, fostering solidarity across lines of difference.[3] Queer silence offers marginalized subjects a way into the chaos of their significations; it offers ways to redirect, resignify, or disidentify with one's rhetorical energies. And as I hope the previous three chapters have made clear, rhetorical energy is as material as it is discursive; or, to borrow from Brennan, "social in origin but biological and physical in effect."[4] In this chapter, I show how the many enactments of queer silence covered thus far, including rhetorical quieting, queer masquerade, and trans silence, might be (and indeed already are) used toward a collective liberation. Pairing Jennifer Nash's notion of "intimacy" with M. Remi Yergeau's "demi-rhetoricity," I argue that queer silence can cultivate intercommunal relationships that blur the boundaries between and among identities. This blurring allows us to move away from goal-oriented agendas that predicate solidarity on shared visions for the future, instead focusing on a mutual desire to occupy our present material conditions differently. In other words, the use value of queer silence to cross-movement work is found less in its ability to change the world than in its capacity to help marginalized folks come together in the meantime, when we're not working, while we're waiting, and when we're tired.

In the next section, I flesh out the cross-movement potential of queer silence and weave together the multiple intellectual conversations that inform my argument. As it has been throughout this book, my intention is to engage these conversations on their own terms and to respect the unique genealogies that inform each perspective therein, as well as to establish new connections across apparently distinct intellectual traditions. These connections bring together queer studies with Black feminism, disability studies, and trans studies in ways that trouble or interrogate the relationship between identity and lived experience. While I acknowledge the importance of honoring the bodyminds who produce particular knowledges, and while I both respect and have benefited from the vocabularies many of us use to collate our bodies alongside similar others, I am skeptical of how neatly siloed these knowledges and vocabularies become in the process of institutionalization. I am likewise curious about the ways that bodyminds, even and perhaps especially in groups, exceed their collective identities, press into other groups' identities, and soften the lines we typically rely on to distinguish one person from another, this movement from that one.

My curiosity, in part, is about intersectionality, about the meshing of identities, and about the political import of organizing intersectionally. But my curiosity is also about nonidentification and difference, about what queer silence offers our collective liberation that cannot necessarily be captured with or explained through the language of identity. Often what queer silence provides cross-movement work goes unrecognized or underappreciated because we expect it to be legible within identity-based frameworks. We hope to identify so much with identity, even though power is itself fundamentally prediscursive and thus irreducible to identity. The coalitional value of queer silence lies in its capacity to establish solidarity among distinct movements while also putting pressure on how those movements have come to distinguish themselves, toggling between the identitarian and the nonidentitarian, the discursive and the prediscursive. My purpose in this chapter is to guide our attention to queer silence's multifaceted, coalitional capacity, both in its existing iterations and in its untapped potentialities. In the second half of this chapter, I offer three examples of cross-movement work, including Bell's performance for Sins Invalid, that are animated by queer silence. Each of the three examples embraces the political necessity of identity, even as each complicates how identity comes to function within and between the spaces of coalition-building. For these collectives, identity is something that comes in handy, even if its handiness is used only to illuminate how little identity can tell us.

Intimating Identity

When I initially set out to write this chapter, I imagined proposing queer silence as a strategy for building queercrip coalitions. Following Nancy J. Hirschmann's observation that queerness and disability are linked by the way "both embody the universal fear that the body is not given, determined, and determinate," I reasoned that rhetorical energy's indeterminability might be a useful correlative for the instability of queer and disabled bodyminds.[5] If "sexuality, like ability, can shift, alter, and change," perhaps queer silence, I figured, could mobilize changeability as the grounds for solidarity.[6] I soon grew uncomfortable, though, with the way this argument legitimized queercrip coalitions on the ironic condition that we don't really know what "queer" and "crip" are: queers are like crips because neither "queer" nor "crip" is a particularly stable identity or state of being. It was an argument not unlike Jasbir K. Puar's "becoming trans," as I discussed in chapter 4, that was primarily rooted in a celebration of shared ambivalence. The reason a queercrip coalition worked well, I implied, was because queers and crips both signify multiply and contradictorily in some contexts. The role of queer silence was to operate as a heuristic, bringing into relief rhetorical energy's shared patterns of movement around queerness and disability and the shared effects of that movement on their slippery significations. Queer silence traced the dots of queerness and disability, making a queercrip coalition appear self-evident, even as "queer" and "crip" are themselves less than stable categories.

I don't disagree with the claim that "queer" and "crip" are unstable, nor do I necessarily doubt the political efficacy of coalitions that harness parallel forms of instability and indeterminability as rhetorical commonplaces. I do, however, worry about a subtle sleight of hand embedded in my original argument that I take to be representative of much scholarship on coalition-building. This sleight of hand at first acknowledges the contingencies of queerness and disability as separate identities but then suddenly ignores those contingencies when queerness and disability are considered together. In other words, queerness and disability are stabilized in the context of a queercrip coalition to make the site of their coalescence legible. The function of queer silence was not merely interpretive but inventive, resuscitating the structure of single-axis identity politics, even as it claimed to do the opposite. This resuscitation not only essentialized queerness and disability as distinct categories but also ignored the indeterminability and fluidity that define rhetorical energy.

Anna Carastathis's work on intersectionality helps to resolve this problem by "conceptualizing identities as coalitions—as internally heterogeneous, complex unities."[7] To imagine an identity as a coalition is to recognize, first, the multiplicity of identities that exist within each movement. Queers contain crips and crips contain queers because some queers are crips and some crips are queers. Second, coalitional identities remind us to shift our focus away from the differences between movements toward the things that we all share, what Carastathis calls "an integrated practice of struggle."[8] Importantly, this shift is not a denial of difference, nor is it a flattening of difference to prioritize similarities; rather, the shift makes evident that difference is always already a part of whom our groups are meant to represent. Conceiving of difference in this way allows for the slipperiness of queerness and disability to remain intact within the context of cross-movement work.

A perfect example of Carastathis's model for coalitional identities occurs in Alison Kafer's *Feminist, Queer, Crip,* where Kafer proposes "coalitions as a process in which the interests and identities themselves are always open to contestation and debate."[9] Here, coalitions not only honor the contingencies of individual identities, including but not limited to queerness and disability, but also put these contingencies in tension with one another to "trouble the boundaries of the constituencies involved."[10] This approach allows Kafer to identify coalitions between disability activism and feminism, trans activism, environmental activism, and reproductive justice that open up the concept of disability, marshaling its instability, to address a variety of identities and situations that are not typically read as relevant to disability studies or activism. Kafer thus demonstrates how the coalitions embedded within disability identity can reveal new coalitions beyond disability; or, as Carastathis puts it, "Differences within us can enable radical alliances among us."[11]

What strikes me as particularly useful about Carastathis's and Kafer's work is how they glimpse an approach to cross-movement organizing that does not do away with identity politics entirely, even as they presume the instability of any given identity category. Indeed, the value of coalitions for Carastathis and Kafer lies in their capacity to reshape the identities that constitute them. The variation of "queer" that enters into a queercrip coalition will not likely be the same variation that emerges on the other side. In fact, when identities are imagined as always already coalitional, there is no "other side" for "queer" to emerge from—there is no "queer" outside of a queercrip coalition; there is no "crip" outside of a queercrip coalition. And the same could be said for any number of marginalized identities that, beneath the surface of their identitarian singularity, are caught up in similar negotiations of power and subjection. While these negotiations manifest differently for each group and for each person within each group, accounting for their similarities (or intersections) helps us to push back against the logic of single-axis organizing that presumes insurmountable differences between groups and depends on a kind of narcissistic reciprocity to justify cross-movement work: *I see myself in you, and you see yourself in me, so let's get to coalition-building.*

Instead, a coalitional model of identity politics that is predicated on difference can generate power from unlikely alliances that do not immediately appear relevant. These alliances do not require explicit justification because it is understood, as Cathy J. Cohen argues, that what decides "one's political comrades" is "one's relation to power, and not some homogenized identity."[12] What's called for is not an end to identity politics but rather a suspicion of the egocentrism underpinning some cross-movement work, an egocentrism that risks foreclosing opportunities for collaboration that have yet to be articulated through the language of identity. Such coalitions remain conditional, a matter of personal relevance, and their value continues to be measured against their contributions to a discrete set of identity-based groups. The purpose of establishing solidarity should not be to overcome differences or to stabilize identities—a kind of gesture to intersectionality that effectively isolates identities into discrete categories. Cross-movement work should, rather, lean into intergroup and intragroup differences to foster forms of togetherness that enable "one to cross naturalized boundaries imposed by systems of oppression."[13] These boundaries include not only physical ones, such as the national borders Carastathis discusses, but also identities, which have been refined by a neoliberal instinct for consumer division. Coalitions as border crossing conjures a vision of collective liberation freed from any existing form of relationality, and it invites us to imagine ways of being together now that are similarly untethered.

In the interest of imagining such coalitional ways of being together, I turn to Jennifer C. Nash's call for "a radical embrace of the political potentiality of intimacy."[14] In *Black Feminism Reimagined: After Intersectionality,* Nash suggests that the concept of intersectionality, which "is part of a cohort of terms that Black Feminists created in order to analyze the interconnectedness of structures of domination," has reached a kind of affective threshold, where its political and intellectual currency is undercut by the emotional labor wrapped up in preserving the concept's integrity.[15] The field of Black feminism is forced into "a largely protective posture, leaving black feminists mired in policing intersectionality's usages, demanding that intersectionality remain located within black feminism, and reasserting intersectionality's 'true' origins in black feminist texts."[16] While Nash acknowledges a "certain kind of agency" enacted by guarding the intellectual property of intersectionality, she nevertheless worries that such "defensiveness" is ultimately "dangerous" because it restricts the creative impulses of Black feminists from pursuing other ideas.[17] As a result, Nash urges "other ways of feeling black feminist, other ways of being black feminist and doing black feminist labor in the academy that eschew defensiveness and its toxicity."[18]

This pivot toward "other ways" comes to a head in the third chapter, where Nash seeks to establish "a conception of intersectionality" that is "expansive, broad, and deterritorialized enough to move with figures beyond 'black woman.'"[19] In moving intersectionality "beyond" Black women, Nash is not denying the centrality of Black women or Black feminism to intersectionality's history, nor is she collapsing differences between and among Black women and other marginalized groups. Instead, Nash opens up intersectionality "to unleash *intimacies*" that might reveal new potentialities for cross-movement work.[20] In some respects, Nash's intimacies mirror the work of Carastathis's and Kafer's coalitions: bringing together two or more groups for a common cause. However, Nash's intimacies take Carastathis's coalitional identities one step further to reveal "the permeability between concepts and their imagined 'origins,' and between bodies."[21] Intimacies, according to Nash, are less about the identitarian differences that divide groups, such as Black women and non-Black women of color, than they are about the opportunities created by "blur[ring] the boundaries of who these analytics 'belong' to, who they can—or should—describe."[22] To imagine cross-movement work as a matter of intimacy is to measure the value of an alliance not by what people have in common but by what their differences can offer one another. It is a way of bringing the concept of diversity to diversity work, acknowledging that different knowledges offer different ways of imagining different worlds.

To build on Nash's project, I'd like to draw attention to the queer resonances of intimacy and intimate activisms. Specifically, I am interested in the role of desire and the way that cultivating cross-movement intimacies might allow groups not only to exchange liberatory visions but also to imagine new forms of liberation together. This kind of desiring-together produces a temporal displacement that shifts our focus from the present we have to the future we want. José Esteban Muñoz famously calls this displacement "seeing queerness as horizon," when "straight time is interrupted or stepped out of" in favor of an "ecstatic time" that "offers queers much more than the meager offerings of pragmatic gay and lesbian politics."[23] For Muñoz, ecstatic time is a kind of double displacement, a "horizontal temporality," that looks ahead toward a queer(er) futurity as a way of renegotiating our relationship to the present. It fosters "a path and a movement to a greater openness to the world."[24] I am arguing that desiring-together, as a kind of cross-movement intimacy, produces a similar kind of renegotiation, wherein our shared desires for the future help us to occupy our current world otherwise. Nash calls this "the possibility of being done and undone through relationality."[25] When our intimacies open up possibilities for dreaming new worlds, our identities begin to unravel, even if temporarily. This is not to suggest that intimacy or desire or dreaming erases all our differences or flattens the power differentials that are still very much present in cross-movement work. But it is to emphasize the ways that desiring-together a different future creates opportunities for us to be differently together right now in the present.

By "differently together," I am referring to this notion of living otherwise or reimagining our relationship to our current material conditions in a way that makes our lives more livable. As the previous chapters have shown, this is the project of queer silence: rerouting and re-regulating and renegotiating our rhetorical energies to help us stay alive, despite not always having the power to change our rhetorical energies entirely. Thus, to engage our rhetorical energies differently together is to suture cross-movement intimacies that do not depend on the coalescence of our identities. It is to push back against the ways we've come to understand our unique experiences and oppressions as irreconcilable with one another. It is to acknowledge that the energies hurtling through all our bodyminds are often energies that we have not chosen, layering us in significations we have no choice but to bear. Queer silence holds space for cross-movement intimacies that don't seem to make sense or to follow any normative organizing logic. Queer silence encourages the coming together of groups and peoples that don't seem to have a reason for doing so. Queer silence invites alliances that pursue ostensibly nonpolitical or lesser political ideals, such as beauty and pleasure. Queer silence promotes the kind of being differently together that allows marginalized folks across the board to take a break from their large-scale, structural organizing labor and, even if just for a few moments, settle into a little joy that we can have right now.

Neuroqueering Cross-Movement Work

In turning away from traditional approaches to cross-movement work that rely on varying degrees of identitarian legibility, and in embracing an approach that furthers more fluid relations/relationships/relationalities, I am making something of a rhetorical argument. Or, more precisely, I am making a demirhetorical argument, to paraphrase M. Remi Yergeau: I am intervening in rhetorical discourse only to ultimately foreclose the rhetoricity of my argument. In *Authoring Autism: On Rhetoric and Neurological Queerness,* Yergeau introduces "demi-rhetoricity" as the defining rhetorical characteristic of autistic people. It refers to ways that clinicians can "argue that autistic people are not autistic enough to make claims about autism" and "likewise argue that autistic people are too autistic to make claims about autism," thrusting autists into an impossible and liminal space between the rhetorical and the nonrhetorical that "incrementally halve[s] autistic rhetoricity."[26] Because some autistic people mirror others' words and behaviors, clinicians presume that autists must necessarily be unable to think and act for themselves. They are, according to this medical model of disability, rhetorical leeches who feed off others' rhetorical agency, who copy and echo instead of empathize and engage. Autistic people are demirhetorical because no matter what they say or do, they are never perceived as rhetorically authentic.

Given this demirhetoricity, Yergeau argues that autistic rhetorics might be described as "asocial," as rhetorics that "bristle against the compulsoriness of interaction, of human engagement, of compliance with the neurotypical."[27] Whereas nondisabled rhetorics presume that all rhetors are intentionally communicating with an audience through symbolic signs and signifiers, autistic demirhetorics embrace the possibility that the rhetor might be their own audience, that a person might perform rhetorical action for themself. This possibility of rhetor-as-audience allows for autistic speech and behavior to be read as rhetorical, regardless of whether or not it is intentional, social, or symbolic. Yergeau links this asocial potentiality to queerness, writing: "Queerness and disability may not be equivalent or even analogical, but they are resonant and interweaving constructs, and they are norm-shattering ways of moving, are ways of disorientating toward the perverse."[28] In pairing neurodivergence (autism, in particular) with queerness, Yergeau instantiates the kind of cross-movement intimacy I am calling for, where the cause for coming together is not based on perceived similarities or differences but on two groups' desiring-together, "their striving toward futurity."[29]

The neuroqueer intimacy that Yergeau envisions, one that necessarily "signifies a generous and inter-bodily gesturing, one that postures beyond brains, bones, and dermis; one that waves in a plurality of identities, orientations, affective stances, and lived experiences," brings into focus the rhetorical (non)implications of queer silence as a strategy for cross-movement organizing.[30] Sometimes neuroqueer intimacies don't produce anything of measurable value. Sometimes neuroqueerness doesn't revolutionize whatever we hope it will. Sometimes neuroqueerness doesn't do the kind of intellectual heavy lifting that people want it to. "What we know and want to know are not necessarily what is prioritized, sentient, or perceived," Yergeau writes; "The thereness of neuroqueer rhetorics is complicated."[31] But like queer silence, the import of neuroqueer rhetorics is in their movement toward an elsewhere, an otherwise, a different future that—in the process of always becoming—jars free new ways of occupying the here and now.

These new ways may not be rhetorically significant; they might be decidedly insignificant, rhetorically speaking. Akin to what Arseli Dokumaci calls "microactivist affordances," neuroqueer intimacies may be "ephemeral" and "impromptu," manifesting as a stim or a tic or a meltdown that means *nothing* or, rather, *means* nothing.[32] Or maybe they will mean something but not to anyone other than the person in motion. "The neuroqueer dwell in continuous, embodied motion," Yergeau says. "Ours are the rhetorics of perseverative loops, cumulative loops, loops that defy rest or sense or logic."[33] This kind of movement, which is indeterminable and undecidable, is the closest we can get to visualizing rhetorical energy—that constellation of discourses surging through our bodyminds. And it's this kind of movement that all cross-movement intimacies would do well to emulate: the kind that keeps on moving. That keeps on dreaming. That keeps on desiring. That keeps on pulsing in ecstatic time toward a future that may never come but that still offers a blueprint for making today a bit more livable.

In advocating that all cross-movement efforts model themselves after neuroqueer rhetorics, I recognize the (mis)appropriative risks. I am aware of the violence done to neurodivergent people when nondisabled folks mock our words, speech, and behaviors. I know of the harm compounded when nondisabled people are hired to act disabled on stage and screen, as if they know how to be us better than we know how to be ourselves.[34] I worry, along with Carrie Sandahl, that "moving too quickly away from disability identity" threatens those disabled folks "who have the most to lose."[35] And I fear, just as many Black feminists fear with intersectionality, being written out of the very discourse that bears our namesake. Yet, I also recognize the rewards of "letting go," as Nash puts it.[36] To let go of neuroqueerness is to move away from "making property of knowledge" and to embrace the unforeseen intimacies that the language and concept of disability may invite.[37] It is also to respect the contingencies of disability itself, as an idea that—as the history of homosexuality's pathologization and as the modern lives of ex-gays surely reveal—depends on where, when, and how a person is. Though having a set of words to call one's own can offer a certain kind of intimacy, it is ultimately an intimacy based on exclusions and assumptions: that we know who qualifies to use the words and who doesn't.

Frankly, I'm too tired for that level of surveillance, but even if I had the energy for it, is neuroqueerness itself not already an amalgamation of identities and experiences? Are there not already contradictions, holes, and elisions wrapped up in neuroqueer rhetorics? And are these contradictions, holes, and elisions not the very essence of *neuroqueer*'s potentiality to "articulate alternate spaces and knowledges for inter/relating"?[38] As Justine E. Egner points out, "neuroqueer" already "obscures delineations of identity categories" through its neologistic grammar, opening up space for new relations through its very utterance.[39] The promise of cross-movement intimacies lies in the yet unimagined alliances, in the heretofore impossible desiring-togethers. Relinquishing neuroqueerness to these intimacies is to trust that disability can come to mean, to quote Margaret Price, a "proliferation."[40] It is to believe in the forward thrust of neuroqueer movement to help carve out more/alternative/better space for us in the present.

As a matter of queer silence, neuroqueer intimacies resemble rhetorical energy: they are in constant motion, they are irreducible, and their purchase is found not in what they mean but in where they're going—that they're going somewhere at all. Yergeau calls this goingness "the motioning of striving."[41] In the context of cross-movement work, rhetorical energy comes to symbolize the potential for eliding identitarian concerns in favor of more dynamic alliances. These alliances are predicated not on what people have in common or on overcoming the differences that divide us but are, instead, invested in a queer(er) set of desires. A set of desires that, in looking toward futures brimming with possibility, unveil the potentialities concealed by the present. Queer silence illuminates the merit of cross-movement work that doesn't appear to get much done, that seems to be a waste of time, that by all straight, cis, and nondisabled accounts would be a failure. As the following three case studies testify, there is enormous value in the labor of doing just enough—doing just enough to survive, just enough to keep going, just enough to feel good enough.

Performing Neuroqueer Intimacies

When selecting examples of neuroqueer intimacy in action, I wanted to strike a balance between offering representation to neuroqueer people and gesturing to a fuller spectrum of cross-movement intimacies that neuroqueerness might inspire. I've thus selected three case studies that progressively move away from *neuroqueer* as it is typically defined—that is, as a kind of queer approach to neurodivergence. This movement is intended to reveal the ways neuroqueerness can invigorate other intimacies that are not, at least superficially, about neurodivergence or queerness. Instead, neuroqueerness comes into focus as an epistemology and politics, a way of knowing, resisting, and remaking in and through the experience of neurological queerness.[42] Collectively, these case studies explore what centering neuroqueerness might do for our activisms. What would it mean to embrace, rather than deny or downplay, the contributions of neurodivergent people in our world-building? How does neuroqueerness affect the worlds we desire-together to build? And most relevant to queer silence, what new understandings of neurodivergence and disability might be produced by cross-movement intimacies modeled after neuroqueerness?

It is noteworthy that all three of the following case studies are from disability-centered performance art groups: the Radical Visibility Collective, Kinetic Light, and Sins Invalid. Though ranging in experience, notoriety, and mission, all three groups share the belief that performance can offer disabled people a way to build and rebuild their relationships with their own bodyminds. While historically disabled performers have been relegated to freak shows that spectacularize the "wondrous and horrifying" disabled body, these groups insist that performance can also offer ways to reclaim or even rewrite the stigmas attached to disability.[43] I will discuss in greater detail how this reclamation process works for each of the respective groups below, but I want to emphasize here that my decision to feature performance art over other forms of disability activism is guided by my desire to dial in on the embodiedness of queer silence as it is enacted in real time, in the spacetime of a single performance. Moreover, I want to draw attention to the variety of ways that collectivity and cross-movement work can be defined and displayed, even within a single medium. As I have said before, the liberation pursued by queer silence contends with our current material conditions, and the following performances illustrate how each moment we share can radically transform the ways we occupy our ever-unfolding present.

Radical Visibility Collective

When Sky Cubacub started Rebirth Garments, their intention was to jumpstart a "QueerCrip dress reform movement" that provided "custom-made gender non-conforming lingerie, wearables and accessories for people on the full spectrum of gender, size and ability," and who likewise wanted to display their queercripness proudly.[44] In a zine created to explain their philosophy of fashion, "A Queercrip Dress Reform Movement Manifesto," Cubacub notes that the mainstream fashion industry puts disabled bodies in an awful position, where they are expected either to pass as nondisabled with clothes made for nondisabled people or to draw attention to their disabilities with clothes that are "geared toward senior citizens," are "not active oriented," and are by and large "dehumanizing."[45] Rebirth Garments, by contrast, is designed to help people "embrace our bodies as they are" by making "our own sexiness that is not based on heteronormative ideas of beauty."[46]

Grounded in what they call "Radical Visibility," Cubacub's line uses a "celebration of color" and "exuberant geometry" to draw attention to queercrip forms.[47] As a custom-only brand, Rebirth Garments' items are designed not only to fit the wearer but also to celebrate the wearer's body, including and especially those parts/pieces of the body that deviate from a nondisabled, cisheteronormative standard. By celebrating the individual body in all its unique nonconformance, Cubacub hopes to reveal the "intersections of identity" that, when left unattended, restrict cross-movement work by isolating those folks who are multiply marginalized.[48] Cubacub's clothes reveal how normative beauty and professionalization standards are premised on the exclusion of racialized, disabled, fat, queer, and gender nonconforming bodies, and that to fundamentally reimagine beauty and comfort requires the Radical Visibility of people from all these groups.[49] "This is why we all need to work together to help each other up," Cubacub writes, "and take care not to base our power by defining ourselves as the negative of the oppressed."[50] Radical Visibility does not seek to realign nonnormative bodies with normative aesthetics but instead crafts intimacies across various expressions of the nonnormative to reinvent what beauty can be.

In 2017, Cubacub extended their work with Rebirth Garments to create the Radical Visibility Collective, in collaboration with musician and performer Jake Vogds and designer Compton Q.[51] The Radical Visibility Collective (RVC) integrates the philosophy of Cubacub's Radical Visibility into what Jhoni Jackson calls "a pioneering, wholly inclusive and immersive fashion experience" that models a fashion show after a futuristic club scene.[52] This scene includes not only the garments designed and constructed by Cubacub and Compton Q but also a playlist of songs specifically written and produced for the performances. The lyrics of the songs are "audio descriptive," meaning that they detail aurally what is occurring onstage, thereby integrating access into the performance itself, rather than adding it as an afterthought.[53] Having staged their first performance in 2018 at the Chicago History Museum and a second performance in 2019 at the Co-Prosperity Sphere, RVC has earned a reputation for offering "not just an act of unveiling new design work but a means to show what fashion can look like and who it can be for."[54]

In both the 2018 and 2019 showcases, the models represented a wide array of Black, brown, fat, femme, gender nonconforming, queer, and disabled bodyminds (Figure 12). In the image, nine people pose for a group picture in front of a printed backdrop of oversized jewelry. In the back row from left to right is someone with light skin and short brown hair wearing a mesh blue top with one arm behind their head; someone with light skin wearing a white and silver headpiece and bodysuit with pink accents; someone with brown skin and brown braids wearing blue lipstick and a pink and gold bodysuit, and using crutches; someone with light skin and brown shoulder-length hair wearing a purple top and a silver skirt; someone with light brown skin and feathered brown hair wearing a purple and blue dress with a wrap composed of purple and red rings; and someone with brown skin and brown, curly hair wearing a silver, orange, and blue mask, harness, and shorts with black knee pads and orange socks and shoes. In the front row from left to right is someone with light skin and short, light brown hair wearing blue lipstick, a pink harness and gloves, and a pink skirt while sitting in a motorized wheelchair; someone with light skin and chest-length brown hair wearing a blue and purple dress; and someone with light skin wearing blue lipstick, a blue and pink headpiece and singlet, and silver platform shoes. While recordings of RVC showcases evidence the models flaunting their clothes for the audience, the interactions between and among the models themselves indicate a different kind of relationship than that typically expected on the runway of a fashion show. Instead of staggering each model to be individually observed and photographed, RVC's showcases fill the performance space with all of the models at once, disrupting the stability of the audience's gaze. Rather than walking onto the runway, the models dance and roll to the music. They bring their service animals, crutches, and canes. They lean against their power chairs to twerk. They move and move with one another; they vibe. As Sunni Johnson writes, "Each Rebirth Garment [*sic*] fashion show is a dance party, not a runway walk."[55] Similar to my discussion of Roland Barthes's studium and punctum in chapter 2, where blank Grindr profiles throw the visuality of the app's interface into crisis, so too does the sociality of RVC models trouble the supposed purpose of the showcase.

It is not that the audience cannot see or access the garments; the audio descriptive lyrics ensure that sighted, blind, and low-vision folks are all aware of the models' attire. Rather, it is unclear whether the fashion is even the point, the studium, or if it is the punctum that draws the eye in service of a grander project. Where to look? What to see? Conventional fashion shows cater to the audience's ability to observe the garments: the structure of the runway, the demeanor and embodymindedness of the models, the timing and organization of the models' movement. RVC's performances, however, seem to displace the priority of the garment in favor of the models themselves.

FIGURE 12. The Radical Visibility Collective at the Museum of Contemporary Art Chicago. Photograph by Sandra Oviedo/Colectivo Mulipolar.

Or, in some cases, the garment is revealed as a prosthetic extension of the model, pulling the model's embodymindedness into relief. The studium of RVC performances is the models themselves. The audience encounters the garments not as the intended focus of the performance but as a punctum that "pricks" the audience into noticing something far more important.[56] Barthes writes that the punctum invites us to grasp "the absolute excellence of a being, body and soul together."[57] Designed as they are to highlight and celebrate nonnormative bodyminds, the garments modeled during RVC performances resignify the rhetorical energies layered onto fat, gender nonconforming, disabled, queer, and racialized bodies, transforming them into the pinnacles of beauty, the ideals.

Equally important, the garments draw the audience's attention to the "kind of blissful eroticism" cultivated by the intimacies on stage.[58] This eroticism works on multiple registers. First, it speaks back to the assumption that disabled performers cannot be sexy or that sexy performances preclude the disabled body.[59] Second, it invites readings of queercrip performance that are attuned to the embodyminded realities of queercrip existence, instead of "the disembodied rhetoric of aesthetic discourse," as Jennifer Richardson notes.[60] These readings do not attempt to (re)align queercrip bodies and movements with nondisabled expectations for what performance should or can be but open up the genre of performance to queercrip reinvention. Third, and most essential to my analysis, the queercrip erotics performed by RVC are rooted in a proliferation of aesthetic ideals, not in a consolidation of the erotic into an alternative, albeit singular, standard. This proliferation and thus diversification of aesthetic ideals requires the participation of many bodymind configurations, emphasizing the value of desiring-together.

The eroticism produced by RVC's performances stems not from the imaginations of Cubacub, Vogds, and Compton Q but from the interanimation of all the models' embodyminded energies. "As avid Chicago queer nightlifers," write Cubacub, Vogds, and Compton Q, "we are both inspired by the experimental and magical atmosphere of parties and critical of how these spaces exclude certain bodies through their structure, architecture, and environment—often giving way to transphobia, misogyny, racism, and ableism. The Radical Visibility Collective combats and dismantles these problematic aspects and brings people together to create the queer utopian space of the future."[61]

RVC's animating potential and, I argue, the source of its queercrip erotics can be found in the forward-looking intimacies it cultivates. It is not only that the models' garments redefine beauty or even that each model's body is resignified as beautiful but that the models, dancing and twerking and vibing, collectively engage in an act of queer silence that gestures toward a different future, "a kind of subtle *beyond*."[62] The garments unleash the models' embodyminded meaning-making potential in such a way that works most powerfully when it is collaborative. The models are each and every one of them beautiful, but together RVC projects an image of another world, another time, another framework for being with and around one another.

RVC models (through its models) what Kafer calls "crip kin-making practices" that facilitate a crip sociality through the appropriation of "deadly serious technologies," such as prosthetics and mobility devices.[63] In "Crip Kin, Manifesting," Kafer explores how "medicalized aesthetics and technologies" might not only adorn and assist disabled bodies in ways that heighten pleasure but also create new paths to intimacy between and among disabled people.[64] Reflecting on her own reaction to seeing boots designed to accentuate "burned, scarred skin," she writes, "I am made aware of the persistence of deeply embodied memories that I have no desire to surface, memories that I fear if awakened will carry me off forever. These fears likely bind me to others encountering these images, a knotted kinship of experiences unspeakable."[65] The material of the boots fosters an invisible, affective magnetism between Kafer and other viewers, producing "deeply intimate and lively relations [that] are not easily reducible to family, or reproduction, or identity."[66] The crip kin Kafer imagines are organized around a queercrip sociality; their intimacies are sutured together through the uneasy and unpredictable relationships between people and things, subjects and objects, you and me and this and that. RVC operates on a similar logic, using custom garments to generate new and erotic, even if uncertain, intimacies.

The most visible of these intimacies are among the models themselves. As Kafer remarks, "The relationship that matters here is not between viewer and viewed, but between artist and artist or even wearer and worn."[67] Likewise, the relationships among the models take precedence over the relationship between the models and the audience, the latter of whom bears witness to the intimacies nurtured within the performance space. We can read these intimacies as explicitly neuroqueer not only because they include queer and neurodivergent people but also because they perform a kind of demirhetoricity that jettisons widespread rhetorical appeal in favor of a "queer utopian space of the future," one that lacks normative legibility. The performance space is at once a portal into a distant, future universe that has been collectively imagined and a window into a parallel dimension that exists right here, right now. RVC makes manifest a glimpse of the world that they desire-together. They mobilize Radical Visibility toward a kind of visible radicalness that, even if it exists only for a few minutes under bright lights with EDM beats, models a way of being here that reminds us of the elsewhere yet to come.

Kinetic Light

Like everyone I know who has seen the show, my first reaction to *DESCENT* was an open mouth and wide eyes. Performed by Alice Sheppard, a Black disabled woman, and Laurel Lawson, a white disabled woman, from the performance ensemble Kinetic Light, *DESCENT* is nothing short of breathtaking. The duet, which explores "what it might mean to build an interracial queer relationship," is set on a distant planet—the performance space initially shadowy with speckled white stars in the background and red and blue craters projected across the floor.[68] The floor itself is composed entirely of a series of interlocking pieces that form a large swooping ramp, which was designed in conversation with Sheppard by Sara Hendren, Yevgeniya Zastavker, and some of their students at Olin College (Figure 13). The image shows a huge ramp as wide as the entire stage sitting against a purple, starry background; shards of sunrise are visible on the left of the image. On the right, the shadowy outline of a figure hangs just above the black peak of the ramp. The main deck of the ramp is covered with projections of rippling blue water. As a wheelchair user, Sheppard was frustrated by the fact that most ramps, while useful for providing her with physical access to spaces, were "almost uniformly utterly unpleasant."[69] "Yes, they ensured our entrances and exits," Sheppard says, "but they isolated us, denied us the company of our lovers and friends, and robbed us of the very pleasures that wheels offer: the joy of the freedom of a descent and pleasure in the labor of ascent."[70] The ramp was built to maximize these pleasures, offering both the performers a space to indulge their bodies' capacity for joy and the audience an opportunity to witness such joyful indulgence.

Whereas ramps designed to facilitate only access are often ugly, hidden, and implicitly linked to incapacitation, the set for *DESCENT* "is sensual, glorious, and inviting," flipping the script on what access is meant to be, do, and serve.[71] In her reflection on the show, Georgina Kleege proposes that the ramp transforms the performance space from an empty vessel that the performance fills into a vital participant in the performance. "In rehearsals, everyone anthropomorphizes the ramp," she writes. "They refer to it as if it is a living, feeling being."[72] Sheppard offers a similar reflection: "The *DESCENT* ramp is an active

FIGURE 13. The Ramp. Kinetic Light Residency, MANCC, 2017. Photograph by Chris Cameron, media specialist.

partner in the dance: its slopes and curves render the dancers utterly vulnerable to gravity."[73] For Kleege and Sheppard, the ramp does not passively provide access to a preexisting structure or space but rather introduces a structure and space that, when interanimated with and by wheeling bodies, produces new pleasures (Figure 14). These pleasures are apparent in the image, where Laurel Lawson, a white woman with short-cropped teal hair, is flying in the air with arms spread wide, wheelchair wheels spinning, supported by Sheppard. Sheppard, a multiracial Black woman with coffee-colored hair, is lifting from the ground below. They are making eye contact and smiling. A burst of white light appears in a dark blue sky. These new and apparent pleasures would be impossible without the ramp, which offers access not to the world nondisabled people already inhabit but to an entirely new and other crip world.

This new, other world teeters between the literal and the figurative. Literally, *DESCENT* is set in another world, on a different planet, and the narrative unfolds as a romance between the Greek goddess Andromeda and the Roman goddess Venus. This other world is fictional and fantastical and, given its extraterrestrial setting, not

FIGURE 14. Alice Sheppard and Laurel Lawson dance. Photograph by Jay Newman / Britt Festival.

immediately accessible. But *DESCENT* also stages a figurative other world that gestures toward crip pleasures we do have access to or, rather, toward crip pleasures that access might help to generate. This figurative other world depends on a variation of the queer masquerade discussed in chapter 3 and serves as a reminder that rhetorical energy animates not only people but also nonhuman animals, things, spaces, and ideas. In chapter 3, ex-gays performed their queer masquerade to resignify their queerness as a disability—a rhetorical maneuver typically intended as a survival strategy within hostile environments. Here, I propose that the ramp enacts another queer(crip) masquerade that resignifies access as a tool to produce and enhance pleasure.

In making this argument, I not only acknowledge the rhetorical energy bound up in objects, such as ramps and wheelchairs, but also insist that the circulation of rhetorical energy troubles the boundaries between these objects and their users. Disabled people have long said that the technologies we use every day, whether they be prosthetic limbs, pharmaceutical drugs, or service animals, are not easily divided from how we understand ourselves.[74] This is not to suggest that all disabled people use or want to use technology, nor is it to suggest that a given technology is used in the same way by all users. As

Kafer suggests, we would do well to adopt a "cripped cyborg theory" that would account for the diversity of relationships disabled people have with technology and biomedical interventions more generally.[75] My point is that the ramp's masquerade calls attention to the rhetorical power engendered by the energetic enmeshment of the dancers' bodies with and in the ramp itself. Much like ex-gays depend on the saturation of evangelical doctrine with homophobic and heterosexist models of gender and sexuality in order to pass as disabled, the ramp relies on the presence, touch, and movement of Sheppard and Lawson to animate its resignification.

The energetic exchange between the dancers and the ramp resonates with what Shannon Walters calls "rhetorical touch," where physical or emotional contact "bring[s] bodies together in dynamic potentials."[76] In this case, the bodies in question include not only Sheppard's and Lawson's human bodies but also the ramp, and all three together constitute a cross-movement intimacy. The role of the ramp is essential to this configuration because, as Sheppard makes clear, *DESCENT* is not merely about an interracial romance but about "normalized assumptions of racialized disabled movement."[77] The ramp comes to symbolize the ways disability and access are racialized issues that disproportionately affect Black, brown, and Indigenous populations. These populations are not only more likely to experience disability through processes of debilitation but also less likely to have access to the technologies and biomedical interventions mentioned above that are intended to alleviate the pain sometimes incurred by disability.[78] The "kinesthetic pleasure" that Sheppard experiences on the ramp is a commentary on whose bodies are allowed to move, to feel pleasure, and to feel pleasure through movement.[79]

The racialized relationship between pleasure and movement also indexes a neuroqueer intimacy that, despite neither Sheppard nor Lawson identifying as neurodivergent, recalls both the pleasure many neuroqueer people glean from perseverating and the pain we experience when our perseverations are policed and punished. Movement is political; pleasure is political. And to indulge either or both is to engage what adrienne maree brown refers to as "pleasure activism," which "asserts that we all need and deserve pleasure and that our social structures must reflect this."[80] In *Pleasure Activism: The Politics of*

Feeling Good, brown argues that not only can liberation work open up avenues for the development and experience of new pleasures but also pleasure itself can be a route to liberation. Brown writes:

> I think a result of sourcing power in our longing and pleasure is abundant justice—that we can stop competing with each other, demanding scarce justice from our oppressors. That we can instead generate power from the overlapping space of desire and aliveness, tapping into an abundance that has enough attention, liberation, and justice for all of us to have plenty.[81]

Shifting the aim of liberation work from securing "scarce justice from our oppressors" to "generat[ing] power" for ourselves echoes the temporal displacement demanded by desiring-together. Instead of "competing" for limited resources in the present, pleasure activism looks ahead to that "overlapping space of desire and aliveness." This overlapping space captures the procedure and purpose of desiring-together: by drawing on shared visions of the future, we can reveal the hidden "abundance" of the present. For brown, abundance is accessed most directly through pleasure, which she recognizes as "a measure of freedom."[82] "Pleasure activism is about learning what it means to be satisfiable," she writes, "to generate, from within and from between us, an abundance from which we can all have enough."[83] Pleasure, in this formulation, is a middle ground between our collective desires and our imagined, future realities. To experience pleasure is to manifest a touch—literally, figuratively—of that which we desire-together.

DESCENT produces this kind of pleasure through the intimacies among Sheppard, Lawson, and the ramp (Figure 15). In this image, Sheppard crawls on her hands with her knees in Lawson's footplate. Lawson is arching her back on the ground as she is dragged along the floor. The dancers' wheelchairs are stacked. A sunset appears behind them, and shadowy figures appear below. The performance displays the dancers' pleasure with and on the ramp, and their experiences of pleasure gesture toward a world where pleasure is freely available and accessible to all. This gesture is particularly explicit near the beginning of the show during a sex(y) scene, when Sheppard removes the strap securing her to her chair. Without the strap in place, she can more

FIGURE 15. Alice Sheppard drags Laurel Lawson in their chairs. Kinetic Light Residency, MANCC, 2017. Photograph by Chris Cameron, media specialist.

easily fall, but she can also more easily move, including move toward, for, and during sex. "The act of strapping oneself into a chair is so familiar to those who are or who know wheelchair users," Sheppard explains. "For the select few who love a wheelchair user, the sound of that Velcro may well recall moments of intimacy. It is such a cultural moment. Resonant. Political. And, I hope, beautiful."[84] This moment of crip erotic foreplay strikes different members of the audience in multiple ways. Many nondisabled and non-wheelchair-using people may miss the moment entirely. Among disabled audience members, Sheppard recounts that some are uncomfortable and put off: "The choice to strap publicly was controversial, too private to show on stage." But other disabled viewers are thrilled: "It was revelatory, a moment of celebration."[85] Thus, the pleasure Sheppard indulges on stage—hearing the sound of the Velcro peeling—is felt communally, even if it is variously received.

The experience and liberation of pleasure is important for disabled people, for whom sexual pleasure in particular is often thought to be incompatible or immoral. As Tobin Siebers describes, "Disabled people experience sexual repression, possess little or no sexual autonomy, and tolerate institutional and legal restrictions on their intimate conduct."[86] It is not that disabled people don't or can't have sex, however we define it for ourselves, but that we face what Michael Carl Gill terms "sexual ableism" that places us into an impossible double bind.[87] On one hand, sexual ableism presumes that disabled people, especially those with intellectual disabilities, are unable to consent to sex and thus too disabled to experience sexual pleasure. On the other hand, sexual ableism conjures up a fear of disabled sexualities that, if left unmitigated, pose a threat to the sexual health of nondisabled others. Notably, this fear is also racialized, echoing models of race and disability that link madness with Blackness and thereby resuscitating the stereotype of (disabled) Black men preying on (nondisabled) white women.[88] Sexual ableism thus casts disabled people as both too sexual and not sexual enough, excess and deficit, a danger to others and yet defenseless against sexual violence.

The pleasure that Sheppard experiences and shares during *DESCENT,* however, turns sexual ableism on its head. Indeed, the foreplay between Sheppard and Lawson—"She flirts; I flirt right back"—models the successful establishment of consent between two disabled people.[89] Then, the sound of the Velcro pulling apart can be read as both masturbatory and exhibitionistic, enacting a kind of sexual agency that queerly resists the (hetero)normative assumptions that underpin sexual ableism. Gill notes that "homophobia and ableism often work together not only to deny the disabled subject the ability to express sexual agency and desire, but also to actively redirect queer sexual desire."[90] As a masturbatory practice, pulling out a strap might seem more restrained than, say, explicit sexual contact to the casual, nondisabled observer, but to the disabled audience member "what it actually means to see and feel strapping on stage, to hear and recognize the sound of Velcro unfurling is different, more complex."[91] For a disabled audience, pulling the strap is not only masturbatory but also exhibitionistic, roping us into a voyeuristic position. Sheppard's sexual (rhetorical) energy is channeled into her strap, and the moment she pulls it loose is the moment she opens herself for all to see: a queer, disabled woman in heat, a queer, disabled woman pleasuring herself, a queer, disabled woman offering her pleasure to us.

To partake in Sheppard's pleasure, and thus to pleasure ourselves, is to build an intimacy. It is an intimacy rooted not in who we are or what we share, besides a familiarity with strapping, but in what we want and who we want to be. In an interview with brown, Una Osato says of burlesque dance that "it's about finding freedom onstage, in my own body, while others watch and experience. It's not just about rehearsing the revolution, it's about creating cracks that show our bodies that we can experience freedom."[92] What cracks does *DESCENT* create? What freedom does Sheppard find onstage? To watch *DESCENT* as a disabled person is to watch a masquerade unfold, to watch a ramp become a world, to watch chairs become rolling altars beneath two disabled dancers who are goddesses. To watch *DESCENT* is to experience the ecstatic joy of desiring-together, reaching into another world to feel in our seats the pleasure that is already rightfully ours.

Sins Invalid

To round out my examples of neuroqueer intimacies, I want to return to the image I used to open this chapter: Rodney Bell, performing for Sins Invalid, dangling from the ceiling in his chair. Though Bell is steadily lowered toward the ground throughout his performance, his vertical motion is hardly noticeable. He appears weightless in space, suspended. Compared to the intensity and movement of the models in the Radical Visibility Collective and the dancers from Kinetic Light, Bell's performance marks a dramatic departure. Bell performs alone, not even occupying the same plane as the rest of the performers that evening. He uses some assistive technologies—his chair and the wire contraption to which he is attached—but the function and figuration of these technologies are up for debate. While in the air, Bell does not necessarily need his chair. And while the wire is essential to the performance, it does not carry the same significations as other assistive technology because the incapacity to levitate is, obviously, not a disability. The social markers nondisabled people typically use to register someone else's disability status are absent from Bell's performance: there are no visible impairments, no other disabled or nondisabled people to whom he can be compared, no technologies that are put to definitively assistive purposes. As I proposed in the introduction to this chapter, Bell's suspended body mirrors the suspension of his disability identity, along with his Indigeneity and immigration status.

I'll argue here that these suspensions open up possibilities to engage and perform cross-movement intimacies.

Importantly, Bell's performance does not render him nondisabled, let alone less Indigenous or less of an immigrant. Despite the fact that disability is contingent on social, cultural, and material contexts, the experience of disability is also deeply embodied, offering some disabled people a kind of ontological status that crosses borders. This ontological status may bear various significations and relations to a disabled subjectivity, but especially in Bell's case, the visibility of a wheelchair marks a departure from abled norms in most cultures. Moreover, decolonial approaches to disability and disability studies insist that the experience of disability is inextricable from settler colonialism, such as that facing the Māori people.[93] The temporary suspension of Bell's impairment might be read less as a commentary on the social dimensions of disability than as a nod to the intersections between his disability and Indigeneity. Zeroing in on the troubled intelligibility of Bell's identities underscores how his embodied significations break from white, Western models of disability. The mingling of his rhetorical energies press up against monolithic representations of how and what disability can come to mean.

To understand the connection between settler colonialism and disability, we must first recognize that the category of "disability" is itself part of a colonial project. Both deficit-based and liberatory models of disability identity come at the expense or exclusion of Indigenous peoples and populations living across the diaspora. Adria L. Imada writes that "the colonized were *always already figured and constituted as disabled,*" regardless of the presence or absence of impairment.[94] In this case, colonialism depends on a deficit-based model of disability to justify "the incarceration, elimination, and removal of unfit colonial Others."[95] Colonized peoples are all disabled; disability is bad; thus, colonized peoples are all bad. More recent and liberatory models attempt to recuperate the category of "disability" as a natural part of human diversity and as one that deserves to be celebrated. These celebratory models, however, ignore the pain and violence bound up with what Jasbir K. Puar calls "debility," or the "constitutive slow death" that is "a banal feature of quotidian existence" for many multiply marginalized populations.[96] While there is tremendous power in reclaiming the immanent value of disabled bodyminds, this reclamation risks effacing the ongoing brutality of settler colonialism. In fact, Helen Meekosha contends that (settler) disability studies depends on the excision of colonized experiences and knowledges from the field.[97] Puar laments, "It is . . . a constitutive and capacitating absence."[98]

Bell's suspension during his performance speaks to this absence by troubling the boundaries between disability and Indigeneity. By removing elements of the built environment that are disabling (indeed, by removing the built environment in its entirety), Bell effectively throws the meaning of impairment into crisis. But by choosing to remain in his chair, Bell draws attention to the persistence of debility in the face of physical access. The other aesthetic elements of the performance—the Māori song choice, the choreography, the body and face paint—foreground Bell's Indigenous identity and connection to his native culture. These elements contextualize the presence of debility, replacing the markers of disability identity that are otherwise stricken from the performance, and theorize his suspension not as an eradication of disability but as an invitation to decolonize it. This decolonization, in part, interrogates the grounds on which some (white, settler) populations come to name and categorize experiences of disability without acknowledging the epistemic violence that attends such naming and categorization in a transnational context. This violence surely affects Bell, whose Māori people have been struggling to reclaim native sovereignty since at least the 1840s.[99] Yet, because he was living in the United States at the time of his performance with Sins Invalid, Bell's experience of disability may have been additionally informed by racist xenophobia. Similar to the ways that colonizers have presumed colonized peoples to be disabled, so too has the process of immigrating to the United States been used to demarcate racialized bodies as disabled, regardless of their disability status.[100] What is striking about Bell's experiences, as a survivor of settler colonialism and racist xenophobia, is that both vectors of ableism affecting his life deny the reality of Bell's actual impairment. That is, despite being figuratively rendered disabled and literally exposed to the violence of debility, Bell's impairment remains illegible. It is in response to this illegibility that the potential for cross-movement intimacies embedded in Bell's performance is articulated most clearly.

Rather than attempt to make his impairment legible to the audience, Bell chooses instead to lean into its given illegibility. Suspending his body and thus the signification of his disability rehearses a variation of trans silence introduced in chapter 4. Certainly, Bell's resistance to a stable disability identity could be read as a kind of disidentification in line with Muñoz's original formulation.[101] Yet, as I discussed in the previous chapter, trans silence builds on disidentification to better account for temporality and the ways that our past, present, and future selves may not always neatly coalesce. While Bell does not to my knowledge identify as trans or gender nonconforming, the interplay among his disability, race, ethnicity, Indigeneity, and immigration status demand a diachronic reading that allows for changes, tensions, and contradictions over time. Moreover, there is little question that Bell's experience of gender and masculinity, regardless of his gender identity, exists in tension with white, abled models of normative gender.[102] Trans silence offers us a way to understand what is necessarily inarticulable about Bell's performance. It provides us a way to honor his impairment's illegibility in the time and place of his suspension while also looking ahead with him toward what decolonizing disability would offer.

Decolonizing disability would, first, pry open the meaning of disability. It would not only engage with the violences of debility produced by settler colonialism, racism, and xenophobia but also attend to how the experience of these violences is compounded by impairment.[103] Second, decolonizing disability would resist the liberal impulse of disability studies and activism to pursue rights and representation over equitable justice. "Any appeal to the state for equal rights," Liat Ben-Moshe reminds us, "is a continuation and legitimization of the occupation and appropriation of land by making the state appear as a sovereign entity with the ability to grant such things as rights or land."[104] In pursuing equitable justice, as opposed to a narrow version of liberal inclusion, decolonizing disability would mean recognizing, along with Nirmala Erevelles, that our own crip desires often hinge on the denial or dismissal of others' crip horrors.[105] That is, decolonization demands a reckoning between what we've come to love about disability and how we've come to love it: whose bodies do we love? Whose bodies have we ignored to grow that love? And on whose ground has this love-born-of-dispossession been nourished? These questions prime the third move of decolonizing disability, which would make visible the intersections among not only ableism, settler colonialism, racism, and xenophobia but also misogyny and cisheterosexism. In making these intersections visible, we would hold space for those people's bodyminds that, like Bell's, sit at the nexus of multiple vectors of subjection. Sins Invalid refers to this work as the "Collective Liberation" of disability justice: "No body or mind can be left behind—only mobbing together can we accomplish the revolution we require."[106]

The work of decolonizing disability moves the category of "disability" beyond the ways we currently know and understand it. It embraces an expansive and recursive approach to the language we use to describe our world as well as the frameworks we employ to make sense of it. Much like Bell's performance models for us, decolonization is in part an act of suspension. It is a freezing, a stopping, a holding of breath. But then, as Bell's descent toward the stage symbolizes, it is also an undoing, unlearning, and unmaking of the institutions and systems that allow settlers to benefit from the ongoing occupation of unceded lands, the racialized and gendered exploitation of workers and children, and the debilitation (and death) of Indigenous peoples and immigrants. Another reading of Bell's descent might suggest that it serves as a reminder of the violence of debility. It could stand in for a white audience's desire for legibility, for Bell's impaired body and wheelchair to "mean" something, for an end to the audience's own suspension. Perhaps Bell's descent is a retelling of his past, how he arrived to that stage told in the air above that same stage. Yet, it might signal something more hopeful too—not a hope bereft of Bell's material conditions but a hope charged with a desire for the safety, stillness, and rest that the earth provides. Maybe it is a trajectory, a foretelling of where he's going or wants to go. And as I've been arguing throughout this chapter, maybe his trajectory is one that we can all long for, that we can all desire-together. Not because we all face the same violences or share the same experiences but because there is world-building power in dreaming together. Desiring is dreaming is moving is mobilizing. These are neuroqueer intimacies in action.

But these are not the only neuroqueer intimacies. The cross-movement and collective potential of queer silence lies in its capacity for and leaning toward the otherwise. While the Radical Visibility Collective, Kinetic Light, and Bell's performance for Sins Invalid gesture toward several intimacies that deploy queer silence to move beyond identity, they are certainly not exhaustive. Neuroqueerness, as I have used it here, is a politic of movement, of moving on. Neuroqueer intimacies likewise move toward new intimacies, even and especially when they don't make sense, when they strut, roll, or suspend in demirhetorical defiance. This defiance, because it doesn't always make sense, might not seem to be all that defiant. Some weird clothes. A cool ramp. Hanging upside down. Who cares? But these little moments, wedged into lives of people who have to fight to live, are brimming with new narratives, new visions, new desires for how they can be in this world. Queer silence is a strategy of resistance, but as Indigenous and Native studies scholars insist, sometimes resistance and survival are one and the same.[107] As a collective manifestation of queer silence, neuroqueer intimacies don't always appear as resistance. They do, however, help folks like Cubacub, Sheppard, and Bell to feel beautiful, to feel pleasure, to feel visible, even in their collective illegibility.

Not all neuroqueer intimacies are performances, such as the ones I discuss, but performance is a useful analogy for the bodyminds of marginalized people who are always on display. For many queer people, being on display is to be simultaneously seen and unseen, to be dripping with rhetorical energy that marks our nonnormativity and simultaneously overdetermines our personhood. We become the sum total of our perceived deficits. We are in excess of lack, overflowing with all that we are not, all that we can't do, all that we can't be, all that we can't become. To push back against these assumptions, discourses, and energies is hard work. It's labor and laborious. It's exhausting to justify our own existence. So neuroqueer intimacies offer a reprieve, a chance to stop pushing back and to take a break, together.

This is not the same as giving up. This is about realizing our collective limits. This is about acknowledging that playing the long game doesn't mean we have to postpone our joy until the final buzzer. To craft intimacies is to love on one another. It's to grab somebody else's hand—somebody else who is hurting too, even if it's a different hurt than your own—and cry at the bus stop. It's to put on silly hats. It's to eat a meal of snacks you all found at the gas station. It's to take a shower together, partly because one of you needs some help getting in and out and partly because why not, it's sexy. It's to see that same tiredness in a stranger's eyes that you've been feeling for longer than you can remember and just giving a nod. Because you both get it. It's to remind yourself that you're not alone, even when you're lonely. It's to stop performing in the middle of this performance we call a life and just fucking scream. Screaming doesn't save the world, at least not usually. Neither does nodding or showering or snacking or crying. Neuroqueer intimacies don't try to fix the stage we're performing on; they just try to change the script of the play a little bit, drawing their inspiration from the liberation we'll all get back to tomorrow. Right now it's about being with, being here, and being alive.

A part of me feels like I'm hedging, as if I'm making excuses for what queer silence can't do. I don't mean to sketch the limits of intimacy too definitively. I don't want to foreclose the radical potentialities laden in neuroqueer desiring-together. I mean only to dwell in the potentialities that don't pass radical muster. I want to see, honor, and celebrate all of the ways that we are collectively surviving. This is a nonhierarchical approach to activism and organizing, informed by a queercrip commitment to each person's boundaries, needs, and limitations. Neuroqueer intimacies and queer silence more broadly understand that world-building is sometimes a matter of world-living, of living and staying alive in this world. There is so much power in the commitment to keep going, even when that going feels like stillness, like stagnation. Liberation work doesn't always feel liberating. Sometimes, perhaps even most of the time, it feels like you're coming up against a wall, like you're going in circles, like you're actually moving backward.[108] After a while, these feelings can wear a person down to a point when they no longer feel like doing the work at all. It can be hard to keep going when it doesn't feel like you've been going anywhere. It's in these moments that neuroqueer intimacies are so important because they invite us to pause our work and return to our dreams, get back to our longings, invest in our desires. They ask us to catch one another's glance, to flirt, to hold hands, to dance. And here, in the space between the world we want and the world we have, is a little joy and a little love. It's not much, but it's enough for now.

Epilogue

Shameful Disattachments and Queer Illegibility

This epilogue contains detailed and graphic depictions of suicide, including the internal monologue of a person experiencing suicidal ideation, the specific methods used in the act of suicide, and the wounds caused by a suicide attempt. I encourage you to engage this epilogue in whatever way is most accessible for you, whether that means reading slowly, reading aloud, reading in fits and starts, reading alone, reading in community, or asking someone else to read it to you. You are also welcome to not read it at all. The narrative that drives this chapter is part of my story—in all of its gore and confusion and shame. I am both grateful and lucky that it is not the end of my story.

At half past eleven, I make my way across campus to the chapel. The wind is thin and sharp, chilling my breath and sending wisps of vapor ahead of my nose. I circle around to the back door, knowing it will be unlocked for other students like myself who find themselves torn between two lives, two dreams, and two gods.

I creep along the rear hallway and into the sanctuary. My eyes follow the moonlight straining through the stained glass. This room is familiar, even in shadows: fourteen rows of wooden pews with a narrow aisle between them, carpet worn from the feet of worshippers holier than me, and an altar composed of nothing but a small table with a cloth draped across it. An empty crucifix hangs from the rafters—no dying man, no savior, no son. Just the cross above the table in a deserted room. It is either quaint or sad, maybe both. If God is here, he isn't speaking. All of creation asleep with its creator.

Prayer seems more powerful to me at night when the stillness of the air sits heavier on my chest. Guilt weighs more in the dark. Shame tastes chalkier. I am less sure of who I am and more confident I am not who I should be. Sitting on my knees a few feet in front of the first pew, I lower my forehead to the floor. A boy prostrate before an absent God.

When Samuel convicts him from beyond the grave, King Saul collapses to the ground. God had abandoned him and his kingdom, and there would soon be nothing left to rule. Not long after, Saul falls on top of his own sword, terrified of what would happen if he didn't. The decision to take your own life is easy when you know it's going to be taken anyway. It's a matter of offering yourself mercy when you know all too well that no one else will.

From my bag, I remove a pocketknife that my grandfather had given me for Christmas several years ago. I'd never used it. The metal feels cold in my palm, and as I open the blade, I am reminded of something he told me when I received it: "There's so much you can do with a knife." He said, "So much you can fix and build." I wondered that Christmas and again at the foot of the altar how much it could also break and destroy. When the knife is your tool, what kind of worlds can you create? If you can only slice into ever smaller chunks, how will you make something whole?

But as Saul knew, and as I whisper to myself with the blade aching against my skin, sometimes fixing and building requires sanding off the rust and clearing the land. Sometimes you have to get rid of what doesn't work before you can repair what does. Worlds aren't crafted by simple addition. Occasionally, you must subtract. *That's what happens to sinners like Saul and me.* We are bound for subtraction. It is macabre, but it is purposeful. Those who off themselves aren't cowards but martyrs, I think, making space for new worlds to come into being.

"Men take responsibility for themselves," my conversion therapist Joe told me. "Men hold themselves accountable to God. They atone."

I attended my final appointment with Joe a month before I started college. One hundred and thirteen days later, I tried to kill myself in the very room in which I had for so long tried to assimilate. I didn't just want to die; I wanted to be a sacrifice. I wanted to give myself back over to God and to let him deliver me from all my shame and all my brokenness. I was done running and done masquerading. I was done lying. My rhetorical energy was undeniable—my queerness trailed me like a stench—and I was too tired to manipulate it anymore. I was eighteen years old, suffocating, and too exhausted to keep fighting for breath.

I share this story not because it reveals something important about me (though it does) or about my use of silence (though perhaps it might) but because the story is a useful framing device for turning the methodological insight of queer silence back on the field of queer studies. I have spent the bulk of this book pointing queer silence outward to illuminate and recover the productive uses of silence among people who exist at the margins of queer politics, whose resistance efforts verge on complicity, dip into misappropriation, and occasionally edge into uselessness. Nevertheless, I've shown that silence can be a form of protection, as it is for some users on Grindr. I've shown it can be mode of sociality, such as it is for ex-gays. It can generate narratives of the self, as it does for some trans elders. And it can bridge difference by facilitating new forms of relationality, as we learned through disability performance projects. I've shown that silence contains many dimensions, including those produced and subsequently ignored by queer studies—a legacy born by gay activism's repudiation of pathology. The conceptual collapse of silence and disability within the gay movement set the stage for *queer* to emerge as a form of politicized nonnormativity predicated on speech and other variations of abled rhetorical presence. Left behind were the disabled people from whom *queer* was purified. Jettisoned were the practices of silence and absence depended on by racialized queers, trans elders, and neuroqueers, among many of the more vulnerable and marginalized queer populations who are disallowed from occupying public space and barred from having a public voice. *Queer* has come to demand a niche instantiation of resistance that is widely inaccessible.

With this epilogue, I'd like to dial in on *queer*'s (in)accessibility to suggest that silence might be not only an external object toward which queer studies should better attend but also a structuring characteristic of the field that must be examined. Unlike previous chapters, where the opening anecdote or narrative provides an example of silence in action, I offer the above story as an exigence to consider not my silence but queer studies' silence, particularly that which makes my suicide attempt difficult to situate within the field. On the surface, my experience would seem to be a perfect fit for *queer* attachment. According to Judith Butler, it has the right players: a marginal subject who is rendered queer vis-à-vis their rubbing up against an oppressive institution. In this case, my queerness is neither claimed nor "conferred," but instead it "*precedes and conditions* the formation of" my subjectivity.[1] My suicide attempt appears open to *queer* attachment because it is only "*through* that shaming interpellation" that my prior self comes into view. This potential for attachment is short-lived, however, because the unfolding of my suicide attempt reveals a politics decidedly less comfortable for queer studies: the subject does not weaponize their marginalization but internalizes it; the oppressive institution is not resisted but acquiesced; the "shaming taboo" of queerness is not opposed but fully embraced.[2] And with regard to the variations of queer silence I've worked to recover throughout this book, there are none worth celebrating. My silence did not save me that night—the janitor did, who caught me minutes before I would have died, called an ambulance, wrapped makeshift bandages around my wrists, and held my head in his lap as I drifted in and out of consciousness. My silence didn't save me, and my shame nearly killed me.

The relationship between silence and shame is an important one that calls attention to a disjunction between the field queer studies promises to be and the one it often turns out to be. This is a disjunction that hinges on silence=disability as an organizing logic to separate speech-based, politically solvent queer objects from silent, apolitical, and thereby pathological ones. While I have worked to reveal silence in each of the preceding chapters through objects that queer studies has heretofore neglected, I offer the example of my suicidal shame to show how silence is already shaping the field's prevailing attachments. In doing so, I pivot the urgency of *Queer Silence* from one that refocuses queer studies onto new objects to one that alters how the field perceives its existing ones. Reconciling with silence involves not only expanding queer studies' horizons but also turning inward to deconstruct its foundations. This is the work of a genealogical critique devoted to absence.

Historicities of Absence

My thinking on queer genealogy is most indebted to the recent work of Kadji Amin, who in *Disturbing Attachments: Genet, Modern Pederasty, and Queer History* attempts to "deidealize" the objects and attachments that, as he argues, bind queer studies to the predominant affects of AIDS activism and queer movements during the 1990s. Building on the genealogical methods introduced by Foucault, Christopher Nealon, Carolyn Dinshaw, and Heather Love, Amin proposes a "method of attachment genealogy" that "excavates earlier and more transnational modes of queer attachment to both historicize and expand *queer*'s current affective orientations."[3] An attachment genealogy seeks to uproot queer studies' existing analytical frameworks that distinguish "good" from "bad" queer objects by contextualizing the processes by which these frameworks have come into being. That is, an attachment genealogy opens queer studies by throwing into relief *queer*'s "disavowed historicity" that delineates the scope of the term's "affective charge."[4] While Amin's ultimate goal is to invite the creation of new frameworks for the field that better reflect "alternative scholarly priorities," he recognizes that the first step toward this goal must be one of exposure, of revealing *queer*'s conceptual limits that dictate "*only certain* forms of nonnormativity."[5] This revelatory step insists that both *queer* and queer studies have histories, temporalities, economies, and geographies that cannot be dismissed or ignored in favor of intellectual fantasies of immaculate conceptions. An attachment genealogy reintroduces queer studies to *queer*'s attachments, susses out "the source of the rub" that renders some objects "bad," and subsequently releases *queer* to pursue those bad objects.[6]

With the intention of extending Amin's project, I propose a *dis*attachment genealogy that holds queer studies accountable for the ways its ideals have been constructed via explicit processes of dispossession. It is not only that *queer* demarcates "good" from "bad" objects, I argue, but also that its criteria for demarcation have been wrought out of a series of affective disavowals that, first, consolidated "homosexuality" into a respectable, nondisabled identity category and that, second, helped to define *queer*'s emergent politics. Even as we encourage queer studies' expansion to consider new objects and attachments—what

Amin calls "chemical reactions with new contexts"—there is also value in mining the field's existing ideals for their residue and excess.[7] A disattachment genealogy attends to what *queer* never meant because it couldn't mean, sketching out the disaffective conditions of *queer*'s creation in "the moment when they remained unrealized."[8] This approach traces the meanderings of all that (and who) were strategically relinquished in an effort to preserve *queer*'s coherence. It is not simply a genealogy of disavowed objects but rather a genealogy of dispossession itself, a mapping of the margins as they are sloughed off from the records of history and ground back into a forgotten past.[9] This is a historicization of field formation by foregrounding the leftovers and throwaways, the broken and the "backward,"[10] the denounced and renounced, as well as the "sublated, repressed, or otherwise disappeared" as they are relegated to their peripheral positions.[11]

But a disattachment genealogy is also about the present. It is a method of understanding what the field of queer studies is doing by attending to who and what the field previously said it's not. Just as Amin tracks *queer*'s affective histories to prepare the field for sponsoring new attachments, so too am I interested in how *queer*'s prior disavowals continue to structure its (dis)orientations now. Lauren Berlant's reading of Henri Bergson's "intuition" is useful here as the space "where affect meets history."[12] Berlant finds in intuition a way to illuminate the discontinuity of history, a way of sensing out that things haven't always been as they are and thus, perhaps, don't have to be the same in the future. Intuition is what guides people toward genealogical critique in the first place: their sinking suspicion that the present they occupy is one of many possible presents all unfolding historiographically—that is, perceived and remembered partially and inaccurately. The intuition fueling disattachment genealogy contends that the historical emergence of *queer* and its attendant ideals contains the ghosts of alternative attachments for the present. These alternatives are found not in new and unfamiliar objects but in objects that were previously and actively discarded. I'm suggesting that by returning to *queer*'s past and perhaps even further to its pathological prehistory, we might discover disattachments that offer us new ways of understanding *queer* as it functions today. Nishant Shahani describes this mobilization of the past as "a reparatively informed hypothetical 'what if' that is inserted back in time," operationalizing "the material conditions that have yet to be fulfilled for more democratic queer futures."[13] This is not a process of romanticizing the past or of simply learning from it; rather, I am calling for an examination of prior erasure in order to map the violence of absence in the present—ultimately with the hope of (re)forming attachments to objects, temporalities, geographies, and positionalities that were previously castrated.

My intention with renewing objects for queer attachment is not to use genealogy in the service of rhetorical translation or affective recapacitation, revealing the inherent queerness of dismissed objects and thereby converting their silence into speech. I am more interested in refining a historiographic sensoria that is sensitive to silence, invisibility, and absence as effects of "the past's own affective volition."[14] A disattachment genealogy makes apparent the presence of absence—a space we can name as space—both as it exists today and as it has been (re)produced over time. It allows us to admire silence for all its minutia and its wiles and its failures while also recognizing the violence that often occasions silence and silencing in the first place. It lets us take in people's quiet irreverence for the world, along with their "feelings of confusion and ambivalence that don't fit into neat models," without expecting or demanding anything more from them.[15] A disattachment genealogy considers the diachronicity of queer silence and its distributed emergence across various rhetorical modes. This method of genealogy calls upon many of the terms and concepts introduced in the preceding chapters in order to chart the rhetorical energy of silence itself as it is produced, structured, remediated, and mined over time. Necessarily, the object of a disattachment genealogy is tricky to observe because we aren't looking to observe an object so much as an object's deferrals. Whereas existing models of queer genealogy and historiography tend to "reinforce our attachment to our own categories of thought and experience" and risk identifying only those variations of *queer* that confirm the ways it is already understood, a disattachment genealogy taps into silence, invisibility, and absence to contend with how *queer* never was, isn't, and has yet to be.[16]

I am thus proposing a simultaneous broadening and undoing of *queer* that expands the term's capacity without claiming that it is entirely nonreferential. The promise of *queer*'s nonreferentiality and infinite mobility remains salient only when the field of queer studies actively disowns its own historicity and affective inheritances.[17] Even if *queer* has no designated objects, it cannot escape its (dis)orientations toward the politics and assemblage of affects from which it emerged. The broadened/undone *queer* I am calling for aligns closely with Eve Kosofsky Sedgwick's understanding of homosexuality as "a space of overlapping, contradictory, and conflictual definitional forces," whereby we might sacrifice *queer*'s sustained coherence for a model more amenable to the coexistence of speech and silence, visibility and invisibility, as well as presence and absence.[18] Unlike Sedgwick, though, I am less interested in denaturalizing the contradictions inherent to *queer*'s various iterations (and thus substituting yet another framework for understanding the term "correctly") than I am in more robustly humanizing the process of *queer*'s rhetorical circulation, acknowledging that its contradictions are a product of the similarly conflicting embodyminded subject positions each of us as queer scholars, activists, educators, agitators, and community builders holds.[19] In other words, I want to approach *queer* not only as that which is impossible to predict but also as that which cannot always be understood right here and now.[20] If *queer* is going to remain useful, I suggest, we will have to surrender any assumptions about the legibility of its rhetoricity, about our own capacity to know what *queer* means. If queer studies wants *queer* to "do new kinds of work with different objects and archives in a range of historical, cultural, and geographic contexts," as imagined by Amin, it will have to do so under no pretenses that its work will always be translatable across these multiple and variegated contexts.[21]

I find it immensely constructive to imagine *queer* as a sensation, in the way Amber Jamilla Musser describes sensation as "both individual and impersonal."[22] On one hand, *queer* is deeply individual and thus contingent and potentially surprising. To this end, queer studies has always recognized *queer*'s "democratizing contestations" as the source of its rhetorical and political power.[23] But on the other hand, as a sensation *queer* has an impersonal dimension also that haunts and feeds each of its individual articulations. Musser refers to the impersonal as sensation's "externality," which "allows us to think about sensation as inhabiting particular forms with a shared (and some might say learned) assumption of the boundaries of each particular category."[24] She uses the color blue as an example, explaining that while each of us "may perceive the color differently," our use of "a shared referent" indicates our collective trust in the "structural aspect of sensation."[25] Blue, in other words, may appear in many shades but remains cataloged as a singular color. Likewise, *queer*-as-sensation brings to mind *queer*'s own externality, its affective structure and arrangement, as revealed by Amin's attachment genealogy. The queer impersonal, as an endlessly updated rubric of inherited affective orientations, is what guides *queer*'s ongoing pursuit of individual attachments.

A disattachment genealogy lays bare the communion between the individual and the impersonal. It highlights the remarkable monochromaticity of queer sensation—the fact that each queer attachment, regardless of how surprising it appears to be, can only be selected for its complementarity to an existing palette—and it brings into relief those attachments that have been neglected, discarded, and disavowed to protect the queer palette's impersonal coherence. The Pride flag, after all, includes only eleven colors. *Queer* remains a singular referent, even if it is capacious, even if it does look different in different contexts, even if it does occupy "a sphere of multiplicity."[26] Sensation operates circuitously: each individual queer attachment shapes the queer impersonal, which in turn conditions all future individual attachments. Amin enriches Musser's sensation with historicity, showing how yesterday's impersonal influences today's individual. I want to insist further that *queer*'s prior deferrals and disavowals—its disattachments—continue to determine its present attachments on both the impersonal and individual registers. What is deferred individually contributes to what is deferred impersonally and thereby truncates, however marginally, the expansiveness of *queer*'s future rhetorical imaginary. We can only sense *queer* to the extent that we agree on what *queer* is allowed to mean.

By calling for a surrender of *queer*'s rhetoricity, I'm acknowledging that in order for *queer*'s circulation to expand, for its objects and attachments to grow in number and diversity, *queer*'s internal coherence (its impersonal) will necessarily fracture. And I'm arguing that *this is okay.* Queer studies is made up of humans, each with our own contexts and raced, gendered, dis/abled, and classed subject positions, and none of us can comprehend all the world in all its complexity all the time, even if we do (as we should) feel ethically compelled to try. Another way of saying this is that *queer* may not always be recognizable to everyone as queer, and that is all right. Not everyone hears every silence. Not everyone sees every apparition. Not everyone feels the empty space left in every other lover's bed. Sometimes one or more of us is going to be left out of the queer joke. Its queerness won't register, but rather than pretend to laugh, we should learn to be comfortable with our position on the outside, realizing that the joke wasn't for us after all. Admittedly, this lesson is more wanting in some people than others, and I am certainly not suggesting that those of us who already find ourselves outside the purview of queer studies should give up on demanding entrance. Instead, I am thinking alongside David L. Eng, Jack Halberstam, and José Esteban Muñoz who suggest that a queer ethics "demands a world in which we must sometimes relinquish not only our epistemological but also our political certitude."[27] A queer ethics, they argue, is also "an ethics of humility."[28]

Perhaps, then, it is under the rubric of humility that we can agree not every queer object is meant to be consumed by all of us. Perhaps it is humility, as a mode of what Musser calls "empathetic reading," that can help queer studies better account for the sway of the queer impersonal. Humility "shifts the focus away from understanding the other as unified and transparently available to us and invites us to experience affinities on a corporeal level *with* others through sensation."[29] This is a way of feeling queer without necessarily knowing what we're feeling or why it's particularly queer. *Queer* has always been inconsistent and on the verge of incomprehensible—thus is the burden of "unrationalized coexistence."[30] I'm suggesting only that queer studies, and all of us very ordinary, very "average," very imperfect people who compose it, own up to our necessarily bounded epistemological limits.[31] Maybe if we were all more comfortable admitting *queer*'s occasional illegibility, admitting that sometimes we just don't understand, it would give us all a chance to ask questions more earnestly, to teach one another more urgently, and to scratch our heads more publicly.

Disability as Queer Disattachment

To a degree, my turn toward humility as an ethical response to *queer*'s fractured rhetoricity resonates with what Eng and Jasbir K. Puar propose as "an emergent 'objectless critique.'"[32] In their special issue of *Social Text,* Eng and Puar introduce objectless critique as an expansion of subjectless critique—that mode of queer analysis intended to decenter sexual minorities in queer studies in order to better capture *queer*'s mobility. Objectless critique, by extension, "focuses on the biopolitics of objects," the ways that queer attachment refurbishes some objects (but not others) into proper subjects.[33] Objectless critique is less interested in the *who* or *what* of queer studies than in the processes by which certain people and things get to become the *who* and *what* of queer studies. Rather than assume a naturalized subject/object distinction, Eng and Puar expect objectless critique to clarify how subjects and objects come to be designated as such and, equally important, how previously designated objects can be rehabilitated "as new subjects for surveillance and governance."[34] A disattachment genealogy complements this project by attending to those objects whose failure to secure queer attachment has become constitutive to the field of queer studies. These expelled objects animate through their absence: their ongoing invisibilization is necessary to other objects' subjectification. As a corollary to what Eng and Puar call an "affective biopolitics," disattachments serve as an affective necropolitics: they can only be ascribed value through their denial and decimation.[35] There can be no recuperation of any new subjects without the processual and perpetual repudiation of most objects. Inclusion only matters so long as it remains exceptional.

Coincidentally, in an attempt to illustrate objectless critique's analytical purchase, Eng and Puar address the role of disability in queer studies. Fearing that disability has come to signal "a legible subject and identity for political rights and representation," they reintroduce Puar's notion of "debility" as a "sublated third term" that generates the polarization between ability and disability.[36] "Debility" works alongside other muted and effectively disattached categories, such as "Indigeneity" and "trans," to shore up the coherence and "discursive consistency" of "politicized binaries," such as abled/disabled, citizen/

noncitizen, and man/woman.[37] Objectless critique pulls these and other third terms into focus as a way to expose liberalism's ideological fragility. According to Eng and Puar, any categorical distinction between "abled" and "disabled" relies on the occlusion of what Puar elsewhere calls "an economy of injury," where the existence of maimed and impaired bodyminds far outpaces the recognition of disabled persons.[38] Within this economy, debility captures disability excess: forms and experiences of disability not described as such because they are quotidian effects of colonial violence and global capitalism or because they are simply illegible within a Western medical model that measures disability by its proximity to whiteness. Debility, through its racialized fungibility, is what engenders disability's appealing plasticity. Disability can only stretch, its edges can only remain porous, in equal proportion to debility's relative anonymity. Disability can only be recuperated as a respectable (and singular) alternative to ability so long as debility continues to be "productively effaced."[39]

In many respects, I agree with Eng and Puar's argument. There is no question that debility's ongoing sublation is necessary to rehabilitate some forms of disability within the liberal state. Nevertheless, I worry that a purely juxtapositional account of debility and disability oversimplifies their relationship. Even within the United States, the rights and privileges made possible by the category of disability are in many ways restricted to white, economically stable, and cisheteronormative individuals who can afford to claim disability for themselves, thereby excluding the much larger category of racialized, poor, trans, and queer persons who come to inhabit the category of disability by alternative means.[40] Many people do not claim disability but are interpellated as disabled by institutions seeking to rid them of their subjectivity—the same subjectivity, I should note, that Eng and Puar contend is made possible by the geopolitics of disability.[41] Though I acknowledge the biopolitical currency of a "crip nationalism"[42] that exceptionalizes U.S. disability policy and pride to subtend colonialist and imperialist agendas,[43] it's worth emphasizing that for many disabled people in the United States, especially those with mental disabilities, the category of disability is not initially embraced willingly but survived under duress within medical or juridical contexts. In these contexts, the category of disability is literally designed to ensure rhetorical incapacitation.[44] Disability, here, is a threat, not a promise. It leads not to our immediate transmogrification into political subjects but, quite the opposite, to our slippage into what Margrit Shildrick calls "bioprecarity," or a person's vulnerability to debility.[45] Not always an escape from debility's "massification,"[46] disability identity can hasten a person's further debilitation through the "political and socioeconomic utility value" of diagnosis.[47] The ontological shift incurred by a person's induction into the medical- or prison-industrial complex (i.e., abled→disabled; civilian→criminal) summons targeted technologies of debilitation under the guise of cure.[48]

Consider, for instance, the number of children who, once appended with an autism diagnosis, are immediately enrolled into Applied Behavior Analysis, wherein their newly attributed disability is adduced to justify a prolonged period of rehabilitative violence.[49] This violence constitutes debilitation because the autistic person's resulting traumas will rarely be regarded as a disability or disabling but, rather, as symptomatic of their alleged pathology, their autism. Or, as another example, we might think about how mental illness is ascribed to incarcerated persons to warrant their indefinite confinement under sexually violent predator statutes. These statutes allow state judiciaries to recommit people who are nearing the end of their existing sentences based on the court's belief that they are at an escalated risk of reoffending. By law, this escalated risk must be linked to a "mental abnormality," which is typically established by forensic psychologists who diagnose defendants with sexual disorders,[50] such as "sexual sadism disorder" or "pedophilic disorder."[51] Rarely are these disorders diagnosed outside of criminal proceedings: the entire class of paraphilic disorders is effectively instrumentalized as a carceral weapon.[52] Similar examples could be given for many people with mental disabilities, especially psychiatric disabilities, whose diagnoses accelerate the threat of incarceration and institutionalization, among other forms of state-sponsored violence.[53]

Medicine and the carceral state manufacture disability as a road to debility: disability doubling up on itself. The category of "disability," in these instances, is not reducible to a privileged subject position but is instead a carefully plotted and expertly crafted iteration of debility that maims through promises of healing or protection. Medical practitioners delivering diagnoses to authorize treatments or condone sentences that themselves cause disabilities never named as such. Extracting the experience of debility from the category of "disability" short-shrifts the latter of its phenomenological range and theoretical depth. If we presume that the category of "disability" only codes for a disabled subject—one who profits off the neoliberal recuperation of the abled/disabled binary—it is more difficult to account for the uneven distribution of subjectivity among those who are identified as disabled, thereby obfuscating the range of bioprecarious intensities within the disability community.

Through their critique of the abled/disabled binary, Eng and Puar inadvertently instantiate a new binary hinged on debility/disability, according to which debility is infused by *queer*'s abject politics in opposition to disability's homonormative resonances. Though Puar initially proposed *debility* as "overlapping" with *disability,* the two terms appear irreconcilable in the introduction to the special issue, where debility's occlusion works to guarantee disability's exceptionality.[54] As such, I find the essay to function as a fascinating example of my larger argument about disability's role in queer studies. By pivoting the field toward debility, Eng and Puar claim to reveal the "relations of production" that capacitate disabled subjectivity.[55] And while perhaps this pivot will "return [queer studies] to questions of embodiment and corporeality," as predicted by Eng-Beng Lim and Tavia Nyong'o, it is a pivot that requires *queer*'s further estrangement from disability.[56]

As it has happened many times before, disability is cast off as politically untenable in favor of an alternative that is more suitable to queer attachment. In this case, Eng and Puar allege that debility's disattachment is what "produce[s], mangage[s], and animate[s] new queer subjects," including disabled subjects.[57] In order to substantiate their argument, the authors distort the category of disability by omitting its dialectic with debility within the medical-industrial complex and criminal punishment system. Disability is straw-manned as a "new queer" subject when, as I have shown, it is neither a stable subject position nor a particularly welcome queer attachment. Queer studies is built on repeated disavowals of disability that have come to insulate *queer*'s institutional politics, making *queer* desirable to disability but never the other way around. Ironically, Eng and Puar limn debility as a sparkly new object for queer attachment by suggesting that disability has already had its turn when, in fact, *queer*'s disability history is much more fraught. In the end, it is not only debility that is disattached but also disability—as always, once again.

It bears repeating that I agree with Eng and Puar that objectless critique is a generative way forward for queer studies. The analytic successfully "provincializes" the field by sketching out its racial, geographic, and capitalistic inheritances.[58] More broadly, the "Left of Queer" special issue charges us to rethink what *queer* means by taking stock of the conditions that surrounded its emergence and guided its evolution. My hope is only that queer studies will engage more robustly with disability's particularities, including all of its nuance, contradictions, and variations that cannot be easily surmised by too clean a separation from debility. Disability is messy and sticky and stretchy and relentless. Even as a disattachment, perhaps especially as one, disability endures. I'm inclined to believe such endurance is what makes disattachment genealogies so necessary: disavowed objects never go away. We might not see them or hear their voices. We might forget about them in their silence. But they're still there, under it all, making what we do see and hear possible, articulable, legible, and comprehensible. This is why they're called disattachments: *dis-* for apart and separate, as in disability itself. Other, outside, beyond. Through their distance, through their difference, leaving the rest of the world feeling whole, familiar, safe, sane, and desirable. We must wonder, don't we, what has been lost in order for *queer* itself to feel the way it does? What ghosts have been forgotten that, through their haunting, make queer studies feel like the house on the hill: home to one family but spooky to the rest of us?

To end, I'd like to pursue these questions by offering an example of a disattachment genealogy for my suicide attempt. When I first drafted this epilogue, I had endeavored to recast my experience in conventionally queer terms that would ally it with a politics, with resistance, and with nonnormativity. I had tried to make queer meaning out of my near death, and I had looked to silence—as I've advocated throughout this project—for insight on where that meaning was located. But in doing so, I focused too intently on the silence of my object, my prior self, while forgetting the silences I was bringing to the analysis, those that, along with more visible expectations, filtered out all the dispossessions, disavowals, and disattachments that had allowed other variations of *queer* to remain legible. By attempting to put my experience in direct conversation with queer studies, I resurrected the very dependence on speech, visibility, and presence that I was trying to contest. Thus, in the following example, I'll begin by drawing attention to the affective attachment that dominates the scene, but then I will consider what this attachment and its disavowals tell us about *queer*'s limits and (im)possibilities.[59]

Pathological Shames

Shame brought me to the church that night. I remember feeling overwhelmed by embarrassment that just a few months out of therapy, I had already fallen into sin. I'd kissed a boy. He'd waited for me in the stairwell after class one afternoon and walked with me to the dining hall. We spent the evening wandering around town before finding our way to a lonely bench at the edge of campus. When we kissed, he put one hand behind my head, and I felt like the luckiest boy in the world. I felt every shiver and tingle that I'd been praying and willing myself to feel toward girls, and in that moment of tender, adolescent pleasure, I realized that there was no going back. I'd been spoiled by an ecstasy unordained by God, and despite all my effort to be good and pure and holy, I knew that this is what I'd always wanted and always would want. I would want to be kissed like this every day for the rest of my life. And therein lay my shame: it was not only that I did something bad—God always forgives behavior—but that it held a mirror up to my essence. I was faced with the fortitude of my own desire. It was a desire so resilient that, even in the midst of believing I was damning myself to hell, I kissed that boy back. I wrapped my arms around his waist. I let him trace a line with his finger from my throat to the button of my jeans, and I gasped—not with pain or regret or confusion but in absolute rapture—when I felt his warmth meet mine. *If this is not God, I don't know God.* I thought as much again three days later, kneeling in the church, fully aware that I would never know God unless I brought my soul to him myself.

The shame I felt that night will be familiar to many queer or otherwise marginalized people who have found their embodyminded desires in conflict with the ideals of their communities. It is a kind of shame experienced in isolation that gnaws away at your senses of belonging and self-worth until both are gone. You're left with nothing but confidence in your total and utter brokenness. This is a shame that is notably distinct from another variation more common within queer studies, which exists not in opposition but in tandem with affirmative models of queerness. David Halperin and Valerie Traub describe this other variation of shame as "continuous with gay pride," where, "because of gay pride, we have become proud enough that we don't need to stand on our pride."[60] Shame in queer studies is generally imbued with its own sociality and offers a way to approach queerness that is not overdetermined by pride but is, instead, more richly interwoven with alternative affective orientations to the self and world.[61] This mixture between pride and shame is the "central turn," according to Heather Love, that defines *queer*: "It is both abject and exalted."[62]

Shame in this context is thus somewhat tongue in cheek. On one hand, queer shame describes a real affective orientation that many queer people experience, but on the other hand, it is invoked from a progressivist position that presumes the coexistence of pride as a mediating affect. Though Sedgwick argues that shame drives an "uncontrollable relationality" without pride's assistance,[63] shame's queer politics depend on the mitigation of an "imperative to affirmation" that, even if intentionally avoided, still structures the discourse.[64] Put differently, no queer scholar earnestly considers queerness to be something of which a person should be ashamed; thus, conversations about shame within the field of queer studies are always already predicated on a degree of playfulness. Shame becomes useful when it no longer poses a threat to the interlocutors. This is, contra my own experience, a defanged shame that reveals more about the affective histories of queer studies and the positionalities of its practitioners than it does about the experience of shame.[65] Shame in the field is a shame begotten by pride, which makes it difficult if not impossible for scholars to account for variations that exist outside of *queer*'s existing political trajectory. What are we meant to do with shame, like mine, that trends not toward "its own powerfully productive and powerfully social metamorphic possibilities" but toward death?[66] In order for queer studies to establish an attachment to shame, what alternative forms of the affect had to be ignored? This is another way of asking Tobin Siebers's question, "Who gets to feel shame" and who doesn't?[67] Or, as Ann Cvetkovich puts it, "Whose feelings count?"[68] Whose don't? And who is not allowed to feel at all?

A disattachment genealogy responds to these questions by sketching out which affects and whose affective orientations have necessarily been surrendered in order for shame to be idealized within queer studies. This approach looks to silence, invisibility, and absence as gaps, elisions, and erasures that were not incidentally forgotten but intentionally produced in order to preserve and consolidate (or perhaps preserve through the consolidation of) *queer*'s intelligibility. In this example, the iterations of shame forcibly excluded from queer studies are those that lack a tether to pride. These shames are reminiscent of older models of stigma, inversion, and internalized heterosexism that preceded and coexisted with the gay movement work of the mid-twentieth century. These are pathological shames characteristically out of time, recalling what Carolyn Dinshaw terms "temporal asynchrony" or "the present's irreducible multiplicity."[69] My suicidal shame doesn't seem to fit within queer studies because it is beholden to another era that does not rhyme with the political impetus of queer shame. Queer shame's politics prefigure a queer subject whose existence affirms the exceptionalism of *queer* and all its affective attachments. That is, shame's idealization requires a self-affirming queer subject who is immune to shame's toxicity.[70] This is a privileged position that exists outside of criminal, medical, and moral jurisdiction. This is an autonomous agent who can wield their shame in public without suffering its material implications in private or at the hands of the state.

As I've argued throughout this book, the notion of queer autonomy relies on the constitutive absence of disability, which by its negation upholds the illusive rationality and health of the liberal queer. Pathological shame threatens the stability of this queer able bodymind, throwing into relief not only the narrow rigidity of *queer*'s affective orientations but also the breadth of affectivities that have been disattached to secure queer shame's political purity. My suicidal shame, for instance, subtends queer shame by making visible one of its original referents, asking, *But what are you ashamed of?* It's worth noting the deep-seated ableism, stemming from conversion therapy and my anxiety over the stigma of mental illness, that informed my own shame. I could not bear the weight of my depraved and deformed sexuality, my perceived brokenness. Queer studies, in its attempt to harness shame's energy, empties the affect of its conditions instead of "taking apart the social processes" that produce it.[71] Pathological shame pulls its conditions and constitutive social processes back into focus by recentering the disabled bodymind that first gave rise to *queer.* "Perhaps this is why disability cannot escape its association with shame," Siebers speculates, because disability is ultimately what queer studies is ashamed of.[72] As I've said before, disability must remain silent in order for *queer* to remain coherent. Likewise, the field's attachment to shame gels only in the absence of a critical interrogation of what makes disability shameful. Disability is the evil ghost that looms over queer shame, simultaneously threatening and engendering its politics. Even if it is reclaimed or conjoined with pride, shame remains indebted to a medical model of queer disability that is rooted in deficiency.

A disattachment genealogy reveals queer shame's implicit dependence on and utter terror of the shamefulness of disability. Here, silence=disability returns as a variation of itself, operating not as a metaphor for silent queers who taint homonormativity with the stain of disability but as a dictum insisting on the absence of disability, the renunciation of the object that bears *queer* and its shame. By illuminating the disability running beneath queer shame, a disattachment genealogy also recovers pathological shame as a refurbished queer attachment. Admittedly, this attachment might not bode well for queer studies. I'm not really sure what happens to a field when it is confronted with the object of its own shame, especially when that object—disability—is still around, as are many people for whom that object is a structuring characteristic of their lives. Maybe, as I suggested earlier, *queer* will diversify itself, breaking off into endless iterations that bear little to no resemblance to one another and, therefore, will maintain no central grammar, no standardized coherence, no guaranteed legibility, no impersonal rhetoricity, no bounded externality. Perhaps when faced with the graveyard of its disattachments, pathological shame among them, *queer* will dissolve back into the referents it has worked so hard to distance itself from. This would not be the end of *queer*'s nonnormativity or its mobility but rather would be its atomic explosion toward multidimensionality, its orgastic release from a delimited political agenda back into the atmosphere as particles and dust that can coat whoever and whatever waves them into their breath or onto its surface. This is a vision of queer studies guided by silence that honors *queer* for what it is, as it is, even when it doesn't appear to be anything at all. *Queer* as an erection for my conversion therapist. *Queer* as blank profiles. *Queer* as ex-gay. *Queer* as a late transition. *Queer* as wheelchairs on the runway. *Queer* as the wrong kind of shame. *Queer* as soiled and inconsistent and devastating. *Queer* as how each of us is getting by, moving on, showing up, and sometimes not. *Queer* as invisibility. *Queer* as absence. *Queer* as silence.

Acknowledgments

I've drafted many iterations of these acknowledgments. Some, several too many pages long; some, an uncomfortably few sentences short. There are certainly many people I am excited to name for their generosity—people who have knowingly and willingly contributed to the formation of this book through their time, labor, compassion, patience, and encouragement. These are people I love, people I aspire to resemble, people who do things with their bodies and with the world that bring me joy. But it seems important for a book on silence, disavowals, and disattachments to also acknowledge the many people whose absence, anonymity, indifference, and hostility also helped to bring this project to fruition. These are people who have, in equal proportions, tried to kill me and survived alongside me, stolen my body and taught me how to find it again, coerced me into speaking and modeled for me the discriminating pleasures of silence. All these people, too, have been crucial to writing *Queer Silence*; all these people, too, flood the pages of this book.

So the question becomes one about the ethics of disclosure. I am rather confident that few of the people I admire will be upset if I name them. These include, in no particular order, my friends: Gavin, Dan, Ruth, Travis, Jackie, Temptaous, Val, Rick, Suban, Cam, and Don James. My siblings, David and Hannah. My mentors, Brian Fehler, Agatha Beins, Cheryl Glenn, Janet Lyon, Debra Hawhee, and especially Hil Malatino for always saying *yes* when I've needed him and for modeling how to *be* when it feels impossible. The reviewers for this book, Robert McRuer and M. Remi Yergeau: Robert, whose work has made mine possible and who supports my research at every opportunity; Remi, who has given me a vocabulary to speak of myself, even in silence. The many, many users on Twitter and other social media platforms who fill my days with laughter, commiseration, and perspectives on issues I know little about. My partner, Darius, who models the kind of feeling deeply that helps me to make sense of my own deep feelings. Vikas, who taught me to love myself even when I didn't know what that meant. Leah Pennywark and the entire staff at the University of Minnesota Press, who believed I had something worth saying. Matthew John Phillips, who curated a brilliant index that offers new ways to enter and navigate the project. Hayden Stern for their gorgeous painting that fills the cover, and Amanda Weiss for her stunning cover design. The Department of Language, Culture, and Gender Studies at Texas Woman's University that helped to fund the costs of this book. The Department of English Language and Literatures at the University of British Columbia and its faculty, who demonstrated excitement for this book before its release. And for all the disability activists and medical professionals who created the protocols, built the care networks, distributed the information, and invented the vaccines that kept me alive during the early years of Covid-19.

Unfortunately, the ethics of disclosure become a little more complicated when I think about those individuals whose contributions to this book were of a different—less direct or less positive—kind. For some of these people, I feel comfortable not naming names. This group includes those fellow queers and survivors who depend on degrees of secrecy and stealth to navigate their lives safely. The kids I met in conversion therapy. The strangers I've cruised. The internet friends who've shared trauma stories with me as a mark of affection and empathic communion. The family members back home who are waiting for their abuser to die because there's no other way for them to leave, to live. In other cases, I want to call a few folks out, even if they would probably prefer to remain unnamed, because their violences trump their preferences for anonymity. There's Joe, my old conversion therapist. There's Marc and Adam, the youth pastors who introduced my parents and me to Joe. There's my father, whose own wounds leave him so angry and scared that he tears apart everyone and everything he doesn't understand. There's Rich and John, the professors I had in graduate school whose intellectual curiosity ended at flesh, at bodies such as mine that didn't think or speak like theirs. There's the other men, the ones I still feel pressing and pulling and scratching, who never gave me their names, who all used different names for me, who opened me up in ways I'll never be able to close. All these folks deserve to be mentioned. They all have earned space here: making worlds with kisses and cum and emoji and tears and blood and bruises and back rubs and video calls and so much love and hate and confusion and fear and hope and prayer to a big sky with a chorus of little voices—I can't stomach it all anymore, but I could at one time, so I did. I heard their silence and suffered their silencing. I made it out, I wrote this book, and now I'm acknowledging them here one last time.

If it's not too self-indulgent, I'd also like to thank John, the last me, the still me but different me, the me who nearly died and kind of actually did die all those years ago. You did your best, and it was good enough.

Notes

Introduction

1. C. Cohen, "Punks, Bulldaggers, and Welfare Queens," 438.
2. Amin, *Disturbing Attachments,* 182.
3. Muñoz, *Cruising Utopia,* 91.
4. Rand, *Reclaiming Queer,* 6.
5. Rand, 164.
6. Duggan, *Twilight of Equality?*; and Snorton and Haritaworn, "Trans Necropolitics."
7. Warner, "Normal and Normaller," 123.
8. J. Cohen, "Queer Crip Sex and Critical Mattering," 153.
9. McRuer, *Crip Theory,* 2.
10. See Schalk, "Coming to Claim Crip"; and Yergeau, *Authoring Autism.*
11. Foucault, *History of Sexuality.*
12. Chauncey, *Gay New York*; and D'Emilio and Freedman, *Intimate Matters.*
13. Vitulli, "Dangerous Embodiments."
14. Halperin and Traub, *Gay Shame*; Love, *Feeling Backward*; and Nealon, *Foundlings.*
15. See Bishop, *Harmful Treatment.*
16. Alexander and Rhodes, "Queer Rhetoric"; Dolmage, *Disability Rhetoric*; and Glenn and Lunsford, "Rhetoric and Feminism."
17. Manning, *Minor Gesture,* 126.
18. Minich, "Enabling Whom?"
19. Schalk, "Critical Disability Studies as Methodology."
20. Nealon, *Foundlings,* 2.
21. Samuels, *Fantasies of Identification,* 3.
22. Kameny's understanding of homosexuality was deeply informed by the clinical and sociological work of Evelyn Hooker, who not only argued for homosexuality's depathologization but also helped to establish the grounds on which later theorists of sexuality, such as Michel Foucault, would historicize the formation of homosexual identity. According to Stephen Molldrem, this connection is important because it foregrounds the contributions of homosexuality's depathologization, rather than its initial medicalization, "to the epistemological and disciplinary origins of social constructionist approaches to sexuality research." "Beyond the Depathologization of Homosexuality," 84. While it is common among queer studies scholars to trace the origination of

homosexuality to nineteenth-century sexology, less remarked on is how the elimination of homosexuality as a diagnostic category "contributed to the conditions" that made humanistic study of sexuality possible (86). See also Minton, *Departing from Deviance.*

23. Kunzel, "Queer History," 315.
24. Kameny, "Does Research into Homosexuality Matter?," 16.
25. Kameny, 16.
26. Kameny, 16–17.
27. Kameny, 17.
28. Kameny, 17.
29. Kameny, 17.
30. Kameny, 17.
31. Bayer, *Homosexuality and American Psychiatry,* 106.
32. Baynton, "Disability and the Justification of Inequality in American History," 26.
33. "Silence = Death," New York Public Library Digital Collections, 1969–1997, Manuscripts and Archives Division, New York Public Library.
34. Finkelstein, *After Silence,* 49.
35. Finkelstein, 2.
36. Cheng, Juhasz, and Shahani, Introduction, 9.
37. Finkelstein, *After Silence,* 3.
38. Román, "Not-about-AIDS," 8.
39. Shahani, "How to Survive," 7.
40. Patton, foreword, viii.
41. Shahani, "How to Survive," 27.
42. Mintz, "Invisibility," 113.
43. Butler-Wall, "Viral Transmissions."
44. McRuer, "Disabling Sex," 109.
45. Kramer, "1,112 and Counting."
46. Kramer.
47. Kramer.
48. Kramer.
49. Kramer.
50. Sedgwick, *Epistemology of the Closet,* 14.
51. Diedrich, *Indirect Action,* 25.
52. Foucault, *History of Sexuality,* 59.
53. Foucault, 20.
54. Foucault, 20.
55. Kramer, "1,112 and Counting."
56. Butler, "Critically Queer," 19.
57. Butler, 20.
58. Butler, *Excitable Speech,* 163.
59. Butler, 108.
60. Amin, *Disturbing Attachments,* 181.
61. See E. Johnson, *No Tea, No Shade*; Driskill et al., *Queer Indigenous Studies*; and Namaste, *Invisible Lives.*
62. Burke, *Language as Symbolic Action.*
63. Eng, *Feeling of Kinship,* 180.
64. Butler, *Excitable Speech,* 108.

65. Love, "Doing Being Deviant," 83.
66. Love, 85.
67. Berger, *Disarticulate,* 157.
68. Gould, *Moving Politics,* 3.
69. McRuer, "Shameful Sites," 186.
70. See Amin, *Disturbing Attachments*; and Castiglia and Reed, *If Memory Serves.*
71. Johnson and McRuer, "Cripistemologies," 142.
72. Malhotra and Carrillo Rowe, *Silence, Feminism, Power,* 1.
73. Brueggemann, *Lend Me Your Ear,* 105–6.
74. Samuels, *Fantasies of Identification,* 6.
75. W. Brown, "In 'the Folds of Our Own Discourse,'" 186.
76. W. Brown, 191.
77. W. Brown, 196.
78. W. Brown, 196.
79. Johnson and Kennedy, Introduction, 162.
80. J. Johnson, "Breaking Down," 182.
81. J. Johnson, 182.
82. Aristotle, *Rhetoric,* 1355b26–27.
83. See Glenn and Ratcliffe, *Silence and Listening as Rhetorical Arts.*
84. Glenn, *Unspoken,* 4.
85. Glenn, 4.
86. Glenn, 13.
87. Rice, "Unframing Models of Public Distribution," 9.
88. Rice, 10.
89. Rice, 13.
90. Foucault, *History of Sexuality,* 20.
91. See Ingraham, "Energy."
92. Hawhee, *Rhetoric in Tooth and Claw,* 42.
93. Campt, *Listening to Images,* 112–13.
94. Campt, 113.
95. Queer silence's implicit critique of subjectivity bears a notable resemblance to Jack Halberstam's "radical passivity," which he proposes as "the refusal quite simply to be." *Queer Art of Failure,* 140. Both queer silence and radical passivity embrace "absence, dis-appearance, and illegibility" to undercut the humanist subject's provincializing claim to agency (142). However, while radical passivity leans into queer studies' "antisocial mode" (140) through "a cleaving to that which seems to shame or annihilate" (144), queer silence embraces a more deeply relational and interdependent model of personhood informed by disability studies and disability justice work (see Kittay, *Love's Labor*; and Piepzna-Samarasinha, *Care Work*). Unlike Halberstam, I am skeptical about how useful the antisocial is for multiply marginalized people, especially those with disabilities, for whom subjectivity is not always granted in the first place. Additionally, Halberstam relies heavily on death and suicide as examples of radical passivity, of which, as I elaborate in the epilogue, I am generally suspicious. Instead, I intend queer silence to showcase the multiple and often invisibilized relations that make subjectivity possible for some and not for others.
96. Davis, *Inessential Solidarity,* 87.
97. Davis, 105–6.

98. Davis, 111.
99. Davis, 2.
100. Davis, 113.
101. See Rhodes, "Becoming Utopias."
102. Halberstam, *Female Masculinity,* 10.
103. Amin, *Disturbing Attachments,* 10.

1. To Speak of Silence

1. See McRuer, *Crip Theory*; Malatino, *Queer Embodiment*; and Ferguson, *Aberrations in Black.*
2. Smilges, "White Squares to Black Boxes."
3. Buehl, *Assembling Arguments,* 24.
4. Derrida, *Writing and Difference,* 54.
5. Foucault, *History of Sexuality,* 27.
6. Derrida, *Writing and Difference,* 54.
7. Foucault, *History of Sexuality,* 27.
8. Glenn and Ratcliffe, *Silence and Listening as Rhetorical Arts,* 2.
9. Glenn, *Unspoken,* 4.
10. Glenn, 7.
11. Glenn, 13.
12. Glenn, 13.
13. Glenn, 155.
14. Vitanza, "Some Meditations-Ruminations," 801.
15. Vitanza, 813.
16. Huffer, *Are the Lips a Grave?,* 132.
17. Huffer, 132.
18. Huffer, 141.
19. Huffer, 141.
20. Huffer, 141.
21. Malhotra and Carrillo Rowe, *Silence, Feminism, Power,* 18.
22. Malhotra and Carrillo Rowe, 15–16.
23. Malhotra and Carrillo Rowe, 18.
24. Malhotra and Carrillo Rowe, 18.
25. Vitanza, "Some Meditations-Ruminations," 801.
26. Glenn, *Unspoken,* 7.
27. Shahani, "I Have a Voice," 77.
28. Treichler, "AIDS, Homophobia, and Biomedical Discourse," 31.
29. Alexander and Rhodes, "Queer Rhetoric."
30. Alexander and Rhodes.
31. Alexander and Rhodes.
32. Brouwer, "Precarious Visibility Politics," 206.
33. Brouwer, 209.
34. Alexander and Rhodes, "Queer Rhetoric."
35. Murray, *Non-discursive Rhetoric,* 2.
36. Murray, 3.
37. Murray, 8.
38. Murray, 9.

39. Ingraham, "Energy," 264.
40. Ingraham, 264.
41. I recognize that not all affect theorists make such a clear distinction between affect and emotion, especially Sara Ahmed. I engage her work carefully in chapter 2.
42. Massumi, *Parables for the Virtual,* 5.
43. Massumi, 21.
44. Massumi, *Politics of Affect,* 54.
45. Massumi, *Parables for the Virtual,* 35.
46. Massumi, 43.
47. Flatley, *Affective Mapping,* 12.
48. Massumi, *Parables for the Virtual,* 21.
49. Brennan, *Transmission of Affect,* 3.
50. Brennan, 75.
51. While Brennan does not make this connection, I think it's important to point out the similarities between the language of transmission and the language of contagion, given the affect(ivity) of AIDS and of disability more generally. Jules Gill-Peterson, in fact, uses the phrase "affective virality" to describe ACT UP demonstrations. See "Haunting the Queer Spaces of AIDS." See also Izard, *Human Emotions*; and Sedgwick, *Touching Feeling.*
52. Brennan, *Transmission of Affect,* 149.
53. Brennan, 149.
54. Verlinden, "On Affect Theory's Hidden Histories," 325.
55. Verlinden, 323, 321.
56. Gorman, "Quagmires of Affect," 311.
57. Gorman, 312.
58. Aho, Ben-Moshe, and Hilton, "Mad Futures," 297–98.
59. Prahlad, *Secret Life of a Black Aspie,* 191, 217, 4.
60. Prahlad, 47, 217.
61. This series of excisions also affects the legibility and valuation of many disabled people's languages, literacies, and methods of communication. For autistic folks who use facilitated communication or other assisted communication technologies, traditional affect theory works to delegitimize rather than recuperate their language as meaningful. Mel Baggs addresses this problem at length in hir video "In My Language."
62. Prahlad, *Secret Life of a Black Aspie,* 162.
63. G. Kennedy, "Hoot in the Dark," 2.
64. G. Kennedy, 6.
65. G. Kennedy, 4.
66. G. Kennedy, 10.
67. G. Kennedy, 4.
68. G. Kennedy, 10.
69. I do not contest that violence can be rhetorical or that rhetorical theory typically informs military strategy (e.g., *The Art of War*). My point is simply that rhetorical skill does not guarantee survival, let alone power.
70. G. Kennedy, "Hoot in the Dark," 10.
71. G. Kennedy, 10.
72. K. Campbell, *Man Cannot Speak for Her,* 1.
73. Hawhee, "Toward a Bestial Rhetoric," 82.

74. Hawhee, 81.
75. Hawhee, 85.
76. Rickert, *Ambient Rhetoric,* x.
77. Rickert, xii.
78. Rickert, 3.
79. Rickert, 198.
80. Chen, *Animacies,* 41.
81. Chen, 5.
82. Chen, 11.
83. Chen, 55.
84. See Bitzer, "Rhetorical Situation."
85. C. Cohen, "Punks, Bulldaggers, and Welfare Queens," 438.
86. Bessette, "Queer Rhetoric In Situ," 157.
87. Bessette, 157.
88. Chávez, *Queer Migration Politics,* 58.
89. Brennan, *Transmission of Affect,* 86.
90. Chávez, *Queer Migration Politics,* 8.
91. Chávez, 147.
92. Chávez, 147.
93. I pick up on the coalitional potential of queer silence in chapter 5.
94. Amin, *Disturbing Attachments,* 10.
95. Amin, 10.
96. Amin, 10.
97. Stryker, "Dungeon Intimacies," 39.
98. Stryker, 42.
99. Stryker, "General Editor's Introduction," 516.
100. Stryker, 516.
101. Stryker, "Dungeon Intimacies," 44.
102. Samuels, *Fantasies of Identification,* 3.
103. Samuels, 6.
104. Prendergast, "On the Rhetorics of Mental Disability," 56.
105. Prendergast, 54.
106. Prendergast, 56.
107. Samuels, *Fantasies of Identification,* 12.
108. Spade, *Normal Life,* 5.
109. Shildrick, *Dangerous Discourses,* 1.
110. Shildrick, 1.
111. Snorton and Haritaworn, "Trans Necropolitics," 67.

2. White Squares to Black Boxes

1. Grindr LLC, Grindr.
2. My use of *tactical strategy* is adopted from Karma R. Chávez's *Queer Migration Politics,* where Chávez herself borrows from María Lugones. For Chávez and Lugones, the tactical strategy "seeks to disrupt the dichotomy between tactic and strategy that Michel de Certeau creates." *Queer Migration Politics,* 158. While de Certeau claims that tactics are for the oppressed while strategies are for oppressors, a tactical strategy contends with the complexity of power

and positionality for marginalized people, as well as the impossibility of stabilizing any one person into a singular role of "oppressed" or "oppressor." Here and throughout *Queer Silence,* I use *tactical strategy* or simply *strategy* to emphasize queer people's agential capacity when working from within and/or against material and embodyminded conditions that make such work nearly impossible. The tactical strategy is how I name the work we do to survive, even and especially when survival is all the work we can do. See also Lugones, *Pilgrimages/Peregrinajes*; and de Certeau, *Practice of Everyday Life.*

3. Campt, *Listening to Images,* 91.
4. Ross, "Beyond the Closet," 162.
5. Fraser, "Queer Closets," 35.
6. Grindstaff, *Rhetorical Secrets,* 126.
7. Faris, "Queering Networked Writing," 143–44.
8. Glenn, *Unspoken,* 7.
9. Olson, Finnegan, and Hope, "Visual Rhetoric in Communication," 3.
10. C. Jones, "Vision of the Quilt," xiv.
11. Finnegan, "Doing Rhetorical History of the Visual," 198.
12. Finnegan, 198.
13. Propen, *Locating Visual-Material Rhetorics,* 23, xvii.
14. Ommen, *Politics of the Superficial,* 7.
15. Propen, *Locating Visual-Material Rhetorics,* 123.
16. Muckelbauer and Hawhee, "Posthuman Rhetorics," 768.
17. Propen, *Locating Visual-Material Rhetorics,* 123.
18. Boyle, Brown, and Ceraso, "Digital," 257.
19. Barthes, "Rhetoric of the Image," 159.
20. Barthes, 159.
21. Barthes, 159.
22. Barthes, *Camera Lucida,* 26–27.
23. Barthes, 43.
24. Barthes, 45.
25. Barthes, 59.
26. Barthes, 53.
27. Glenn, *Unspoken,* 4.
28. Hatfield, "Queer Kairotic," 44.
29. Cárdenas, "Dark Shimmers," 169.
30. Massumi, *Parables for the Virtual,* 35.
31. Ahmed, *Cultural Politics of Emotion,* 208.
32. Flatley, *Affective Mapping,* 12.
33. Ahmed, *Promise of Happiness,* 230.
34. Ahmed, 230.
35. Ahmed, 231.
36. J. Campbell, *Getting It On Online,* 6.
37. J. Campbell, 55, 57.
38. J. Campbell, 11.
39. J. Campbell, 20.
40. J. Campbell, 150.
41. Weise, "Dawn of the 'Tryborg.'"
42. Kafer, *Feminist, Queer, Crip,* 119.
43. Mowlabocus, *Gaydar Culture,* 15.

44. Campbell, *Getting It On Online,* 53.
45. Mowlabocus, *Gaydar Culture,* 15. It is somewhat surprising how quickly outdated most queer studies scholarship has become with regard to queer internet cultures, especially with the rise of mobile apps designed to facilitate queer sex. In 2009, just over a decade ago, Tim Dean worried that "cruising online . . . transforms public space into private, thereby reducing the contact sport of cruising to a practice of networking." *Unlimited Intimacy,* 194. I would first point out that this concern ignores the diverse access needs of many marginalized queer persons, who may struggle to play the traditional "contact sport" variation of cruising safely or successfully. But more relevantly to the evolution of online cruising, Dean's perspective failed to predict the invention of mobile internet devices, such as smartphones, that don't privatize public space but more radically destabilize the boundary between public and private. For instance, one new app, Sniffies, invites users to anonymously broadcast their location to other anonymous users with the intention of creating and populating new cruising sites. Contra Dean's fear that "everyone who traverses city streets while talking on his or her cell phone . . . abets the degeneration of contact space into network space," this app actively renetworks space into new contact space (194).
46. Martin Stempfhuber and Michael Liegl call this phenomenon the "interface-to-space connection," suggesting that Grindr can function "as a mapping device for the reading of urban space and the writing of urban fiction." "Intimacy Mobilized," 66. They are referring to users' abilities to both locate other users and, in doing so, construct an imagined space where those users are together.
47. Blackwell, Birnholtz, and Abbott, "Seeing and Being Seen," 1,126.
48. Mowlabocus, *Gaydar Culture,* 79, 82.
49. Mowlabocus, 52.
50. Mowlabocus, 81.
51. Mowlabocus, 104, 103.
52. Mowlabocus, 103.
53. Mowlabocus, 104–5.
54. McGlotten, *Virtual Intimacies,* 3.
55. McGlotten, 63.
56. Rodriguez, "One Brutal Truth."
57. O. Jones, "No Asians, No Black People."
58. Holland, *Erotic Life of Racism,* 42.
59. Holland, 9, 5.
60. Holland, 6.
61. Lorenzo, "On Being Black and Gay."
62. Snorton, *Nobody Is Supposed to Know,* 23.
63. Snorton, 18.
64. Snorton, 18.
65. McGlotten, *Virtual Intimacies,* 72.
66. Gosine, "Brown to Blonde at Gay.com," 141.
67. Every, "Trans Guy and a Femme Guy."
68. Potts, "Navigating Grindr as a Non-binary Trans Boy."
69. DeafBuzzy, "Man Reveals the Shocking Abuse He Received."
70. Strudwick, "This Is What Dating Is Like."

71. Galassi, "Should I Include That I Am Disabled in My Dating Profile?"
72. Potts, "Navigating Grindr as a Non-binary Trans Boy."
73. Cameron, "How to Scruff a Trans Guy."
74. Pritchard, *Fashioning Lives*, 206.
75. Cedillo, "Disabled and Undocumented," 206.
76. McGlotten, *Virtual Intimacies*, 73.
77. McGlotten, 76.
78. McGlotten, 76.
79. Glenn, *Rhetorical Feminism*, 197.
80. Glenn, 206.
81. McGlotten, *Virtual Intimacies*, 77.
82. McGlotten, 77.
83. Hepple, "If You're a Disabled, Gay Twentysomething."
84. McGlotten, *Virtual Intimacies*, 8.
85. McGlotten, 8.
86. Mowlabocus, *Gaydar Culture*, 103.
87. Barthes, *Camera Lucida*, 27.
88. Mowlabocus, *Gaydar Culture*, 108.
89. Stockton, *Beautiful Bottom, Beautiful Shame*, 129.
90. Stockton, 130.
91. Barthes, *Camera Lucida*, 51.
92. Stockton, *Beautiful Bottom, Beautiful Shame*, 129.
93. Hodgson, *Post-Digital Rhetoric and the New Aesthetic*, 155.
94. Something I do not explore in this chapter but that deserves further consideration is catfishing, or when a user pretends to be someone they're not—typically by posting or sharing images of a person who they fraudulently claim to be. There are many reasons a person might choose to disguise themselves, just as there are many reasons a person might choose not to reveal themselves at all. In either case, whether catfishing or entirely invisible, a user's bodymind is digitized as *queer* through their operation of the app, regardless of whether they can be correctly identified as themselves. What distinguishes a catfishing profile from a blank profile is the former's appropriation of desirability politics, its deployment of a particular image because it carries an erotic charge or cultural currency that resonates with how the user sees themself or wishes others would see them. I discuss similar attempts to strategically resignify one's own rhetorical energy in chapter 3.
95. Barthes, *Camera Lucida*, 53.
96. I use the word *attention* as an oblique reference to Rosemarie Garland-Thomson, who argues that recorded images have largely superseded older models of "live staring encounters" offered by freak shows and circuses that would feature disabled, racialized, gender nonconforming, and otherwise nonnormatively embodyminded performers. *Staring*, 165. The long gaze aimed toward deviance is one owed to the stigmas, discourses, and narratives that come to signify queerness. As Garland-Thomson puts it, "story structures staring" because queer bodyminds are at once "unfamiliar as flesh and too familiar as narrative" (167). Queer persons remain foreign, even as their queer rhetorical energy circulates widely. On Grindr, staring reconciles what a user believes (is appealing, attractive, desirable, fuckable) with what they perceive (bodies that don't look like their own, bodies that deviate from their ideals of

beauty, bodies that stretch their imagination). Often, homonormative fantasy rubs up against deviant corporeality, edging on the violence of surveillance. But I am admittedly left wondering about the stares of queer users directed toward other queers, when fantasy is exploded by the revelation of new corporeal possibilities, by the encounter with visual evidence that a person can look like this, that a body can be desirable for this, and that I, too, might occupy my bodymind like this. In these cases, the stare is not reducible to violence but is a generator of new ways to understand oneself and the world. Also see Clarke, "Disability, Spectatorship, and *The Station Agent.*"

97. Barthes, *Camera Lucida,* 59.
98. Mowlabocus, *Gaydar Culture,* 108.
99. Barthes, *Camera Lucida,* 27.
100. Sawicki, *Disciplining Foucault,* 43.
101. See Koyama, "Transfeminist Manifesto"; and Sins Invalid, "10 Principles of Disability Justice."
102. Alexander and Rhodes, "Queer Rhetoric."
103. Faris, "Queering Networked Writing," 129.
104. I feel compelled to note that Herring actually mentions the town in which I attended graduate school in his book *Another Country.* I'll let the reader dig up the town's name if they are so inclined, but Herring refers to it as "cosmopolitan," which I think is very generous. *Another Country,* 155.
105. Herring, 13.
106. One of the readers for the initial draft of this book wondered whether the context of a college town raises questions about the age of consent and the taboo of faculty/student relationships. I think, in short, yes: the reasons a person may choose to withhold their identity online are many and, on Grindr, include the desire to use the app before they are eighteen (as I once did), to browse while remaining unnoticed by students, professors, or employers, or to perhaps pursue encounters with people who are significantly older or younger without unnecessarily exposing themselves. Quieting, in this way, allows users to access intergenerational sex and sex across institutionalized power differentials that could be against university policy, be illegal, or—far worse—cause sexual harm. While I am certainly opposed to nonconsensual sexual activity, I am also hesitant to universally condemn desires and sexual activities that conflict with homonormative tastes. Instead, I am persuaded by what Joseph J. Fischel and Hilary O'Connell in *Screw Consent* call "sexual autonomy" or "the *capability to co-determine sexual relations*" that holds space for the multiplicity of desire while also ensuring that "all parties can plan the existence, directions, and trajectories of their sexual relations." "Cripping Consent," 237. This model is attentive to the power dynamics that can increase risks of coercion and sexual harm without prematurely foreclosing opportunities for sexual pleasure. See also Fischel, *Sex and Harm in the Age of Consent.*
107. Herring, *Another Country,* 23.
108. Vidali, "Seeing What We Know."
109. Burke, *Language as Symbolic Action,* 45.

3. Queer(crip) Masquerading

1. TLC, "My Husband's Not Gay."
2. Barton, *Pray the Gay Away,* 116.
3. Bolles, "More than 70,000 Call."
4. Rodriguez-Jimenez, "Is *My Husband's Not Gay* an Ad?"
5. Rodriguez-Jimenez.
6. Chambers, *Leaving Homosexuality,* 23.
7. Fletcher, *Preaching to Convert,* 297.
8. Sedgwick, *Epistemology of the Closet,* 19.
9. See Halperin, *One Hundred Years of Homosexuality* and *How to Do the History of Homosexuality.*
10. Siebers, "Disability as Masquerade," 5.
11. Nicolosi, "Why Gays Cannot Speak for Ex-Gays." Technically, the phrase *reparative therapy* was coined by British psychologist Elizabeth Moberly in *Homosexuality: A New Christian Ethic* (1983)—some eight years prior to Nicolosi's *Reparative Therapy of Male Homosexuality: A New Clinical Approach* (1991). Though Nicolosi cites Moberly, he is largely responsible for the wide circulation of both the terminology and the clinical practice of reparative therapy.
12. Throckmorton, "Alan Chambers."
13. Nicolosi, *Reparative Therapy of Male Homosexuality,* 218.
14. Nicolosi, 200.
15. Bayer, *Homosexuality and American Psychiatry,* 39.
16. Though it's not the focus of this chapter, I would be remiss if I did not point out that the medicalization of homosexuality has long been entangled with the pathologization of gender nonconformance. Even as mainstream medical organizations, such as the APA, have stopped diagnosing nonheterosexualities as disorders, they continue to find reasons to police forms of gender variance often associated with homosexuality, such as feminine boys and masculine girls. This explains why Karl Bryant argues that the ongoing pathologization of trans experience, most recently as "gender dysphoria" in the *DSM-V,* is "one of the sites where forms of homosexuality, especially respectable homonormative forms of homosexuality, are *produced.*" "In Defense of Gay Children?," 464. That gender remains beholden to medical oversight, while sexuality does not, suggests, in part, that only a narrow range of nonheterosexual expressions are tolerated. Those sexualities that press up against cisnormativity are quickly and neatly repathologized.
17. Drescher, "Queer Diagnoses," 451.
18. Erzen, *Straight to Jesus,* 54. While there are indeed ex-gay therapies available for women, they are not nearly as popular and they lack clinical documentation. Often, reparative therapists view lesbian and bisexual women as "asexual" and their same-gender relationships as "emotionally dependent" (152).
19. Alliance for Therapeutic Choice and Scientific Integrity, "Alliance Statement on Sexual Orientation Change."
20. Alliance for Therapeutic Choice and Scientific Integrity.
21. Alliance for Therapeutic Choice and Scientific Integrity.
22. Rosik, "Sexual Attraction Fluidity Exploration in Therapy," 1.
23. It is worth noting that Alliance has recently endorsed a new clinical practice

called "the Reintegrative Protocol" that was invented by Nicolosi's son. Nicolosi Jr., "Resolving Trauma and Addiction." This new "treatment" is advertised as "a method of trauma resolution" (59) wherein "changes in sexuality are a byproduct, not the goal" (60). Perhaps as a way to bypass legislation that bans licensed therapists from practicing conversion therapy, Nicolosi Jr. explicitly denounces his father's work—"Reintegrative Therapy itself and this protocol are categorically separate from 'conversion therapy' or 'sexual orientation change efforts'" (60)—but he adopts wholesale his father's assumption that "addictive behavior," such as persistent homoerotic desire, is "a deficit-driven phenomenon" propelled into existence by childhood traumas (68). Reintegrative therapy promises to be a last ditch effort to resurrect reparative therapy. It's conversion therapy with a new coat of paint.

24. Rosik, "Sexual Attraction Fluidity Exploration in Therapy," 2.
25. Rosik, 2.
26. Alliance for Therapeutic Choice and Scientific Integrity, "Guidelines for the Practice," 7.
27. The irony, of course, is that this fluidity is only intended to go in one direction (i.e., gay→straight).
28. Erzen, *Straight to Jesus,* 218.
29. Sociologist Bernadette Barton writes that "how Bible Belt gays *identify* is less significant than how we are *perceived by others.*" *Pray the Gay Away,* 19. She goes on to explain that bisexual and homosexual identities are irrelevant so long as the individual is not "engaging in a homosexual lifestyle" (20).
30. Erzen, *Straight to Jesus,* 14.
31. Gerber, "Opposite of Gay," 10.
32. Harris, *Slouching toward Gaytheism,* 75.
33. Sedgwick, *Epistemology of the Closet,* 8.
34. Butler, "Critically Queer," 29.
35. Butler, 19.
36. Erzen, *Straight to Jesus,* 14.
37. Yarhouse and Tan, *Sexual Identity Synthesis.*
38. Snyder and Mitchell, *Cultural Locations of Disability,* 5–6.
39. Eiesland, *Disabled God,* 70.
40. Eiesland, 70–71.
41. Creamer, "Disability Theology," 340.
42. DasGupta, "Medicalization," 120.
43. Gerber, "Opposite of Gay," 18.
44. Gerber, 18.
45. Appropriating a medical model of disability to shore up a dimorphic model of (hetero)sex differentiation brings to mind the politics surrounding the pathologization of intersexuality. As Alyson K. Spurgas explains, the shift away from the language of "intersex" among clinicians and toward "disorders of sex development" (DSD) was driven by the desire to protect normative gender and sexuality. "(Un)Queering Identity." For DSD, disability functions as a rhetorical sponge to soak up the stigma attached to sex differentiation while simultaneously sparing intersex people's capacity to operate within the gender binary. As it is for ex-gays, disability is imagined by so-called medical experts and some intersex activists to be preferable over sexual and gender queerness. Framing intersexuality as a disability introduces "the idea that there may be a

physical disorder present," but it "in no way compromises normative gender identity and certainly does not compromise heteronormative sexual desire and lifestyle" (106). For both ex-gays and intersex people, disability is meant to shoulder the cisheterosexism that makes queerness undesirable.

46. Waidzunas, *Straight Line,* 25.
47. Waidzunas, 25.
48. Gerber, "Opposite of Gay," 21.
49. Alliance for Therapeutic Choice and Scientific Integrity, "Guidelines for the Practice," 12.
50. Gerber, "Opposite of Gay," 21.
51. Alliance for Therapeutic Choice and Scientific Integrity, "Three Guiding Principles."
52. Phelan, Whitehead, and Sutton, "What Research Shows," 53.
53. Phelan, Whitehead, and Sutton, 81, 85.
54. Hobbes, "Together Alone."
55. Hobbes.
56. M. Brown, "Why 'Gay Marriage.'"
57. Fletcher, *Preaching to Convert,* 4.
58. Fletcher, 3.
59. Fletcher, 23.
60. Fletcher, 266.
61. Fletcher, 283.
62. Fletcher, 18.
63. Goffman, *Stigma,* 102.
64. Goffman, 102.
65. Siebers, "Disability as Masquerade," 4.
66. Siebers, 5.
67. K. Kennedy, "'I Forgot I'm Deaf!,'" 187.
68. Siebers, "Disability as Masquerade," 8.
69. Siebers, 1.
70. Siebers, 19.
71. Siebers, 19–20.
72. Wilson and Lewiecki-Wilson, "Disability, Rhetoric, and the Body," 6.
73. Dolmage and Lewiecki-Wilson, "Refiguring Rhetorica," 27.
74. Siebers, "Disability as Masquerade," 19.
75. Selzer, "Habeas Corpus," 8.
76. Alliance for Therapeutic Choice and Scientific Integrity, "Holding Therapy Techniques."
77. Most ex-gays abbreviate this diagnosis as SSA (same-sex attraction).
78. R. Cohen, *Coming Out Straight,* xi.
79. Just the Facts Coalition, "Just the Facts"; and Boodman, "Conversion Therapist's Unusual Odyssey."
80. Erzen, *Straight to Jesus,* 92.
81. R. Cohen, *Coming Out Straight,* 10.
82. R. Cohen, 1.
83. R. Cohen, 1.
84. R. Cohen, 24.
85. As mentioned in a previous note, most ex-gay practitioners collapse gender nonconformance and homoeroticism into the same queer category. Both are

said to be wounds, addictions, or symptomatic of other underlying psychiatric disabilities or mental illnesses that affect a person's ability to maintain a healthy relationship with their gender and with people who share their gender. Alliance's website includes a "Transgender Resources" page that rehearses popular talking points among gender critical feminists, including "concerns" about the "psychological, medical, and societal risks" transitioning poses to trans people, especially children. Alliance for Therapeutic Choice and Scientific Integrity, "Transgender." The page additionally includes testimonies from people who have detransitioned, an array of articles on the pathology of trans experience, and a series of manuals instructing parents on why and how to de-trans their children. Among the few classic ex-gay texts that address trans experience is Charles W. Socarides and Abraham Freedman's edited collection *Objects of Desire: The Sexual Deviations,* which includes a final section on "Tranvestitism." In it, there are two chapters, one titled "Prehomosexual Child" and another titled "Transvestite Behavior in a Preschool Boy." Both resonate with Richard Green's *The "Sissy Boy Syndrome" and the Development of Homosexuality,* resurrecting Freud's assumption that gender variance indicates sexual immaturity, which ultimately leads to homoeroticism.

86. R. Cohen, *Coming Out Straight,* 25.
87. Wyler, *Then & Now,* 4.
88. Ponticelli, "Crafting Stories," 169–70.
89. Ponticelli, 168.
90. R. Cohen, *Coming Out Straight,* 103.
91. Ponticelli, "Crafting Stories," 168.
92. R. Cohen, *Coming Out Straight,* 104.
93. Ponticelli, "Crafting Stories," 169.
94. R. Cohen, *Coming Out Straight,* 104.
95. R. Cohen, 105.
96. Ponticelli, "Crafting Stories," 170.
97. R. Cohen, *Coming Out Straight,* 115.
98. Fletcher, *Preaching to Convert,* 265.
99. Linton, "Reassigning Meaning," 225.
100. Linton, 228.
101. Clare, *Exile and Pride,* 84.
102. Siebers, "Disability as Masquerade," 8.
103. Siebers, 20.
104. Siebers, 18.
105. Siebers, 18.
106. Perhaps my language is a bit strong here. Siebers would surely have been familiar with transabled folks who are nondisabled but feel as though they should be disabled (Baril, "Needing to Acquire") and with devotees, or disability fetishists, who occasionally feign disabilities to get closer to their fetish objects (Kafer, "Desire and Disgust"). While there is probably a lot that could be written about the fetishization of disability in ex-gay circles—how the disavowal of one form of queerness ultimately engenders another; how the castigation of same-gender desire imbues homoeroticism with a new, perverse edge; how ex-gays model a kind of pathological erotics that at once pathologizes desire and desires pathologization, etc.—I'm not doing any of that shit right now. Maybe in the next book.

107. R. Cohen, *Coming Out Straight,* 60.
108. McRuer, *Crip Theory,* 2.
109. McRuer, 2.
110. McRuer, 41.
111. McRuer, 41.
112. McRuer, 41.
113. McRuer, 37.
114. McRuer, 53.
115. McRuer, 57.
116. McRuer, 56.
117. McRuer, 53.
118. McRuer, 76.
119. McRuer, 76.
120. McRuer, 37.
121. Gerber, "Grit, Guts, and Vanilla Beans," 38.
122. Erzen, *Straight to Jesus,* 71.
123. I return to and expand on this provocation in the epilogue.
124. Siebers, "Disability as Masquerade," 7.

4. Disidentifying Silence

1. Intentionally, I leave age-related terms, such as *old, middle age,* and *young,* ambiguous. In doing so, I shift the focus of the terms away from quantifiable ages and toward the constellation of experiences that often accompany the various stages of our lives (e.g., education, career, retirement).
2. Dugan and Fabbre, *To Survive on This Shore,* 13.
3. Dugan and Fabbre, 82.
4. Stryker, *Transgender History,* 1.
5. Gallop, *Sexuality, Disability, and Aging,* 102.
6. Despite Eve Kosofsky Sedgwick introducing disidentification to queer theory in *Tendencies,* my discussion draws from Muñoz's later development of the term in *Disidentifications: Queers of Color and the Performance of Politics.*
7. Human Rights Campaign Foundation, *Transgender Visibility,* 2.
8. The It Gets Better Project was launched in 2008 as a campaign of user-uploaded videos to YouTube, all of which revolved around the alleged guarantee that queer and trans lives improve as people age. The intention behind the project was to motivate and encourage queer and trans youth, but it has received criticism for failing to address the systemic and institutionalized forms of violence that marginalize queer and trans folks at all ages. See Doyle, "Does 'It Gets Better' Make Life Better?"
9. Human Rights Campaign Foundation, *Transgender Visibility,* 4.
10. Serrano, *Whipping Girl,* 36–37.
11. See Samuels, *Fantasies of Identification.*
12. Rowling, "J. K. Rowling."
13. For instance, the trans Grindr users I cite in the chapter 2 struggle to articulate their transness without disclosing the particularities of their genitalia. Ex-gays, similarly, do not distinguish between gender and sexuality, often assuming that homoerotic desire is linked to a "gender deficit."

14. Snorton and Haritaworn, "Trans Necropolitics," 67.
15. Gill-Peterson, *Histories of the Transgender Child,* 4.
16. Gill-Peterson, 4.
17. Gill-Peterson, 35.
18. Gill-Peterson, 35.
19. Gill-Peterson, 56.
20. Meadow, *Trans Kids,* 73.
21. Meadow, 197.
22. Beauchamp, *Going Stealth,* 96.
23. Beauchamp, 96.
24. Schuller and Gill-Peterson, "Introduction," 3.
25. Schuller and Gill-Peterson, 4.
26. Schuller and Gill-Peterson, 6.
27. Halberstam, *Trans**, 53.
28. Travers, *Trans Generation,* 180.
29. Beauchamp, *Going Stealth,* 39.
30. Castañeda, "Childhood," 61.
31. Meadow, *Trans Kids,* 58.
32. Halberstam, *Trans**, 64.
33. Halberstam, 64.
34. See Ford, "Cartoon Depicts Transgender Rights."
35. Vitto and Edevane, "Photo of Young Transgender Girl."
36. Morrison, "Trans Girl's Anti-North Carolina Photo."
37. See Robertson, *Growing Up Queer.*
38. Beauchamp, *Going Stealth,* 106.
39. Beauchamp, 105.
40. Edelman, *No Future,* 3.
41. Dyer, *Queer Aesthetics of Childhood,* 48.
42. Gullette, *Aged by Culture,* 7.
43. Gullette, *Ending Ageism,* 5.
44. Gullette, 10.
45. Ippolito and Witten, "Aging," 477.
46. Beauchamp, *Going Stealth,* 31.
47. Gullette, *Aged by Culture,* 107.
48. See Rawson, "Accessing Transgender."
49. Malatino, "Future Fatigue," 644.
50. Malatino, 642.
51. Fischer, *Terrorizing Gender,* 16.
52. Malatino, "Future Fatigue," 641.
53. Barad, "Transmaterialities," 401.
54. Barad, 402.
55. Barad, 411.
56. Barad, 413.
57. Barad, 400.
58. Barad, 411.
59. Barad, 413.
60. Barad, 413.
61. Barad, 411.
62. Enke, "Education of Little Cis," 243.

63. Gullette, *Aged by Culture,* 124.
64. Gullette, 125.
65. Gullette, 143.
66. Barad, "Quantum Entanglements," 244.
67. Dugan and Fabbre, *To Survive on This Shore,* 34.
68. Snorton, *Black on Both Sides,* 74.
69. Snorton, 74.
70. Snorton, 74.
71. My understanding of mutual aid is informed by trans and disability justice organizing that not only addresses people's needs directly but also identifies those needs as effects of institutional failure and seeks to address that failure at the systemic level. Unlike charities, which tend to reinforce class, racial, and geographic hierarchies, mutual aid efforts instead "are participatory, solving problems through collective action." Spade, *Mutual Aid,* 16.
72. Ahmed, "Affinity of Hammers," 228.
73. Muñoz, *Disidentifications,* 176.
74. Muñoz, 161.
75. Muñoz, 161.
76. I use the name "Ricardo," and the attendant masculine pronouns, to reflect Sara/Ricardo's gender at the time of his death. In line with my commitment to a model of longitudinal gender that honors the flux of gender over time, I am choosing to use the most recent iteration of Ricardo's gender rather than to fall back on the transnatural assumption that he was essentially trans and, thus, a woman. I understand that the conditions surrounding Ricardo's gender during the final months of his life were not free of coercion or manipulation; nevertheless, I do not want to further undermine the agency he wielded to disidentify with those conditions.
77. Muñoz, *Disidentifications,* 163.
78. McRuer, *Crip Theory,* 124.
79. Muñoz, *Disidentifications,* 178.
80. McRuer, *Crip Theory,* 141.
81. McRuer, 145.
82. Muñoz, *Disidentifications,* 179 (emphasis added).
83. Muñoz, 170.
84. Muñoz, 179.
85. Dugan and Fabbre, *To Survive on This Shore,* 52.
86. Dugan and Fabbre, 52.
87. Muñoz, *Disidentifications,* 167.
88. Though my focus in this chapter is on trans elders' lived experiences of disability and on disability as a vector of trans pathologization, disability also plays a role in the aesthetics of aging that deserves further attention. As Sally Chivers explains, "Looking old means *being* old, which, in this discourse, means being ill. To age visibly means to admit ill health. By this logic, healthy aging is an imitation of youth and so images that reveal wrinkles suggest ill health." *Silvering Screen,* 8. I am left wondering about how much of gender plasticity is tethered to a person's perceived age, rather than their actual age, as yet another degree of separation from their embodyminded capacity to undergo medical transition. What are the aesthetics of plasticity? How are these aesthetics governed by logics of age, in addition to race, class, and disability?

And, just as important, how are these dominant aesthetics contested and accommodated by the desirability politics espoused by trans elders themselves?

89. Malatino, *Queer Embodiment,* 176.
90. Malatino, 179.
91. Clare, *Brilliant Imperfection,* 175.
92. Puar, "Bodies with New Organs," 47.
93. Halberstam, *Trans**, 60.
94. Puar, *Right to Maim,* 56.
95. Puar, 56.
96. Puar, 56.
97. Puar, 57.
98. Puar, 58, 60.
99. Clare, *Brilliant Imperfection,* 177.
100. Puar, *Right to Maim,* 60.
101. See Alexandre Baril's work for a more thorough reflection on the insufficiency of disability studies' "social model" for trans experience, including for Baril himself whose "transness has been and continues to be a debilitating and disabling component of [his] life." "Needing to Acquire," 111.
102. Puar, *Right to Maim,* 55.
103. Puar, 46.
104. Puar, 49 (emphasis added), 45.
105. Puar, 46.
106. Puar, 58.
107. Rai, "Race Racing," 73; Puar, *Right to Maim,* 58.
108. Puar, 58–59.
109. Puar, 58, 59.
110. Puar, 61.
111. Puar, 46.
112. Puar, 58.
113. It is also important to recognize that a gender transition, no matter which technologies are used to facilitate it, cannot by itself produce a transnormative subject. Transnormativity, as Snorton and Haritaworn explain, is linked to a "universalized trajectory of coming out/transition, visibility, recognition, protection, and self-actualization." "Trans Necropolitics," 67. This trajectory may be greased by a person's economic and geographic access to biomedical intervention, but it is not initiated or sustained by transitioning alone. Lest we forget: there are many trans of color, trans disabled, poor trans, and otherwise marginalized trans people who pursue gender transitions with or without formalized medical oversight. (See Spade, *Normal Life*; and Malatino, *Trans Care.*) And these folks are not suddenly imbued with "health and attendant registers of bodily prowess" following a year on testosterone, a top surgery, or a new vagina—all of which, mind you, are generally only accessible via heavily securitized and often criminalized technologies. Puar, *Right to Maim,* 49. There is something deeply concerning about portraying the transsexual as more normative (and thus more complicit with cissexism) than anyone else when transsexual people, especially transsexual women, are among the most at-risk populations to face economic precarity, medical violence, and homicide.
114. Puar, *Right to Maim,* 49.

115. Puar, 56, 50.
116. Puar, 60.
117. Riddell, "Divided Sisterhood," 154.
118. Clare, *Brilliant Imperfection,* 183.
119. Muñoz, *Disidentifications,* 179.
120. Preciado, "Pharmaco-pornographic Politics," 115.
121. Bailey, "On the Impossible."
122. Bailey.
123. Clare, *Brilliant Imperfection,* 184.
124. Dugan and Fabbre, *To Survive on This Shore,* 50.

5. Neuroqueer Intimacies

1. Sins Invalid, "Mission & Vision."
2. Sins Invalid.
3. Brennan, *Transmission of Affect,* 3.
4. Brennan, 3.
5. Hirschmann, "Queer/Fear," 141.
6. Hirschmann, 141.
7. Carastathis, "Identity Categories as Potential Coalitions," 942.
8. Carastathis, 944.
9. Kafer, *Feminist, Queer, Crip,* 150–51.
10. Kafer, 151.
11. Carastathis, "Identity Categories as Potential Coalitions," 960.
12. C. Cohen, "Punks, Bulldaggers, and Welfare Queens," 438.
13. Carastathis, *Intersectionality,* 182.
14. Nash, *Black Feminism Reimagined,* 104.
15. Nash, 6.
16. Nash, 3.
17. Nash, 26, 27.
18. Nash, 32.
19. Nash, 104.
20. Nash, 106.
21. Nash, 107.
22. Nash, 107.
23. Muñoz, *Cruising Utopia,* 32.
24. Muñoz, 25.
25. Nash, *Black Feminism Reimagined,* 107.
26. Yergeau, *Authoring Autism,* 32–33.
27. Yergeau, 71.
28. Yergeau, 84.
29. Yergeau, 84.
30. Yergeau, 86.
31. Yergeau, 86.
32. Dokumaci, "Theory of Microactivist Affordances," 493.
33. Yergeau, *Authoring Autism,* 76.
34. Siebers, "Disability as Masquerade," 17.
35. Sandahl quoted in McRuer and Johnson, "Proliferating Cripistemologies," 157.

36. Nash, *Black Feminism Reimagined,* 3.
37. Nash, 3.
38. Yergeau, *Authoring Autism,* 87.
39. Egner, "Disability Rights Community," 143.
40. Price quoted in McRuer and Johnson, "Proliferating Cripistemologies," 153.
41. Yergeau, *Authoring Autism,* 75.
42. Johnson and McRuer, "Cripistemologies," 141.
43. Clare, *Exile and Pride,* 86.
44. Cubacub, "Queercrip Dress Reform Movement Manifesto."
45. Cubacub.
46. Cubacub.
47. Cubacub.
48. Cubacub.
49. Hubrig, "Negotiating Crip Comfort," 142.
50. Cubacub, "Queercrip Dress Reform Movement Manifesto."
51. See Rebirth Garments, "Radical Visibility Collective."
52. Jackson, "Collective Making Intersectional Future-Fashion Accessible."
53. Rebirth Garments, "Radical Visibility Collective."
54. S. Johnson, "Chicago's Radical Visibility Collective."
55. S. Johnson.
56. Barthes, *Camera Lucida,* 27.
57. Barthes, 59.
58. Barthes, 59.
59. Milbrodt, "Sexy Like Us," 380.
60. Richardson, "Creative Production and the Schizophrenia Spectrum," 285.
61. Rebirth Garments, "Radical Visibility Collective."
62. Barthes, *Camera Lucida,* 59.
63. Kafer, "Crip Kin, Manifesting," 7, 13.
64. Kafer, 4.
65. Kafer, 28.
66. Kafer, 29.
67. Kafer, 27.
68. Sheppard, "I Dance Because I Can."
69. Sheppard, "Staging Bodies, Performing Ramps," 8.
70. Sheppard, 7.
71. Sheppard, 8.
72. Kleege, "What the Ramp Teaches."
73. Sheppard, "Staging Bodies, Performing Ramps," 10.
74. Shildrick, "Why Should Our Bodies End at the Skin?," 16.
75. Kafer, *Feminist, Queer, Crip,* 119.
76. Walters, *Rhetorical Touch,* 35.
77. Sheppard, "Ramp Magic."
78. Puar, *Right to Maim,* 72.
79. Sheppard, "Ramp Magic."
80. A. brown, *Pleasure Activism,* 10.
81. A. brown, 9.
82. A. brown, 3.
83. A. brown, 10.
84. Sheppard, "I Dance Because I Can."

85. Sheppard.
86. Siebers, "Sexual Culture for Disabled People," 38.
87. Gill, *Already Doing It,* 7.
88. Pickens, *Black Madness,* 29.
89. Sheppard, "I Dance Because I Can."
90. Gill, *Already Doing It,* 185.
91. Sheppard, "I Dance Because I Can."
92. A. brown, *Pleasure Activism,* 254.
93. Block et al., "Occupying Disability," 9.
94. Imada, "Decolonial Disability Studies?"
95. Imada.
96. Puar, *Right to Maim,* 16.
97. Meekosha, "Decolonising Disability," 667.
98. Puar, *Right to Maim,* 89. In the epilogue, I return to the idea of a "capacitating absence" to further complicate the relationship between debility and disability. Recent interest in the concept of debility among queer studies scholars, I argue, risks reigniting the field's legacy of disavowing disability.
99. Walker, "The Genesis of Maori Activism."
100. Dolmage, *Disabled upon Arrival,* 7.
101. Muñoz, *Disidentifications,* 176.
102. See Snorton, *Black on Both Sides*; and Tyburczy, "Leather Anatomy."
103. Soldatic and Grech, "Transnationalizing Disability Studies."
104. Ben-Moshe, "Movements at War?," 50–51.
105. Erevelles, "Thinking with Disability Studies."
106. Sins Invalid, "10 Principles of Disability Justice."
107. Vizenor, *Manifest Manners,* vii.
108. Ahmed, *What's the Use?,* 60.

Epilogue

1. Butler, "Critically Queer," 18.
2. Butler, 18.
3. Amin, *Disturbing Attachments,* 28.
4. Amin, 184.
5. Amin, 31, 184.
6. Amin, 31.
7. Amin, 188.
8. Foucault, "Nietzsche, Genealogy, History," 76.
9. Love, *Feeling Backward,* 162.
10. I owe the inspiration for this sentence to Lee Edelman's comment that among the effects of reproductive futurity is an "oblig[ation] to keep[] turning time into history." Edelman in Dinshaw et al., "Theorizing Queer Temporalities," 181.
11. Eng and Puar, "Introduction," 16.
12. Berlant, *Cruel Optimism,* 52.
13. Shahani, *Queer Retrosexualities,* 18–19.
14. Bessette, *Retroactivism in the Lesbian Archives,* 149.
15. Cvetkovich, *Archive of Feelings,* 314.

16. Halperin, *How to Do the History of Homosexuality,* 3.
17. Amin, *Disturbing Attachments,* 184.
18. Sedgwick, *Epistemology of the Closet,* 45.
19. Sedgwick, 48.
20. See Eng, Halberstam, and Muñoz, "What's Queer about Queer Studies Now?," 3.
21. Amin, *Disturbing Attachments,* 187.
22. Musser, *Sensational Flesh,* 2.
23. Butler, "Critically Queer," 19.
24. Musser, *Sensational Flesh,* 1.
25. Musser, 2.
26. Musser, 2.
27. Eng, Halberstam, and Muñoz, "What's Queer about Queer Studies Now?," 15.
28. Eng, Halberstam, and Muñoz, 15.
29. Musser, *Sensational Flesh,* 25.
30. Sedgwick, *Epistemology of the Closet,* 47.
31. Martin, "Extraordinary Homosexuals," 123.
32. Eng and Puar, "Introduction," 16.
33. Eng and Puar, 16.
34. Eng and Puar, 17.
35. Eng and Puar, 9.
36. Eng and Puar, 17, 12.
37. Eng and Puar, 15.
38. Puar, *Right to Maim,* xvii.
39. Eng and Puar, "Introduction," 17.
40. Mingus, "Moving toward the Ugly."
41. Christina Crosby and Janet R. Jakobsen introduce "a geopolitical model of disability" that interrogates not only the fallacy of independence but also the supposition that interdependence can appear as mutual independence. "Disability, Debility, and Caring Queerly," 78. They show how care is stratified across racial, class, gender, and geographic lines in such a way "that the survival of those in need of care depends on caring labor done by persons struggling to survive" (89). Disability's geopolitics expose the designation of disability as a switch point between the encouraged receipt or demanded extraction of care labor.
42. Markotić and McRuer, "Leading with Your Head," 167.
43. Puar, *Right to Maim,* 71–72.
44. See Prendergast, "On the Rhetorics of Mental Disability."
45. Shildrick, "Neoliberalism and Embodied Precarity," 597.
46. Puar, *Right to Maim,* xvii.
47. Shildrick, "Neoliberalism and Embodied Precarity," 600–01.
48. Clare, *Brilliant Imperfection,* 70.
49. Yergeau, *Authoring Autism,* 132–33.
50. See Holoyda, "Admissibility of Other Specified Paraphilic Disorder."
51. American Psychiatric Association, *Diagnostic and Statistical Manual of Mental Disorders,* 5th ed. https://doi.org/10.1176/appi.books.9780890425596.
52. The horrors of both the category of paraphilic disorders and SVP statutes far exceed the parameters of this project. For those interested in learning more, I recommend Mottier and Duschinsky, "DSM-5"; Moser, "DSM-5, Paraphilias, and the Paraphilic Disorders"; O'Donohue and Bromberg, *Sexually Violent*

Predators; and my chapter in Jonathan Alexander and Jacqueline Rhodes's forthcoming *Routledge Handbook of Queer Rhetoric* (Smilges, "Pathological Desire, Perverse Erotics").

53. Bruce, *How to Go Mad,* 34.
54. Puar, *Right to Maim,* 72.
55. Eng and Puar, "Introduction," 17.
56. Lim and Nyong'o, "Afterword," 153.
57. Eng and Puar, "Introduction," 2.
58. Eng and Puar, 5.
59. Though shame is the example I've chosen to use, it should go without saying that I welcome and encourage additional disattachment genealogies for other rejected and disappeared objects. One topic in particular that interests me (and one of the reviewers for this book) is asexuality, given its dominant representation as an absent or silent sexuality. There are important connections between asexuality and disability, upheld by both the sheer existence of asexual disabled people and the more malicious process of desexualization that feeds an ableist cultural imaginary wherein disabled people are incapable of having sexual desire or consenting to sexual activity. This latter process brings to mind the disavowal of disability in gay activism and during the institutionalization of queer studies. The parallel makes me wonder to what degree the desexualization of disability and disabled people has served as a structuring characteristic of modern sexuality itself. Eunjung Kim argues that it was certainly an important contributor. See Kim, "Asexualities and Disabilities" and "Asexuality in Disability Narratives"; also Gupta, "Asexuality and Disability."
60. Halperin and Traub, *Gay Shame,* 10.
61. Halperin and Traub, 4.
62. Love, *Feeling Backward,* 3.
63. Sedgwick, *Touching Feeling,* 37.
64. Halperin and Traub, *Gay Shame,* 11.
65. The distinction I draw here between institutionalized shame and the shame experienced outside queer studies bears some familiarity with Dana Seitler's analysis of suicidal tropes in queer literature. For her, it is both useful and important to separate out "actual acts of suicide" from "the fantasy of undoing," which, within the context of narrative, can oxymoronically function "as a tactic of survival." "Suicidal Tendencies," 606.
66. Sedgwick, *Touching Feeling,* 65.
67. Siebers, "Sex, Shame, and Disability Identity," 202.
68. Cvetkovich, *Archive of Feelings,* 308.
69. Dinshaw et al., "Theorizing Queer Temporalities," 190.
70. Halberstam, "Shame and White Gay Masculinity," 230.
71. Halberstam, 224.
72. Siebers, "Sex, Shame, and Disability Identity," 213.

Bibliography

Ahmed, Sara. "An Affinity of Hammers." In *Trap Door: Trans Cultural Production and the Politics of Visibility,* edited by Tourmaline, Eric A. Stanley, and Johanna Burton, 221–34. Cambridge, Mass.: MIT Press, 2017.

Ahmed, Sara. *Cultural Politics of Emotion.* Edinburgh: Edinburgh University Press, 2014.

Ahmed, Sara. *The Promise of Happiness.* Durham, N.C.: Duke University Press, 2010.

Ahmed, Sara. *What's the Use? On the Uses of Use.* Durham, N.C.: Duke University Press, 2019.

Aho, Tanja, Liat Ben-Moshe, and Leon J. Hilton. "Mad Futures: Affect/Theory/Violence." *American Quarterly* 69, no. 2 (2017): 291–302.

Alexander, Jonathan, and Jacqueline Rhodes. "Queer Rhetoric and the Pleasures of the Archive." *Enculturation* (2012): http://enculturation.net/queer-rhetoric-and-the-pleasures-of-the-archive.

Alliance for Therapeutic Choice and Scientific Integrity. "Guidelines for the Practice of Sexual Attraction Fluidity Exploration in Therapy." *Journal of Human Sexuality* 9 (2018).

Alliance for Therapeutic Choice and Scientific Integrity. "Alliance Statement on Sexual Orientation Change." Therapeutic Choice. January 25, 2012. https://a20ceadd-0fb7-4982-bbe2-099c8bc1e2ae.filesusr.com/ugd/ec16e9_1d6108cfa05d4a73921e0d0292c0bc91.pdf.

Alliance for Therapeutic Choice and Scientific Integrity. "'Holding Therapy Technique': Official Position Statement." Therapeutic Choice. November 2006. https://a20ceadd-0fb7-4982-bbe2-099c8bc1e2ae.filesusr.com/ugd/ec16e9_b7d4def46eda4cc29d594f7894c927e7.pdf.

Alliance for Therapeutic Choice and Scientific Integrity. "Three Guiding Principles." Therapeutic Choice. Accessed September 7, 2020, https://www.therapeuticchoice.com/three-guiding-principles.

Alliance for Therapeutic Choice and Scientific Integrity. "Transgender." Therapeutic Choice. Accessed September 7, 2020, https://www.therapeuticchoice.com/transgender.

Amin, Kadji. *Disturbing Attachments: Genet, Modern Pederasty, and Queer History.* Durham, N.C.: Duke University Press, 2017.

Aristotle. *The Rhetoric and the Poetics of Aristotle.* Translated by W. Rhys Roberts. New York: Random House, 1984.

Baggs, Mel. "In My Language." Silentmiaow. January 14, 2007. YouTube video, 8:36. https://youtu.be/JnylM1hl2jc.

Bailey, Courtney W. "On the Impossible: Disability Studies, Queer Theory, and the Surviving Crip." *Disability Studies Quarterly* 39, no. 4 (2019): http://dx.doi.org/10.18061/dsq.v39i4.6580.

Barad, Karen. "Quantum Entanglements and Hauntological Relations of Inheritance: Dis/continuities, SpaceTime Enfoldings, and Justice-to-Come." *Derrida Today* 3, no. 2 (2010): 240–68.

Barad, Karen. "Transmaterialities: Trans*/Matter/Realities and Queer Politics Imaginings." *GLQ* 21, no. 2–3 (2015): 387–422.

Baril, Alexandre. "Needing to Acquire a Physical Impairment/Disability: (Re)Thinking the Connections between Trans and Disability Studies through Transability." Translated by Catriona Lebanc. *Hypatia* 30, no. 1 (2015): 30–48.

Barthes, Roland. *Camera Lucida: Reflections on Photography.* Translated by Richard Howard. New York: Hill and Wang, 1981.

Barthes, Roland. "Rhetoric of the Image." *Visual Rhetoric in a Digital World: A Critical Sourcebook,* edited by Carolyn Handa, 152–63. Boston: Bedford/St. Martin's, 2004.

Barton, Bernadette. *Pray the Gay Away: The Extraordinary Lives of Bible Belt Gays.* New York: NYU Press, 2012.

Bayer, Ronald. *Homosexuality and American Psychiatry.* New York: Basic, 1981.

Baynton, Douglas C. "Disability and the Justification of Inequality in American History." In *The Disability Studies Reader,* edited by Lennard J. Davis, 17–33. Abingdon, U.K.: Routledge, 2013.

Beauchamp, Toby. *Going Stealth: Transgender Politics and U.S. Surveillance Practices.* Durham, N.C.: Duke University Press, 2019.

Ben-Moshe, Liat. "Movements at War? Disability and Anti-occupation Activism in Israel." In *Occupying Disability: Critical Approaches to Community, Justice, and Decolonizing Disability,* edited by Pamela Block, Devva Kasnitz, Akemi Nishida, and Nick Pollard, 47–61. New York: Springer, 2016.

Berger, James. *The Disarticulate.* New York: NYU Press, 2014.

Berlant, Lauren. *Cruel Optimism.* Durham, N.C.: Duke University Press, 2011.

Bessette, Jean. "Queer Rhetoric In Situ." *Rhetoric Review* 35, no. 2 (2016): 148–64.

Bessette, Jean. *Retroactivism in the Lesbian Archives: Composing Pasts and Futures.* Carbondale: Southern Illinois University Press, 2018.

Bishop, Amie. *Harmful Treatment: The Global Reach of So-Called Conversion Therapy.* New York: OutRight Action International, 2019.

Bitzer, Lloyd F. "The Rhetorical Situation." *Philosophy and Rhetoric* 1 (1968): 1–14.

Blackwell, Courtney, Jeremy Birnholtz, and Charles Abbott. "Seeing and Being Seen: Co-situation and Impression Formation Using Grindr, a Location-Aware Gay Dating App." *New Media & Society* 17, no. 7 (2015): 1,117–1,136, https://doi.org/10.1177/1461444814521595.

Block, Pamela, Devva Kasnitz, Akemi Nishida, and Nick Pollard. "Occupying Disability: An Introduction." In *Occupying Disability: Critical Approaches to Community, Justice, and Decolonizing Disability,* edited by Pamela Block, Devva Kasnitz, Akemi Nishida, and Nick Pollard, 3–14. New York: Springer, 2016.

Bolles, Alexandra. "More Than 70,000 Call on TLC to Cancel 'My Husband's Not Gay.'" GLAAD. January 6, 2015. www.glaad.org/blog/more-70000-call-tlc-cancel-my-husbands-not-gay.

Boodman, Sandra G. "A Conversion Therapist's Unusual Odyssey." *Washington Post,* August 16, 2005. www.washingtonpost.com/wp-dyn/content/article/2005/08/15/AR2005081501063.html.

Boyle, Casey, James J. Brown, and Steph Ceraso. "The Digital: Rhetoric Behind and Beyond the Screen." *Rhetoric Society Quarterly* 48, no. 3 (2018): 251–59.

Brennan, Teresa. *The Transmission of Affect.* Ithaca, N.Y.: Cornell University Press, 2004.

Brouwer, Dan. "The Precarious Visibility Politics of Self-Stigmatization: The Case of HIV/AIDS Tattoos." *Text and Performance Quarterly* 18, no. 2 (1998): 114–36, https://doi.org/10.1080/10462939809366216.

brown, adrienne maree. *Pleasure Activism: The Politics of Feeling Good.* Oakland, Calif.: AK Press, 2019.

Brown, Michael. "Why Gay 'Marriage' Has Not Cured Gay Loneliness." Townhall. March 5, 2017. https://townhall.com/columnists/michaelbrown/2017/03/05/why-gay-marriage-has-not-cured-gay-loneliness-n2294208.

Brown, Wendy. "In the 'Folds of Our Own Discourse': The Pleasures and Freedoms of Silence." *University of Chicago Law School Roundtable* 3, no. 1 (1996): 185–97.

Bruce, La Marr Jurelle. *How to Go Mad without Losing Your Mind: Madness and Black Radical Creativity.* Durham, N.C.: Duke University Press, 2021.

Brueggemann, Brenda Jo. *Lend Me Your Ear: Rhetorical Constructions of Deafness. Washington, D.C.:* Gallaudet University Press, 1999.

Bryant, Karl. "In Defense of Gay Children? 'Progay' Homophobia and the Production of Homonormativity." *Sexualities* 11, no. 4 (2008): 455–75.

Buehl, Jonathan. *Assembling Arguments: Multimodal Rhetoric and Scientific Discourse.* Columbia: University of South Carolina Press, 2016.

Burke, Kenneth. *Language as Symbolic Action: Essays on Life, Literature, and Method.* Oakland: University of California Press, 1966.

Butler, Judith. "Critically Queer." *GLQ* 1, no. 1 (1993): 17–32.

Butler, Judith. *Excitable Speech: A Politics of the Performative.* Abingdon, U.K.: Routledge, 1997.

Butler-Wall, Karisa. "Viral Transmissions: Safer Sex Videos, Disability, and Queer Politics." *Disability Studies Quarterly* 36, no. 4 (2016): http://dx.doi.org/10.18061/dsq.v36i4.5325.

Cameron, Nic. "How to Scruff a Trans Guy." Advocate. June 7, 2016. https://www.advocate.com/commentary/2016/6/07/how-scruff-trans-guy.

Campbell, John Edward. *Getting It On Online: Cyberspace, Gay Male Sexuality, and Embodied Identity.* New York: Harrington Park, 2004.

Campbell, Karlyn Kohrs. *Man Cannot Speak for Her: A Critical Study of Early Feminist Rhetoric.* Vol 1. New York: Praeger, 1989.

Campt, Tina M. *Listening to Images.* Durham, N.C.: Duke University Press, 2017.

Carastathis, Anna. "Identity Categories as Potential Coalitions." *Signs* 38, no. 4 (2013): 941–65.

Carastathis, Anna. *Intersectionality: Origins, Contestations, Horizons.* Lincoln: University of Nebraska Press, 2016.

cárdenas, micha. "Dark Shimmers: The Rhythm of Necropolitical Affect in Digital Media." In *Trap Door: Trans Cultural Production and the Politics of Visibility,* edited by Tourmaline, Eric A. Stanley, and Johanna Burton, 151–82. Cambridge, Mass.: MIT Press, 2017.

Castañeda, Claudia. "Childhood." *TSQ* 1, no. 1–2 (2014): 59–61.

Castiglia, Christopher, and Christopher Reed. *If Memory Serves: Gay Men, AIDS, and the Promise of the Queer Past.* Minneapolis: University of Minnesota Press, 2011.

Cedillo, Christina V. "Disabled and Undocumented: In/Visibility at the Borders of Presence, Disclosure, and Nation." *Rhetoric Society Quarterly* 50, no. 3 (2020): 203–11.

Chambers, Alan. *Leaving Homosexuality: A Practical Guide for Men and Women Looking for a Way Out.* Eugene, Ore.: Harvest House, 2009.

Chauncey, George. *Gay New York: Gender, Urban Culture, and the Making of the Gay Male World, 1890–1940.* New York: Basic Books, 1994.

Chávez, Karma R. *Queer Migration Politics: Activist Rhetoric and Coalitional Possibilities.* Urbana: University of Illinois Press, 2013.

Chen, Mel Y. *Animacies: Biopolitics, Racial Mattering, and Queer Affect.* Durham, N.C.: Duke University Press, 2012.

Cheng, Jih-Fei, Alexandra Juhasz, and Nishant Shahani. Introduction to *AIDS and the Distribution of Crises,* edited by Jih-Fei Cheng, Alexandra Juhasz, and Nishant Shahani, 1–28. Durham, N.C.: Duke University Press, 2020.

Chivers, Sally. *The Silvering Screen: Old Age and Disability in Cinema.* Toronto: University of Toronto Press, 2011.

Clare, Eli. *Brilliant Imperfection: Grappling with Cure.* Durham, N.C.: Duke University Press, 2017.

Clare, Eli. *Exile and Pride: Disability, Queerness and Liberation.* Vol. 10. Cambridge, Mass.: South End Press, 2009.

Clarke, Michael Tavel. "Disability, Spectatorship, and *The Station Agent.*" *Disability Studies Quarterly* 34, no. 1 (2014): http://dx.doi.org/10.18061/dsq.v34i1.3310.

Cohen, Cathy. "Punks, Bulldaggers, and Welfare Queens: The Radical Potential of Queer Politics?" *GLQ* 3 (1997): 437–65.

Cohen, Jeffrey Jerome. "Queer Crip Sex and Critical Mattering." *GLQ* 21, no. 1 (2015): 153–62.

Cohen, Richard. *Coming Out Straight: Understanding and Healing Homosexuality.* Winchester, Virginia: Oakhill, 2000.

Creamer, Deborah Beth. "Disability Theology." *Religion Compass* 6, no. 7 (2012): 339–46.

Crosby, Christina, and Janet R. Jakobsen. "Disability, Debility, and Caring Queerly." *Social Text* 38, no. 4 (2020): 77–103.

Cubacub, Sky. "A Queercrip Dress Reform Movement Manifesto." Rebirth Garments. 2015. http://rebirthgarments.com/radical-visibility-zine.

Cvetkovich, Ann. *An Archive of Feelings: Trauma, Sexuality, and Lesbian Public Cultures.* Durham, N.C.: Duke University Press, 2003.

DasGupta, Sayantani. "Medicalization." In *Keywords for Disability Studies,* edited by Rachel Adams, Benjamin Reiss, and David Serlin, 120–21. New York: NYU Press, 2015.

Davis, Diane. *Inessential Solidarity: Rhetoric and Foreigner Relations.* Pittsburgh: University of Pittsburgh Press, 2010.

DeafBuzzy. "Man Reveals the Shocking Abuse He Receives on Grindr for Being Deaf—PinkNews." DeafBuzzy. September 19, 2019. https://deafbuzzy.com/2019/09/13/man-reveals-the-shocking-abuse-he-receives-on-grindr-for-being-deaf-pinknews/ (site inactive).

Dean, Tim. *Unlimited Intimacy: Reflections on the Subculture of Barebacking.* Chicago: University of Chicago Press, 2009.

de Certeau, Michel. *The Practice of Everyday Life.* Oakland: University of California Press, 2011.

D'Emilio, John, and Estelle B. Freedman. *Intimate Matters: A History of Sexuality in America.* 3rd ed. Chicago: University of Chicago Press, 2012.

Derrida, Jacques. *Writing and Difference.* Chicago: University of Chicago Press, 1978.

Diedrich, Lisa. *Indirect Action: Schizophrenia, Epilepsy, AIDS, and the Course of Health Activism.* Minneapolis: University of Minnesota Press, 2016.

Dinshaw, Carolyn, Lee Edelman, Roderick A. Ferguson, Carla Freccero, Elizabeth Freeman, Jack Halberstam, Annamarie Jagose, Christopher S. Nealon, and Tan Hoang Nguyen. "Theorizing Queer Temporalities: A Roundtable Discussion." *GLQ* 13, no. 2–3 (2007): 177–95.

Dokumaci, Arseli. "A Theory of Microactivist Affordances: Disability, Disorientations, and Improvisations." *South Atlantic Quarterly* 118, no. 3 (2019): 491–519.

Dolmage, Jay Timothy. *Disability Rhetoric.* Syracuse, N.Y.: Syracuse University Press, 2014.

Dolmage, Jay Timothy. *Disabled upon Arrival: Eugenics, Immigration, and the Construction of Race and Disability.* Columbus: Ohio State University Press, 2018.

Dolmage, Jay Timothy, and Cynthia Lewiecki-Wilson. "Refiguring Rhetorica: Linking Feminist Rhetoric and Disability Studies." In *Rhetorica in Motion: Feminist Rhetorical Methods & Methodologies,* edited by Eileen E. Schell and K. J. Rawson, 23–38. Pittsburgh: University of Pittsburgh Press, 2010.

Doyle, Sady. "Does 'It Gets Better' Make Life Better for Gay Teens?" *Atlantic,* October 7, 2010. https://www.theatlantic.com/entertainment/archive/2010/10/does-it-gets-better-make-life-better-for-gay-teens/64184/.

Drescher, Jack. "Queer Diagnoses: Parallels and Contrasts in the History of Homosexuality, Gender Variance, and the Diagnostic and Statistical Manual." *Archive of Sexual Behavior* 39 (2010): 427–60.

Driskill, Qwo-Li, Chris Finley, Brian Joseph Gilley, and Scott Lauria Morgensen, eds. *Queer Indigenous Studies: Critical Interventions in Theory, Politics, and Literature.* Tucson: University of Arizona Press, 2011.

Dugan, Jess T., and Vanessa Fabbre. *To Survive on This Shore: Photographs and Interviews with Transgender and Gender Nonconforming Older Adults.* Heidelberg, Germany: Kehrer, 2018.

Duggan, Lisa. *The Twilight of Equality? Neoliberalism, Cultural Politics, and the Attack on Democracy.* Boston: Beacon, 2003.

Dyer, Hannah. *The Queer Aesthetics of Childhood: Asymmetries of Innocence and the Cultural Politics of Child Development.* New Brunswick, N.J.: Rutgers University Press, 2020.

Edelman, Lee. *No Future: Queer Theory and the Death Drive.* Durham, N.C.: Duke University Press, 2004.

Egner, Justine E. "'The Disability Rights Community Was Never Mine': Neuroqueer Disidentification." *Gender & Society* 33, no. 1 (2019): 123–47.

Eiesland, Nancy L. *The Disabled God: Toward a Liberatory Theology of Disability.* Nashville, Tenn.: Abingdon Press, 1994.

Eng, David L. *The Feeling of Kinship: Queer Liberalism and the Racialization of Intimacy.* Durham, N.C.: Duke University Press, 2010.

Eng, David L., Jack Halberstam, and José Esteban Muñoz. "What's Queer about Queer Studies Now?" *Social Text* 23, no. 3–4 (2005): 1–17.

Eng, David L., and Jasbir K. Puar. "Introduction: Left of Queer." *Social Text* 38, no. 4 (2020): 1–23.

Enke, A. Finn. "The Education of Little Cis: Cisgender and the Discipline of Opposing." *The Transgender Studies Reader 2,* edited by Susan Stryker and Aren Z. Aizura, 234–47. Abingdon, U.K.: Routledge, 2015.

Erevelles, Nirmala. "Thinking with Disability Studies." *Disability Studies Quarterly* 34, no. 2 (2014): http://dx.doi.org/10.18061/dsq.v34i2.4248.

Erzen, Tanya. *Straight to Jesus: Sexual and Christian Conversions in the Ex-Gay Movement.* Berkeley: University of California Press, 2006.

Every, Jace. Interview by Arisce Wanzer. "A Trans Guy and a Femme Guy Swap Profiles on Grindr: What the Flip Season 2 Ep 5." Grindr. January 29, 2019. YouTube video, 18:14. https://www.youtube.com/watch?v=OnahTm_-pyY&t=557s.

Faris, Michael J. "Queering Networked Writing: A Sensory Autoethnography of Desire and Sensation on Grindr." *Re/Orienting Writing Studies: Queer Methods, Queer Projects,* edited by William P. Banks, Matthew B. Cox, and Caroline Dadas, 127–49. Logan: Utah State University Press, 2019.

Ferguson, Roderick. *Aberrations in Black: Toward a Queer of Color Critique.* Minneapolis: University of Minnesota Press, 2003.

Finkelstein, Avram. *After Silence: A History of AIDS through Its Images.* Oakland: University of California Press, 2018.

Finnegan, Cara A. "Doing Rhetorical History of the Visual: The Photograph and the Archive." In *Defining Visual Rhetorics,* edited by Charles A. Hill and Marguerite Helmers, 195–214. Mahwah, N.J.: Lawrence Erlbaum Associates, 2004.

Fischel, Joseph J. *Sex and Harm in the Age of Consent.* Minneapolis: University of Minnesota Press, 2016.

Fischel, Joseph J., and Hilary O'Connell. "Cripping Consent: Autonomy and Access." In *Screw Consent: A Better Politics of Sexual Justice,* by Joseph J. Fischel, 135–71. Oakland: University of California Press, 2019.

Fischer, Mia. *Terrorizing Gender: Transgender Visibility and the Surveillance Practices of the U.S. Security State.* Lincoln: University of Nebraska Press, 2019.

Flatley, Jonathan. *Affective Mapping: Melancholia and the Politics of Modernism.* Cambridge, Mass.: Harvard University Press, 2009.

Fletcher, John. *Preaching to Convert: Evangelical Outreach and Performance Activism in a Secular Age.* Ann Arbor: University of Michigan Press, 2013.

Ford, Rachel. "Cartoon Depicts Transgender Rights as a Threat to Women and Children." Friendly Atheist. March 1, 2016. https://friendlyatheist.patheos.com/2016/03/01/cartoon-depicts-transgender-rights-as-a-threat-to-women-and-children/.

Foucault, Michel. *The History of Sexuality.* Vol. 1, *An Introduction.* New York: Knopf Doubleday, 2012.

Foucault, Michel. "Nietzsche, Genealogy, History." In *The Foucault Reader,* edited by Paul Rabinow, 76–100. New York: Pantheon, 1984.

Fraser, Vikki. "Queer Closets and Rainbow Hyperlinks: The Construction and Constraint of Queer Subjectivities Online." *Sexuality Research and Social Policy* 7, no. 1 (2010): 30–36, https://doi.org/10.1007/s13178-010-0006-1.

Galassi, Josh. "Should I Include That I Am Disabled in My Dating Profile?" Queerty. September 17, 2017. https://www.queerty.com/include-disabled-dating-profile-20170917.

Gallop, Jane. *Sexuality, Disability, and Aging: Queer Temporalities of the Phallus.* Durham, N.C.: Duke University Press, 2019.

Garland-Thomson, Rosemarie. *Staring: How We Look.* Oxford: Oxford University Press, 2009.

Gerber, Lynne. "Grit, Guts, and Vanilla Beans: Godly Masculinity in the Ex-Gay Movement." *Gender and Society* 29, no. 1 (2015): 26–50.

Gerber, Lynne. "The Opposite of Gay: Nature, Creation, and Queerish Ex-Gay Experiments." *Nova Religio: The Journal of Alternative and Emergent Religions* 11, no. 4 (2008): 8–30.

Gill, Michael. *Already Doing It: Intellectual Disability and Sexual Agency.* Minneapolis: University of Minnesota Press, 2015.

Gill-Peterson, Jules. "Haunting the Queer Spaces of AIDS: Remembering ACT UP/New York and an Ethics for an Endemic." *GLQ* 19, no. 3 (2013): 279–300.

Gill-Peterson, Jules. *Histories of the Transgender Child.* Minneapolis: University of Minnesota Press, 2018.

Glenn, Cheryl. *Rhetorical Feminism and This Thing Called Hope.* Carbondale: Southern Illinois University Press, 2018.

Glenn, Cheryl. *Unspoken: A Rhetoric of Silence.* Carbondale: Southern Illinois University Press, 2004.

Glenn, Cheryl, and Andrea Lunsford. "Rhetoric and Feminism." In *The Oxford Handbook of Rhetorical Studies,* edited by Michael J. MacDonald, 583–98. Oxford: Oxford University Press, 2014.

Glenn, Cheryl, and Krista Ratcliffe. *Silence and Listening as Rhetorical Arts.* Carbondale: Southern Illinois University, 2011.

Goffman, Erving. *Stigma: Notes on the Management of Spoiled Identity.* New York: Simon & Schuster, 1963.

Gorman, Rachel. "Quagmires of Affect: Madness, Labor, Whiteness, and Ideological Disavowal." *American Quarterly* 69, no. 2 (2017): 309–13.

Gosine, Andil. "Brown to Blonde at Gay.com: Passing White in Queer Cyberspace." In *Queer Online: Media, Technology, & Sexuality,* edited by Kate O'Riordan and David J. Phillips, 139–53. New York: Peter Lang, 2007.

Gould, Deborah. *Moving Politics: Emotion and ACT UP's Fight against AIDS.* Chicago: University of Chicago Press, 2009.

Green, Richard. *The "Sissy Boy Syndrome" and the Development of Homosexuality.* New Haven, Conn.: Yale University Press, 1987.

Grindr LLC. Grindr. Apple App Store, v. 7.15.2. Grindr LLC, 2021.

Grindstaff, Davin Allen. *Rhetorical Secrets: Mapping Gay Identity and Queer Resistance in Contemporary America.* Tuscaloosa: University of Alabama Press, 2006.

Gullette, Margaret Morganroth. *Aged by Culture.* Chicago: University of Chicago Press, 2004.

Gullette, Margaret Morganroth. *Ending Ageism, or How Not to Shoot Old People.* New Brunswick, N.J.: Rutgers University Press, 2017.

Gupta, Kristina. "Asexuality and Disability: Mutual Negation in *Adams v. Rice* and New Directions for Coalition Building." In *Asexualities: Feminist and Queer Perspectives,* edited by Karli June Cerankowski and Megan Milks, 551–86. New Brunswick, N.J.: Routledge, 2014.

Halberstam, Jack. *Female Masculinity.* Durham, N.C.: Duke University Press, 1998.

Halberstam, Jack. *The Queer Art of Failure.* Durham, N.C.: Duke University Press, 2011.

Halberstam, Jack. "Shame and White Gay Masculinity." *Social Text* 23, no. 3–4 (2005): 219–33.

Halberstam, Jack. *Trans*: A Quick and Quirky Account of Gender Variability.* Oakland: University of California Press, 2018.

Halperin, David. *How to Do the History of Homosexuality.* Chicago: University of Chicago Press, 2002.

Halperin, David. *One Hundred Years of Homosexuality: The New Ancient World and Other Essays on Greek Love.* Abingdon, U.K.: Routledge, 1990.

Halperin, David, and Valerie Traub, eds. *Gay Shame.* Chicago: University of Chicago Press, 2009.

Harris, W. C. *Slouching toward Gaytheism: Christianity and Queer Survival in America.* New York: SUNY Press, 2014.

Hatfield, Joe Edward. "The Queer Kairotic: Digital Transgender Suicide Memories and Ecological Rhetorical Agency." *Rhetoric Society Quarterly* 49, no. 1 (2019): 25–48.

Hawhee, Debra. *Rhetoric in Tooth and Claw: Animals, Language, Sensation.* Chicago: University of Chicago Press, 2016.

Hawhee, Debra. "Toward a Bestial Rhetoric." *Philosophy & Rhetoric* 44, no. 1 (2011): 81–87.

Hepple, Josh. "If You're a Disabled, Gay Twentysomething, Grindr Is a Godsend." *Guardian,* December 1, 2016. https://www.theguardian.com/commentisfree/2016/dec/01/disabled-gay-twentysomething-grindr-cerebral-palsy.

Herring, Scott. *Another Country: Queer Anti-urbanism.* New York: NYU Press, 2010.

Hirschmann, Nancy J. "Queer/Fear: Disability, Sexuality, and the Other." *Journal of Medical Humanities* 34 (2013): 139–47.

Hobbes, Michael. "Together Alone: The Epidemic of Gay Loneliness." Huffington Post. March 2, 2017. https://highline.huffingtonpost.com/articles/en/gay-loneliness/.

Hodgson, Justin. *Post-Digital Rhetoric and the New Aesthetic.* Columbus: Ohio State University Press, 2019.

Holland, Sharon Patricia. *The Erotic Life of Racism.* Durham, N.C.: Duke University Press, 2012.

Holoyda, Brian. "The Admissibility of Other Specified Paraphilic Disorder (Non-consent) in Sexually Violent Predator Proceedings." *Behavioral Sciences & the Law* 38 (2020): 173–85.

Hubrig, Adam. "Negotiating Crip Comfort: Dispatches from My (Involuntarily) Subversive Wardrobe." *Journal of Multimodal Rhetorics* 3, no. 2 (2020): 140–53.

Huffer, Lynne. *Are the Lips a Grave? A Queer Feminist on the Ethics of Sex.* New York: Columbia University Press, 2013.

Human Rights Campaign Foundation. *Transgender Visibility: A Guide to Being You.* Washington, D.C.: HRC, 2014.

Imada, Adria L. "A Decolonial Disability Studies?" *Disability Studies Quarterly* 37, no. 2 (2017): http://dx.doi.org/10.18061/dsq.v37i3.5984.

Ingraham, Chris. "Energy: Rhetoric's Vitality." *Rhetoric Society Quarterly* 48, no. 3 (2018): 260–68.

Ippolito, Joe, and Tarynn M. Witten. "Aging." In *Trans Bodies, Trans Selves: A Resource for the Transgender Community,* edited by Laura Erickson-Schroth, 476–97. Oxford: Oxford University Press, 2014.

Izard, Carroll. *Human Emotions.* New York: Springer US, 1977.

Jackson, Jhoni. "The Collective Making Intersectional Future-Fashion Accessible to All." *Paper,* April 23, 2018. https://www.papermag.com/radical-visibility-collective-2562641347.html.

Johnson, E. Patrick, ed. *No Tea, No Shade: New Writings in Black Queer Studies.* Durham, N.C.: Duke University Press, 2016.

Johnson, Jenell. "Breaking Down: On Publicity as Capacity." *Rhetoric Society Quarterly* 50, no. 3 (2020): 175–83.

Johnson, Jenell, and Krista Kennedy. "Introduction: Disability, In/Visibility, and Risk." *Rhetoric Society Quarterly* 50, no. 3 (2020): 161–65.

Johnson, Merri Lisa, and Robert McRuer. "Cripistemologies: Introduction." *Journal of Literary & Cultural Disability Studies* 8, no. 2 (2014): 127–47.

Johnson, Sunni. "Chicago's Radical Visibility Collective Return for Their Second Showcase." *Wussy,* September 9, 2019. https://www.wussymag.com/all/2019/9/9/chicagos-radical-visibility-collective-return-for-their-second-showcase.

Jones, Cleve. "A Vision of the Quilt." In *Remembering the AIDS Quilt,* edited by Charles E. Morris III, xi–xxxvi. East Lansing: Michigan State University Press, 2011.

Jones, Owen. "No Asians, No Black People: Why Do Gay People Tolerate Blatant Racism?" *Guardian,* November 24, 2016. https://www.theguardian.com/commentisfree/2016/nov/24/no-asians-no-blacks-gay-people-racism.

Just the Facts Coalition. "Just the Facts about Sexual Orientation and Youth: A Primer for Principals, Educators, and School Personnel." Washington, D.C.: American Psychological Association, 2008. https://www.apa.org/pi/lgbt/resources/just-the-facts.

Kafer, Alison. "Crip Kin, Manifesting." *Catalyst* 5, no. 1 (2019): 1–37.

Kafer, Alison. "Desire and Disgust: My Ambivalent Adventures in Devoteeism." In *Sex and Disability,* edited by Robert McRuer and Anna Mollow, 331–54. Durham, N.C.: Duke University Press, 2012.

Kafer, Alison. *Feminist, Queer, Crip.* Bloomington: Indiana University Press, 2013.

Kameny, Franklin E. "Does Research into Homosexuality Matter?" *Ladder: A Lesbian Review* 9, no. 8 (1965): 14–20.

Kennedy, George A. "A Hoot in the Dark: The Evolution of General Rhetoric." *Philosophy & Rhetoric* 25, no. 1 (1992): 1–21.

Kennedy, Krista. "'I Forgot I'm Deaf!': Passing, Kairotic Space, and the Midcentury Cyborg Woman." *Rhetoric Society Quarterly* 50, no. 3 (2020): 184–93.

Kim, Eunjung. "Asexualities and Disabilities in Constructing Sexual Normalcy." In *Asexualities: Feminist and Queer Perspectives,* edited by Karli June Cerankowski and Megan Milks, 484–550. Abingdon, U.K.: Routledge, 2014.

Kim, Eunjung. "Asexuality in Disability Narratives." *Sexualities* 14, no. 4 (2011): 479–93.

Kittay, Eva Feder. *Love's Labor: Essays on Women, Equality and Dependency.* Abingdon, U.K.: Taylor & Francis, 2020.

Kleege, Georgina. "What the Ramp Teaches." Alice Sheppard (website). June 18, 2018. http://alicesheppard.com/what-the-ramp-teaches-by-georgina-kleege/.

Koyama, Emi. "The Transfeminist Manifesto." In *Catching a Wave: Reclaiming Feminism for the 21st Century,* edited by Rory Dicker and Alison Piepmeier, 244–62. Boston: Northeastern University Press, 2003.

Kramer, Larry. "1,112 and Counting." *New York Native,* March 14–27, 1983.

Kunzel, Regina. "Queer History, Mad History, and the Politics of Health." *American Quarterly* 69, no. 2 (2017): 315–19.

Lim, Eng-Beng, and Tavia Nyong'o. "Afterword: Queer Reconstellations." *Social Text* 38, no. 4 (2020): 149–56.

Linton, Simi. "Reassigning Meaning." *Disability Studies Reader,* edited by Lennard J. Davis, 223–36. Abingdon, U.K.: Routledge, 2010.

Lorenzo, Anthony. "On Being Black and Gay." HuffPost UK. October 16, 2016. https://www.huffingtonpost.co.uk/anthony-lorenzo-/on-being-black-and-gay_b_8302598.html?guccounter=1.

Love, Heather. "Doing Being Deviant: Deviance Studies, Description, and the Queer Ordinary." *differences* 26, no. 1 (2015): 74–95.

Love, Heather. *Feeling Backward: Loss and the Politics of Queer History.* Cambridge, Mass.: Harvard University Press, 2007.

Lugones, María. *Pilgrimages/Peregrinajes: Theorizing Coalition against Multiple Oppressions.* Lanham, Md.: Rowman & Littlefield, 2003.

Malatino, Hil. "Future Fatigue: Trans Intimacies and Trans Presents (or How to Survive the Interregnum)." *Trans Studies Quarterly* 6, no. 4 (2019): 635–58.

Malatino, Hil. *Queer Embodiment: Monstrosity, Medical Violence, and Intersex Experience.* Lincoln: University of Nebraska Press, 2019.

Malatino, Hil. *Trans Care.* Minneapolis: University of Minnesota Press, 2020.

Malhotra, Sheena, and Aimee Carrillo Rowe, eds. *Silence, Feminism, Power: Reflections at the Edges of Sound.* London: Palgrave Macmillan, 2013.

Manning, Erin. *The Minor Gesture.* Durham, N.C.: Duke University Press, 2016.

Markotić, Nicole, and Robert McRuer. "Leading with Your Head: On the Borders of Disability, Sexuality, and the Nation." In *Sex and Disability,* edited by Robert McRuer and Anna Mollow, 165–82. Durham, N.C.: Duke University Press, 2012.

Martin, Biddy. "Extraordinary Homosexuals and the Fear of Being Ordinary." *differences* 6, no. 2–3 (1994): 100–25.

Massumi, Brian. *Parables for the Virtual: Movement, Affect, Sensation.* Durham, N.C.: Duke University Press, 2002.

Massumi, Brian. *Politics of Affect.* Cambridge: Polity, 2015.

McGlotten, Shaka. *Virtual Intimacies: Media, Affect, and Queer Sociality.* Albany: SUNY Press, 2013.

McRuer, Robert. *Crip Theory: Cultural Signs of Queerness and Disability.* New York: NYU Press, 2006.

McRuer, Robert. "Disabling Sex: Notes for a Crip Theory of Sexuality." *GLQ* 17, no. 1 (2011): 107–17.

McRuer, Robert. "Shameful Sites: Locating Queerness and Disability." In *Gay Shame,* edited by David M. Halperin and Valerie Traub, 181–87. Chicago: University of Chicago Press, 2009.

McRuer, Robert, and Merri Lisa Johnson. "Proliferating Cripistemologies: A Virtual Roundtable." *Journal of Literary & Cultural Disability Studies* 8, no. 2 (2014): 149–69.

Meadow, Tey. *Trans Kids: Being Gendered in the Twenty-First Century.* Oakland: University of California Press, 2018.

Meekosha, Helen. "Decolonising Disability: Thinking and Acting Globally." *Disability & Society* 26, no. 6 (2011): 667–82.

Milbrodt, Teresa. "Sexy like Us: Expanding Notions of Disability and Sexuality through Burlesque Performance." *Journal of Literary & Cultural Disability Studies* 13, no. 4 (2019): 377–92.

Mingus, Mia. "Moving toward the Ugly: A Politic beyond Desirability." *Leaving Evidence* (blog). August 22, 2011. https://leavingevidence.wordpress.com/2011/08/22/moving-toward-the-ugly-a-politic-beyond-desirability/.

Minich, Julie Avril. "Enabling Whom? Critical Disability Studies Now." *Lateral* 5, no. 1 (2016): https://doi.org/10.25158/L5.1.9.

Minton, Henry L. *Departing from Deviance: A History of Homosexual Rights and Emancipatory Science in America.* Chicago: University of Chicago Press, 2001.

Mintz, Susannah B. "Invisibility." In *Keywords for Disability Studies,* edited by Rachel Adams, Benjamin Reiss, and David Serlin, 113. New York: NYU Press, 2015.

Moberly, Elizabeth R. *Homosexuality: A New Christian Ethic.* Guernsey, U.K.: Guernsey Press, 1983.

Molldrem, Stephen. "Beyond the Depathologization of Homosexuality: Reframing Evelyn Hooker as a Boundary Shifter in Twentieth-Century US Sex Research." *Journal of the History of Sexuality* 30, no. 1 (2021): 48–91.

Morrison, Aaron. "Trans Girl's Anti–North Carolina Photo Goes Viral for All the Wrong Reasons." *Yahoo! News,* April 18, 2016. https://news.yahoo.com/trans-girls-anti-north-carolina-143400175.html.

Moser, Charles. "DSM-5, Paraphilias, and the Paraphilic Disorders: Confusion Reigns." *Archives of Sexual Behavior* 48 (2019): 681–89.

Mottier, Véronique, and Robbie Duschinsky, eds. "DSM-5: Classifying Sex." Introduction to special section. *Archives of Sexual Behavior* 44 (2015): 1,087–90.

Mowlabocus, Sharif. *Gaydar Culture: Gay Men, Technology and Embodiment in the Digital Age.* Farnham, U.K.: Ashgate, 2010.

Muckelbauer, John, and Debra Hawhee. "Posthuman Rhetorics: 'It's the Future, Pikul.'" *JAC* 20, no. 4 (2000): 767–74.

Muñoz, José Esteban. *Cruising Utopia: The Then and There of Queer Futurity.* New York: NYU Press, 2009.

Muñoz, José Esteban. *Disidentifications: Queers of Color and the Performance of Politics.* Minneapolis: University of Minnesota Press, 1999.

Murray, Joddy. *Non-discursive Rhetoric: Image and Affect in Multimodal Composition.* Albany: SUNY Press, 2009.

Musser, Amber Jamilla. *Sensational Flesh: Race, Power, and Masochism.* New York: NYU Press, 2014.

Namaste, Vivian K. *Invisible Lives: The Erasure of Transsexual and Transgendered People.* Chicago: University of Chicago Press, 2000.

Nash, Jennifer C. *Black Feminism Reimagined: After Intersectionality.* Durham, N.C.: Duke University Press, 2019.

Nealon, Christopher. *Foundlings: Lesbian and Gay Historical Emotion Before Stonewall.* Durham, N.C.: Duke University Press, 2001.

Nicolosi, Joseph. *Reparative Therapy of Male Homosexuality: A New Clinical Approach.* Lanham, Md.: Rowman & Littlefield, 1991.

Nicolosi, Joseph. "Why Gays Cannot Speak for Ex-Gays." Exgay Calling. June 7, 2017. https://exgaycalling.com/2017/07/06/why-gays-cannot-speak-for-ex-gays/.

Nicolosi, Joseph, Jr. "Resolving Trauma and Addiction: The Reintegrative Protocol™." *Journal of Human Sexuality* 9 (2018): 59–73.

O'Donohue, William T., and Daniel S. Bromberg, eds. *Sexually Violent Predators: A Clinical Science Handbook.* New York: Springer, 2019.

Olson, Lester C., Cara A. Finnegan, and Diane S. Hope. "Visual Rhetoric in Communication: Continuing Question and Contemporary Issues." In *Visual Rhetoric: A Reader in Communication and American Culture,* edited by Lester C. Olson, Cara A. Finnegan, and Diane S. Hope, 1–14. Thousand Oaks, Calif.: SAGE, 2008.

Ommen, Brett. *The Politics of the Superficial: Visual Rhetorics and the Protocol of Display.* Tuscaloosa: University of Alabama Press, 2016.

O'Toole, Corbett Joan. *Fading Scars: My Queer Disability History.* Fort Worth, Texas: Autonomous, 2015.

Patton, Cindy. “Foreword.” *AIDS and the Distribution of Crises,* edited by Jih-Fei Cheng, Alexandra Juhasz, and Nishant Shahani, vii–xvi. Durham, N.C.: Duke University Press, 2020.

Phelan, James E., Neil Whitehead, and Philip M. Sutton. “What Research Shows: NARTH's Response to the APA Claims on Homosexuality.” *Journal of Human Sexuality* 1 (2009): 1–121.

Pickens, Therí Alyce. *Black Madness :: Mad Blackness.* Durham, N.C.: Duke University Press, 2019.

Piepzna-Samarasinha, Leah Lakshmi. *Care Work: Dreaming Disability Justice.* Vancouver, B.C.: Arsenal Pulp, 2018.

Ponticelli, Christy M. “Crafting Stories of Sexual Identity Reconstruction.” *Social Psychology Quarterly* 62, no. 2 (1999): 157–72.

Potts, Morgan. “Navigating Grindr as a Non-binary Trans Boy.” *Nope Book: Online Feminist Lifestyle Magazine,* August 19, 2017. http://www.thenopebook.com/lifestyle/trans-boy-grindr/.

Prahlad, Anand. *The Secret Life of a Black Aspie: A Memoir.* Fairbanks: University of Alaska Press, 2017.

Preciado, Paul. “Pharmaco-pornographic Politics: Towards a New Gender Ecology.” *Parallax* 14, no. 1 (2008): 105–17.

Prendergast, Catherine. “On the Rhetorics of Mental Disability.” In *Embodied Rhetorics: Disability in Language and Culture,* edited by James C. Wilson and Cynthia Lewiecki-Wilson, 45–60. Carbondale: Southern Illinois University Press, 2001.

Pritchard, Eric Darnell. *Fashioning Lives: Black Queers and the Politics of Literacy.* Carbondale: Southern Illinois University Press, 2016.

Propen, Amy D. *Locating Visual-Material Rhetorics: The Map, the Mill, and the GPS.* Anderson, S.C.: Parlor, 2012.

Puar, Jasbir K. “Bodies with New Organs: Becoming Trans, Becoming Disabled.” *Social Text* 33, no. 3 (2015): 45–73.

Puar, Jasbir K. *The Right to Maim: Debility, Capacity, Disability.* Durham, N.C.: Duke University Press, 2017.

Rai, Amit S. “Race Racing: Four Theses on Race and Intensity.” *Women's Studies Quarterly* 40, no. 1–2 (2012): 64–75.

Rand, Erin J. *Reclaiming Queer: Activist and Academic Rhetorics of Resistance.* Tuscaloosa: University of Alabama Press, 2014.

Rawson, K. J. “Accessing Transgender // Desiring Queer(er?) Archival Logics.” *Archivaria* 68 (2009): 123–40.

Rebirth Garments. “Radical Visibility Collective.” http://rebirthgarments.com/radical-visibility-collective.

Rhodes, Jacqueline. “Becoming Utopias: Toward a Queer Rhetoric of Instantiation.” In *Making Future Matters,* edited by Rick Wysocki and Mary P. Sheridan. Logan, Utah: Computers and Composition Digital

Press, 2018. https://ccdigitalpress.org/book/makingfuturematters/rhodes-intro.html.
Rice, Jenny. "Unframing Models of Public Distribution: From Rhetorical Situation to Rhetorical Ecologies." *Rhetoric Society Quarterly* 35, no. 4 (2005): 5–24.
Richardson, Jennifer (Eisenhauer). "Creative Production and the Schizophrenia Spectrum: The Politics and Rhetorics of Inclusion." *Journal of Literary & Cultural Disability Studies* 13, no. 3 (2019): 273–87.
Rickert, Thomas. *Ambient Rhetoric: The Attunements of Rhetorical Being.* Pittsburgh: University of Pittsburgh Press, 2013.
Riddell, Carol. "Divided Sisterhood: A Critical Review of Janice Raymond's *The Transsexual Empire.*" In *The Transgender Studies Reader,* edited by Susan Stryker and Stephen Whittle, 144–58. Abingdon, U.K.: Routledge, 2006.
Robertson, Mary. *Growing Up Queer: Kids and the Remaking of LGBTQ Identity.* New York: NYU Press, 2019.
Rodriguez, Mathew. "The One Brutal Truth Every White Gay Man Needs to Hear." Mic. June 17, 2016. https://www.mic.com/articles/144985/here-s-one-brutal-truth-every-white-gay-man-needs-to-hear.
Rodriguez-Jimenez, Jorge. "Is *My Husband's Not Gay* an Ad for the 'Ex-Gay' Industry?" *Advocate,* January 6, 2015. https://www.advocate.com/arts-entertainment/television/2015/01/06/my-husbands-not-gay-ad-ex-gay-industry.
Román, David. "Not-about-AIDS." *GLQ* 6, no. 1 (2000): 1–28.
Rosik, Christopher. "Sexual Attraction Fluidity Exploration in Therapy (SAFE-T): Creating a Clearer Impression of Professional Therapies That Allow for Change." Alliance for Therapeutic Choice and Scientific Integrity. May 27, 2016. https://www.therapeuticchoice.com/why-the-alliance-supports-safe-ther.
Ross, Marlon B. "Beyond the Closet: As Raceless Paradigm." In *Black Queer Studies: A Critical Anthology,* edited by E. Patrick Johnson and Mae G. Henderson, 161–89. Durham, N.C.: Duke University Press, 2005.
Rowling, J. K. "J. K. Rowling Writes about Her Reasons for Speaking Out on Sex and Gender Issues." J. K. Rowling (website). June 10, 2020. https://www.jkrowling.com/opinions/j-k-rowling-writes-about-her-reasons-for-speaking-out-on-sex-and-gender-issues/.
Samuels, Ellen. *Fantasies of Identification: Disability, Gender, Race.* New York: NYU Press, 2014.
Sawicki, Jana. *Disciplining Foucault: Feminism, Power, and the Body.* Abingdon, U.K.: Routledge, 1991.
Schalk, Sami. "Coming to Claim Crip: Disidentification with/in Disability Studies." *Disability Studies Quarterly* 33, no. 2 (2013): http://dx.doi.org/10.18061/dsq.v33i2.3705.

Schalk, Sami. "Critical Disability Studies as Methodology." *Lateral* 6, no. 1 (2017): https://doi.org/10.25158/L6.1.13.

Schuller, Kyla, and Jules Gill-Peterson. "Introduction: Race, the State, and the Malleable Body." *Social Text* 143, no. 2 (2020): 1–17.

Sedgwick, Eve Kosofsky. *Epistemology of the Closet.* Oakland: University of California Press, 2008.

Sedgwick, Eve Kosofsky. *Tendencies.* Durham, N.C.: Duke University Press, 1993.

Sedgwick, Eve Kosofsky. *Touching Feeling.* Durham, N.C.: Duke University Press, 2003.

Seitler, Dana. "Suicidal Tendencies: Notes toward a Queer Narratology." *GLQ* 25, no. 4 (2019): 599–616.

Selzer, Jack. "Habeas Corpus: An Introduction." In *Rhetorical Bodies,* edited by Jack Selzer and Sharon Crowley, 3–15. Madison: University of Wisconsin Press, 1999.

Serrano, Julia. *Whipping Girl: A Transsexual Woman on Sexism and the Scapegoating of Femininity.* Emeryville, Calif.: Seal, 2007.

Shahani, Nishant. "How to Survive the Whitewashing of AIDS: Global Pasts, Transnational Futures." *QED* 3, no. 1 (2016): 1–33.

Shahani, Nishant. "'I Have a Voice': Speech, Silence and the Rehabilitation of Empire." *Postcolonial Studies* 18, no. 1 (2015): 67–84.

Shahani, Nishant. *Queer Retrosexualities: The Politics of Reparative Return.* Bethlehem, Penn.: Lehigh University Press, 2011.

Sheppard, Alice. "I Dance Because I Can." *New York Times,* February 27, 2019. https://www.nytimes.com/2019/02/27/opinion/disability-dance-alice-sheppard.html.

Sheppard, Alice. "Ramp Magic." Alice Sheppard (website). October 26, 2017. http://alicesheppard.com/ramp-magic/#longdesc-return-737/.

Sheppard, Alice. "Staging Bodies, Performing Ramps: Cultural-Aesthetic Disability Technoscience." *Catalyst* 5, no. 1 (2019): 1–12.

Shildrick, Margrit. *Dangerous Discourses of Disability, Subjectivity, and Sexuality.* London: Palgrave, 2012.

Shildrick, Margrit. "Neoliberalism and Embodied Precarity: Some Crip Responses." *South Atlantic Quarterly* 118, no. 3 (2019): 595–613.

Shildrick, Margrit. "'Why Should Our Bodies End at the Skin?': Embodiment, Boundaries, and Somatechnics." *Hypatia* 30, no. 1 (2015): 13–29.

Siebers, Tobin. "Disability as Masquerade." *Literature and Medicine* 23, no. 1 (2004): 1–22.

Siebers, Tobin. "Sex, Shame, and Disability Identity: With Reference to Mark O'Brien." In *Gay Shame,* edited by David M. Halperin and Valerie Traub, 201–18. Chicago: University of Chicago Press, 2009.

Siebers, Tobin. "A Sexual Culture for Disabled People." In *Sex and Disability,* edited by Robert McRuer and Anna Mollow, 37–53. Durham, N.C.: Duke University Press, 2012.

Sins Invalid. "10 Principles of Disability Justice." Sins Invalid. September 17, 2015. https://www.sinsinvalid.org/blog/10-principles-of-disability-justice?rq=disability%20justice.

Sins Invalid. "Mission & Vision." Sins Invalid. Accessed May 28, 2020. https://www.sinsinvalid.org/mission.

Smilges, J. Logan. "Pathological Desire, Perverse Erotics, and Paraphiliac Entelechies." In *The Routledge Handbook of Queer Rhetoric,* edited by Jacqueline Rhodes and Jonathan Alexander. Abingdon, U.K.: Routledge, 2022.

Smilges, J. Logan. "White Squares to Black Boxes: Grindr, Queerness, Rhetorical Silence." *Rhetoric Review* 38, no. 1 (2019): 79–92.

Snorton, C. Riley. *Black on Both Sides: A Racial History of Trans Identity.* Minneapolis: University of Minnesota Press, 2017.

Snorton, C. Riley. *Nobody Is Supposed to Know: Black Sexuality on the Down Low.* Minneapolis: University of Minnesota Press, 2014.

Snorton, C. Riley, and Jin Haritaworn. "Trans Necropolitics: A Transnational Reflection on Violence, Death, and the Trans of Color Afterlife." In *The Transgender Studies Reader 2,* edited by Susan Stryker and Aren Z. Aizura, 66–76. Abingdon, U.K.: Routledge, 2015.

Snyder, Sharon, and David Mitchell. *Cultural Locations of Disability.* Chicago: University of Chicago Press, 2010.

Socarides, Charles W., and Abraham Freedman, eds. *Objects of Desire: The Sexual Deviations.* Madison, Conn.: International Universities Press, 2002.

Soldatic, Karen, and Shaun Grech. "Transnationalizing Disability Studies: Rights, Justice, and Impairment." *Disability Studies Quarterly* 34, no. 2 (2014): http://dx.doi.org/10.18061/dsq.v34i2.4249.

Spade, Dean. *Mutual Aid: Building Solidarity during This Crisis (and the Next).* London: Verso, 2020.

Spade, Dean. *Normal Life: Administrative Violence, Critical Trans Politics, and the Limits of Law.* Durham, N.C.: Duke University Press, 2015.

Spurgas, Alyson K. "(Un)Queering Identity: The Biosocial Production of Intersex/DSD." In *Critical Intersex,* edited by Morgan Holmes, 97–122. Farnham, U.K.: Ashgate, 2009.

Stempfhuber, Martin, and Michael Liegl. "Intimacy Mobilized: Hook-Up Practices in the Location-Based Social Network Grindr." *Österreich Z Soziol* 41, no. 1 (2016): 51–70, https://doi.org/10.1007/s11614-016-0189-7.

Stockton, Kathryn Bond. *Beautiful Bottom, Beautiful Shame: Where "Black" Meets "Queer."* Durham, N.C.: Duke University Press, 2006.

Strudwick, Patrick. "This Is What Dating Is Like When You're LGBT and Disabled." *BuzzFeed News,* October 11, 2015. https://www.buzzfeednews.com/article/patrickstrudwick/this-is-what-its-like-coming-out-when-youre-disabled.

Stryker, Susan. "Dungeon Intimacies: The Poetics of Transsexual Sadomasochism." *Parallax* 14, no. 1 (2008): 36–47.

Stryker, Susan. "General Editor's Introduction." *Transgender Studies Quarterly* 5, no. 4 (2018): 515–17.

Stryker, Susan. *Transgender History.* Emeryville, Calif.: Seal, 2008.

Throckmorton, Warren. "Alan Chambers: 99.9% Have Not Experienced a Change in Their Orientation." *Warren Throckmorton* (blog). January 9, 2012. https://www.wthrockmorton.com/2012/01/09/alan-chambers-99-9-have-not-experienced-a-change-in-their-orientation/.

TLC. "My Husband's Not Gay: 'Can I Order Off the Menu?'" February 25, 2015. YouTube video, 1:20. https://www.youtube.com/watch?v=trOt2BJXBeA.

Travers, Ann. *The Trans Generation: How Trans Kids (and Their Parents) are Creating a Gender Revolution.* New York: NYU Press, 2018.

Treichler, Paula A. "AIDS, Homophobia, and Biomedical Discourse: An Epidemic of Signification." *October* 43 (1987): 31–70.

Tyburczy, Jennifer. "Leather Anatomy: Cripping Homonormativity at International Mr. Leather." *Journal of Literary & Cultural Disability Studies* 8, no. 3 (2014): 275–93.

Verlinden, Jasper J. "On Affect Theory's Hidden Histories: Toward a Technological Genealogy." *American Quarterly* 69, no. 2 (2017): 321–26.

Vidali, Amy. "Seeing What We Know: Disability and Theories of Metaphor." *Journal of Literary & Cultural Disability Studies* 4, no. 1 (2010): 33–54.

Vitanza, Victor J. "Some Meditations-Ruminations on Cheryl Glenn's 'Unspoken: A Rhetoric of Silence.'" *JAC* 27, no. 3/4 (2007): 793–818.

Vitto, Laura, and Gillian Edevane. "Photo of Young Transgender Girl Sends Important Message about North Carolina's Bathroom Laws." *Mashable,* April 27, 2016. https://mashable.com/article/corey-maison-meg-bitton-facebook#mcYAAbvnriqb.

Vitulli, Elias Walker. "Dangerous Embodiments: Segregating Sexual Perversion as Contagion in US Penal Institutions." *Feminist Formations* 30, no. 1 (2018): 21–45.

Vizenor, Gerald. *Manifest Manners: Narratives on Postindian Survivance.* Lincoln: University of Nebraska Press, 1999.

Waidzunas, Tom. *The Straight Line: How the Fringe Science of Ex-Gay Therapy Reoriented Sexuality.* Minneapolis: University of Minnesota Press, 2015.

Walker, R. J. "The Genesis of Maori Activism." *Journal of Polynesian Society* 93, no. 3 (1984): 276–82.

Walters, Shannon. *Rhetorical Touch: Disability, Identification, Haptics.* Columbia: University of South Carolina Press, 2014.

Warner, Michael. "Normal and Normaller: Beyond Gay Marriage." *GLQ* 5, no. 2 (1999): 119–71.

Weise, Jillian. "The Dawn of the 'Tryborg.'" *New York Times,* November 30, 2016. https://www.nytimes.com/2016/11/30/opinion/the-dawn-of-the-tryborg.html.

Wilson, James C., and Cynthia Lewiecki-Wilson. "Disability, Rhetoric, and the Body." In *Embodied Rhetorics: Disability in Language and Culture,* edited by James C. Wilson and Cynthia Lewiecki-Wilson, 1–24. Carbondale: Southern Illinois University Press, 2001.

Wyler, Rich, ed. *Then & Now: How My Sexual Attractions Have Changed.* Ruckersville, Va.: People Can Change, 2015.

Yarhouse, Mark, and Erica S. N. Tan. *Sexual Identity Synthesis: Attributions, Meaning-Making, and the Search for Congruence.* Lanham, Md.: University Press of America, 2004.

Yergeau, M. Remi. *Authoring Autism: On Rhetoric and Neurological Queerness.* Durham, N.C.: Duke University Press, 2018.

Index

J. Logan Smilges is assistant professor of English language and literatures at the University of British Columbia.